D1162465

LYRIC AND POLEMIC

LYRIC AND

The Literary Personality of Roy Campbell

McGill–Queen's University Press

POLEMIC

ROWLAND SMITH

MONTREAL AND LONDON 1972

© McGill–Queen's University Press 1972
International Standard Book Number: 0 7735 01215
Library of Congress Catalog Card Number: 72-82245
Legal Deposit 3rd quarter 1972

This book has been published with the help of a grant from
the Humanities Research Council of Canada, using funds
provided by the Canada Council.

Designed by Mary Cserepy

Printed in Canada by John Deyell Ltd.

for Ann

CONTENTS

PREFACE

This study is primarily literary, dealing with Campbell's writing and the personality revealed in it. Although I have used biographical information wherever possible, my emphasis is always on Campbell as a writer rather than on Campbell as a man. I have not attempted to discuss his translations, but have concentrated on his original works. I have been given invaluable assistance by the poet's daughter, Mrs. Teresa Custódio, and by his wife, Mrs. Mary Campbell. Both Mrs. Custódio and Mrs. Campbell answered numerous questions, and Mrs. Custódio went to considerable trouble to sort out, for my own use, letters from the poet to her mother and herself. Photocopies of these letters were made by the Centro de Estudos Históricos Ultramarinos in Lisbon, with the courteous cooperation of the Director and of Dr. A. da Silva Rego. Other material I found in Durban, in the library of the late Dr. Killie Campbell, which contains a collection of early Campbell manuscripts, original letters, and typed copies of other letters.

Mr. William Plomer was most helpful in providing me with information on the writing of "Tristan da Cunha."

Before his death, the late W. H. Gardner was writing a detailed, critical biography of Roy Campbell. He was an untiring and meticulously careful reader of an earlier version of this work, and my debt to him is considerable.

Whenever I have quoted from a private document, I have given its source immediately after the quotation. Thus [KC] indicates a document in the library of Dr. Killie Campbell, [MC] indicates a document in the possession Mrs. Mary Campbell, and [TC] indicates a document in the possession of Mrs. Teresa Custódio.

Unless otherwise stated, all references to Campbell's poetry are to Collected Poems (London: Bodley Head), volume 1, 1949; volume 2, 1957; and volume 3, 1960.

ACKNOWLEDGEMENTS

I wish to thank the following for permission to reprint selections from the works of Roy Campbell and others:

Allan Bevan, Editor, *Dalhousie Review,* for permission to use some of the material from my article, "The Spanish Civil War and the British Literary Right" (*Dalhousie Review*, 1971).

Chandler B. Beall, Editor, *Comparative Literature,* for permission to use some of the material from my article, "Roy Campbell and His French Sources" (*Comparative Literature*, 1970).

The Bodley Head, to quote from *The Georgiad, Flowering Reeds, Mithraic Emblems, Flowering Rifle, Light on a Dark Horse, Broken Record, Portugal,* "Letter from San Mateo," "Félibre," and "Rhapsody of the Man in Hospital Blues."

Mrs. Mary Campbell, for permission to quote from Roy Campbell's unpublished material.

Jonathan Cape, on behalf of the Executors of the Roy Campbell Estate, for selections from *The Wayzgoose* and *The Flaming Terrapin.*

Curtis Brown, on behalf of the Estate of Roy Campbell, for selections from *The Flaming Terrapin* and *Adamastor.*

Faber and Faber, for permission to reprint selections from *Talking Bronco.*

Editions Gallimard, for extracts from Paul Valéry's *Oeuvres,* published in 1957.

D. R. Gillie, for permission to quote his translation of "Tristan d'Acunha" by Johannes Kuhlemann.

Hogarth Press, for the passage from the Introduction by Laurens van der Post to *Turbott Wolfe* by William Plomer.

Mrs. Wyndham Lewis, for permission to quote from *The Apes of God* and *The Letters of Wyndham Lewis.*

William Morrow and Company, for the passage from Laurens van der Post's Introduction to *Turbott Wolfe* by William Plomer. Introduction © Laurens van der Post 1965.

Frederick Muller Ltd., for passages from *The Mamba's Precipice*.

Nigel Nicolson, for permission to quote from *The Land* by Victoria Sackville-West.

William Plomer, for permission to quote from his article, "Voorslag *Days"* (*London Magazine,* 1959).

Henry Regnery Company, for permission to quote from "After the Horse-Fair," *Flowering Rifle, The Georgiad*, and *Light on a Dark Horse.*

Miss Ann Wolfe and the *New Statesman,* for permission to quote from "The Ranciad" by Humbert Wolfe.

INTRODUCTION

To those who remember him, Roy Campbell usually appears an enigmatic figure whose frequent changes of loyalty are confusing and contradictory. His literary career was built around changing allegiances, publicly proclaimed, and usually accompanied by a change of environment. Throughout his adult life he was on the move. As a young man of seventeen he first left his native South Africa to attempt to gain admission to Oxford University. Unsuccessful in that academic endeavour, he led an irregular, Bohemian life, married romantically without parental consent, and completed his first major work. In 1924 that first poem, *The Flaming Terrapin,* brought him an acclaim and standing enjoyed by few young, one-volume poets. From this point, apparently contradictory changes of face follow in rapid succession. Campbell returned to South Africa, and almost at once found himself at odds with that colonial culture. His own, wild, "African" personality had been an essential part of his writing in Europe, and yet, when back in Africa, he was in a state of constant estrangement. Returning to England three years later, he began to publish poems bitterly critical of South African culture. English life, however, was proving to be as confining to the poet's personality as South African life had been, and he again uprooted his family by moving to Provence.

This was a major change and brought with it a new sense of values. Up to this point he had shared many of the "progressive" views of the English intellectuals with whom he was mixing. After leaving England, however, he became increasingly conservative in outlook. His growing conservatism, and the fact that he was living outside England were both likely to isolate him from the mainstream of English literary life which was entering the thirties with a growing social conscience. What isolated him more decisively, however, was his own satire on the English literary establishment, *The Georgiad,* published in 1931. After the publication of *The Georgiad,* he was ostracized in literary circles, and his conservative voice became increasingly strident as he commented on the increasingly turbulent political situation in Europe. Campbell had moved to Spain and had become a Roman Catholic when the Spanish civil war broke out. His passionate support of Franco further alienated him from the overwhelming majority of English writers, who supported the Spanish Republic. By the end of the Spanish war, he had gained the reputation of being a fascist, and was himself bitterly critical of British democracy. Once the Second World War broke out, however, he again realigned his loyalties, left Spain for England, and enlisted in the British army. In manner he proudly adopted the persona of a worldly-wise British N.C.O., and remained in England for several years after the war, accepted once more on the English scene. His new sense of belonging was not sufficient to keep him there, however, and he moved to Portugal in the early fifties, where he died, still an arch-conservative, in 1957.

These changes in loyalty and outlook affect Campbell's writing. He never fully realized the promise shown by his first volume. The lyric power, so clearly evident from the opening lines of *The Flaming Terrapin,* continued to delight readers of his subsequent volumes, but his colourful and incisive talent became increasingly diverted into polemical and satirical writing as he grew older. By turning more frequently to polemic as his political and personal feuds multiplied, he neglected his distinctive lyrical gift which is at its best when capturing his inward reactions to stress or beauty. His later obsession with argument could only lead him away from the vivid expression of subjective values, and into statements and comments which are open to more objective assessment.

In this study I discuss what Campbell's values were, and the extent to which they affect his lyrical and polemical works. The marked variations in tone and manner in the works themselves call for a careful separation between what is excessive and ineffectual in his responses, and that which gives the distinctive vitality and beauty to his best poems. When considered in relation to the events in his life, his beliefs and loyalties are less enigmatic than might at first appear. Without attempting to force his life and work into an oversimplified pattern, my study traces the effects of his colonial background, and his resulting sense of being an outsider from the time of his first contacts with English life. Once his unhappy return to South Africa seemed to cut him off from his native culture, his own feeling of isolation grew more intense. Many of his subsequent allegiances are an inevitable result of his steadily increasing alienation throughout the thirties. His need to justify himself and the values he had adopted became more acute.

Campbell's isolation affects his work in two ways. It drove him into self-justifying polemic, and finally to a predictable, public response. At the same time, however, it gives his writing a remarkable intensity when he uses his lyrical gift to communicate the personal tensions and values which lie behind the less successful, public poems. After he was finally accepted, albeit as an eccentric, on the English literary scene, his lyrical fervour left him. His last volume of original poems was published in 1946. Between 1946 and his death, he published several volumes of translations, for which he won great acclaim, and four prose works. In his role of the rugged individualist he was likely to appear (perhaps a little unsteadily) on public occasions dressed in his army bush-hat or as an Iberian cattleman. His repertoire of tall stories was unlimited. Yet his distinctive lyrical power had gone, and his few original poems show none of the burning intensity which so distinguished his work during his long period of isolation.

CHAPTER ‖

YOUTH AND
THE FLAMING TERRAPIN

Roy Campbell was born in Durban on October 2, 1901. He himself describes his family as one of "soldiers, scholars, athletes, poets, doctors and farmers," and the pride of his frequent references to the achievements of his family in Natal is justified by the local prestige and standing of the Campbells.

Campbell's grandfather, a Scots railway engineer, was one of the early settlers in Natal, and soon established himself as a prominent member of the community. His son, Sir Marshall Campbell, Roy's uncle, was one of the first to introduce sugar cultivation on the Natal north coast, and made a fortune by turning vast tracts of subtropical bush into cane fields. Sir Marshall Campbell's daughter, Dr. Killie Campbell, on her death left to the city of Durban and the University of Natal her house, together with the world-famous museum and library of Africana which it contains, and which represented her life's work. Roy's father, Dr. Samuel George Campbell, was one of the younger brothers of Sir Marshall. He was educated as a doctor at the University of Edinburgh, and lived the life of a member of the professional upper middle class. It was into this class that his children were born. Samuel Campbell was a popular and prominent figure in Durban society, and assisted in the founding of Durban Technical College and of Howard College, which was later to become the Durban section of the University of Natal. Roy's elder brother, George, who is a prominent Durban doctor, was for many years chairman of the Council of the University of Natal and was installed as chancellor in 1967. Like his father before him, George Campbell was awarded an honorary doctorate by the University of Edinburgh for his contribution to the life of Durban.

The local prestige of the Campbells and their history in the early days of a growing colony, where the semi-feudal landowners were also automatically soldiers and administrators, are an important part of Roy Campbell's own intellectual and emotional background. Although he himself lived a life of comparative poverty, without a fixed occupation for an extended period, the poet constantly expressed his belief in aristocratic, "equestrian" forms of life and civilization, and attacked bourgeois, urban civilization, which he equated with "counter jumping" or "shopkeeping" attitudes. The way his dislike of modern urban civilization is linked to his pride in the superior pursuits of his own family can be seen in one of the early passages from his first autobiography, *Broken Record:* "My father's family were among the first settlers of Natal. My grandfather, William Campbell, was the first polemist we had, and wrote very lively verse. I still have his copy of Burns, over a hundred years old, intelligently marked and much-handled. He was always coming to blows with the shopkeeping, and missionising part of the community: and it has remained a family tradition, except for my brief collaboration with *Voorslag* [a South African magazine], for we have never had a shop-keeper, lawyer, politician, or parson in our family, only soldiers, scholars, athletes, poets, doctors and farmers" (p. 12). A genuine sense of pride in the distinguished family history and the humane values of the family tradition is counterbalanced here in typical fashion by an unsettling disregard for shopkeepers. A disturbing assumption of superiority is often an inevitable part of Campbell's forthright views, and gives a harshness to this passage which, for all its bravura, is firmly based on an instinctive belief in standards of behaviour that are not commercialized or vulgarized.

He is always at his best when capturing the positive value of his "aristocratic" view, and often shows similar insensitivity when the impetus behind his writing is to attack those who do not share his outlook. There is no sense of harshness in a passage a few pages later in *Broken Record,* in which he elaborates on the exceptional quality of his family background: "My father educated us primarily so that we should be able to enjoy our lives; success was only a sideline. Unlike a bourgeois father, he raised no objection to my being a poet, but flung every possible advantage at me, sharing and cherishing the ambition as much as myself. He took as much care of our physical and athletic education as of our intellectual, and all my brothers have been fine athletes. We had the run of vast tracts of wild country both on the Natal estates and in Rhodesia, with horses, guns and as many books as we wanted to buy, except novels. My monthly account at the bookshops was something tremendous, but he always paid it without a word" (p. 17).

He does not attack the "bourgeois father" in this passage, but gives a sincerely appreciative assessment of the difference between his own background and that of a conventional, bourgeois youth. The result is that the very real values of the life of the Campbells are an impressive part of the writing, which embodies much of the aristocratic spaciousness of the poet's ideal world, without the crabbed tone that creeps into his attacks on those who do not share his ideals. In all his reminiscences he describes his boyhood with the same lyric delight. A very early letter to his cousin Dora from the young Roy on holiday in Rhodesia shows that his memories of a carefree, open-air existence

are probably not exaggerated. The letter is decorated with
a drawing of a kneeling man firing at a leaping buck, and
reads:

My dear Dora,

How are you? I have just been shooting with my big
gun and I shot a hadadah. I really was going to shoot
an eagle that had been eating the fowls. A hadadah is
a bird about three feet high with a long beak and legs
and its wings when stretched out are four feet. It is
nice eating. There are not many snakes here but the
other day we saw three. I am sending you a box of
stuffed birds. Do not expect them yet as I will be a
month in getting them. I have got one nice one for you
so far. It is a black bird with a scarlet collar on its neck
and tail nine inches long and the body is two inches.
I will try and get you a snake's skin too. There are lots
of buck here but we cant shoot them because it is out
of season. It has been bitterly cold here and the tem-
perature was 59. I must end up now as I want to go
and hunt birds with sticks.

From your affectionate cousin,
Roy
[KC]

Cultivated freedom of the kind enjoyed by the Campbells was exceptional even in Natal at that time. It certainly
was very different from the life in postwar Europe which
the poet encountered in 1919. The fact that he never
adapted completely to modern English life gave an added
intensity to the memories of his youth. This idyllic outdoor
life in the subtropical paradise of the Natal coast mingled
with sterner moments when he attended the Durban Boys'
High School. The dour, public-school ethic imposed on
the school by its headmaster, A. S. Langley, was anathema
to the young poet, and his schooldays were unhappy. At
the age of sixteen he made an unsuccessful attempt to enlist in the South African armed forces. In the following

year he ended an undistinguished school career by ma-
triculating in the third class.

A combination of wide-ranging literary interests and
exuberant outdoor activities was already beginning to put
its unique stamp on his personality, however, and the few
extant poems written before he left South Africa for England in 1919 reflect a passion for action and a heroic pose,
which are characteristic of much of his early published
verse. The unpublished poem, "To the Poet, R. W. Service,"
shows flashes of the poetic genius which was to burst out
in *The Flaming Terrapin*:

> I have roved the hush of the soundless snows
>> In the spell of thy magic lines;
> I have heard the rune of the lonely loon
>> And the moan of the arctic pines.
> It seems I have camped on thy blazoned peaks
>> By the flickering camp-fire's glow
> When the Northern Glories shot their streaks
>> O'er the shuddering ribs of snow;
> When the wild winds wafted their frosty spice
>> And the west was a crimson dye,
> And the ranges lifted their tusks of ice
>> To rip at the frenzied sky.
> Oh! it's there I would have you cast me loose
>> And give me my ancient gun:
> And I'll share my home with the lordly moose
>> In the land of the midnight sun!
> There in the silence undefiled
>> Let me fight to the bitter end,
> Grip to grip with the naked Wild,
>> "The Wild that would crush and rend."
>>> [KC]

The romantic gesture is made in a more restrained mood in
another unpublished schoolboy poem, "Shadows":

> Shadows and shadows from my pale grey trees,
>> My twilight trees about me closely press;
> Stirring dream-fragrant in a scented breeze,
>> Peaceful, and silent, and so meaningless!

I love ye, O pale shadows, more than life,
      More than all things. Say not I love in vain!
For in the midst of battle, and of strife
      Your peace within my spirit shall remain.

With the fierce legions I must cross the sea:
      Dust into dust, our proud platoons will roll!
And I will die. And God will smile to see
      The peace of many shadows in my soul.

                                                    [KC]

Another incomplete, untitled remnant of the poetry of this
period does not have the typical stoicism of "Shadows" or
"To the Poet, R. W. Service," but it does show evidence of
Campbell's distinctive poetic gifts:

Calm is the hour: the night is still
And sprayed with stars, and splashed with dew:
Cool nightwinds breathe about the hill,
And trailing mists perplex the view.

Till a mysterious ecstasy,
Born of the night of stars and wind,
Awakens in the heart of me:
Forth leaps my spirit unconfined!

And with a fervour nothing mars
I leave the silence of the woods
And plunge through shoals of sleepy stars
To scour the skies infinitudes.

And out beyond the swirling suns,
Beyond the tides of time and space,
To find, more far than fancy runs,
The white dream-splendour of your face.

And then in dreamy rapture roll
Our trembling spirits, pale and high,
And heart to heart, and soul to soul,
Are blown about the midnight sky!

                                                    [KC]

The indulgence in this adolescent poetry, and the vagueness of its emotions, distinguish it from Campbell's published work. It was not until he arrived at Oxford and came under the influence of modern French poetry, guided by his friend T. W. Earp, that he really began to embody a hard, clear outline in his verse.

Campbell left South Africa in 1919 and went to Oxford to study for Responsions. As in Durban, he made little progress in his formal academic studies and failed to learn enough Greek to qualify for entry to the university. This first year at Oxford was typical of his uneasy relations with English life. On the one hand it ended in his exclusion from the university, accompanied by an inevitable sense of being an alien, and in addition an alien who fails. In other ways, however, it was extremely fruitful, and established him (at eighteen) among a group of bright young intellectuals who treated him as an equal. He read avidly during his stay at Oxford and totally immersed himself in the life of one of the literary circles. The group included Edgell Rickword, later to become well known as one of the editors of the *Calendar of Modern Letters,* and T. W. Earp, the president of the Oxford Union, and later art critic for the *New Statesman.* Among Campbell's Oxford friends was the young William Walton, who introduced him to the Sitwells and Wyndham Lewis. In *Broken Record* Campbell describes the excitement of his relationship with Walton: "I was surprised and delighted to find that he, though my junior, was already famous; that he knew the Sitwells, whom I had begun to imitate with fervour. The appearance of *Wheels 1919* was a great event. We took up the Sitwell cause violently amongst the undergraduates: besides Earp, there was no one to champion the new poetry of Eliot, and the new prose of Lewis, who had only written *Tarr* at that period" (p. 35).

Avid reading of Elizabethan poetry and drama mingled with play readings and attendance at Union debates during this period. In *Oxford Poetry 1920* two poems by Campbell appeared alongside those of Rickword and other, better-known Oxford friends. A letter written by Roy from Oxford to his father captures the mood of his Oxford experience with great charm and energy:

My dear Father,

With regard to a degree, I find that Oxford with its lectures etc., interferes very much with my work. I cannot conscientiously apply valuable time to such a subject, for instance, as Anglo Saxon. If I were to take a degree and become a schoolmaster, or a professor, could you imagine me in that kind of job? First of all there would be my fellow professors—could you imagine my giving out dogmas to a crowd of gaping students, hour after hour, day after day? Could you imagine my being friendly with the type of person who does that kind of thing? I would be half-way across the Pacific after two months of it. As far as money goes I am very sorry to be so expensive. It is unnecessary to tell you how grateful I am to you. I will try to reward your kindness by making my future as great as your past. Thanks very much for your letters which are a great pleasure.

Love to all,
Roy[1]

The nature of the "work" with which Oxford lectures interfered was wide reading, animated discussion, and the writing of poetry. In another letter to his father from Oxford, he explains his attitude towards work. Speaking of the "school" of "very young people like Rickword and myself," he writes:

We apply our work closely to the life that goes on around us. We read the French symbolists, modern futurists, the Elizabethans, modern scientists, the Roman poets and as much as we can of the Greeks. No one can say we are not as widely read as any of the Georgians or Futurists, most of whom turn their backs on science. I have now read about three-quarters of Darwin and Freud, a good deal of Huxley, and seven volumes of Nietzche [sic]. Please forgive this egoism. I am taking myself as an example just to show where our interest lies.[2]

1. Ethel Campbell, *Sam Campbell: A Story of Natal*, p. 355.
2. Ibid.

The range of his interests while at Oxford and his total immersion in the intellectual life of his circle were soon to bear fruit in the exceptional success of his first work published in 1924. In 1920, however, his lack of progress in Greek forced him to leave Oxford after an eventful holiday with Earp in Paris. This holiday made a deep impression on the young poet. He came across the work of Valéry for the first time, returning to Oxford with most of the poems later printed in *Charmes*. Many of the *Charmes* poems were to be freely adapted into original poems by Campbell in *Flowering Reeds,* over ten years later.

On leaving Oxford he went to London, mingling with literati and intellectuals. Augustus John was one of the circle. He describes meeting Campbell and Earp in the Café Royal at a time when a private detective was constantly stationed at the door to observe suspicious-looking "bohemians": "Roy Campbell's connection with Oxford had been less distinguished: unable to adapt himself to the routine and manners of the university, and pining for the more bracing air of his native Zambesi, he took to beer in a big way, till, pulling himself together, he sent himself down and came to London. Later on I was lucky enough to be of some service to this Jingo of genius."[3]

During this period Campbell was called "Zulu" by his friends, and Wyndham Lewis uses the poet as his model for the boisterous "Zulu Blades" in part three of *The Apes of God*. Although clearly an aspect of Lewis's grotesque enlargement of Bloomsbury life, the portrait of Zulu Blades, "a person of very mixed race, and probably low and confused antecedents," gives a clear enough impression of the effect Campbell's personality had at the time. In the novel, the archetypally virginal Matthew makes these "reflections" as he passes Blades's door: "During the ascent he beguiled the time with topical reflections. In the main they were concerned with Zulu Blades. The man's enterprising nature gave Matthew no peace day or night—Blades was the 'black beast,' an evil neighbour: what with his upstart disrespect as well for his metropolitan betters, since he had brought the hearty habit of the african out-stations

3. Augustus John, *Chiaroscuro*, p. 77.

into their midst, here. His skill with women was natural, it was true he roped them in like steers, he must be working off ten years' solitary confinement in the Veldt (p. 85)." The relationship begun at this time with Wyndham Lewis was to be extremely important. When the poet left England in 1928, the "progressive" and "humanist" period of his life was over, and the conservatism of his later life, as well as his opposition to intellectual cliques or fads of any kind, owe a great deal to the writings of Wyndham Lewis between the wars.

Campbell's periods in London alternated with holidays in the south of France, where he boosted his regular parental income with odd jobs as a deck hand on short cruises. A letter written to his mother in July 1921 from Cassis, Bouches-du-Rhône, vividly captures the ease and freedom of the poet's life on the Mediterranean coast:

My dear Mother,

Please excuse my not writing for so long, but I have been on board since my last letter—I got an ordinary working job on an Italian schooner in Marseilles as they were short-handed. We went to Corsica and Genoa and I got off here at Cassis, where I am going to take a rest. I feel very fit.

After a few days I'm going to look for something that will take me over to North Africa. I want to get into the interior for a few days. It is very amusing down there: this time I'm going to Tangier or Tunis as I know Algiers more or less. . . .

When I got here I only had two days' pay left and I was so shabby from the trip that no hotel would take me. I paid for two days' lodgings and only had three francs more. So I went into a small restaurant to get a bite. There I entered into conversation with the proprietor, a young man of about twenty-three. I amused him and he amused me so we sat talking all afternoon. He then asked me where I was staying—I said I thought in one of the caves among the cliffs. He then invited me to stay at his place—if my money came, as a lodger: but if it didn't come I could stay as a guest. He turned out to be a very well educated, quiet, decent fellow who had had to take up the restaurant to make a living. He had been an officer in the Flying Corps and contemplates going out to South Africa to make a better living.

My money came today, so I fixed him up, but am staying on. Uncle Jim says our account's overdrawn, so if I am to get my August money at the right time, would you please send it straight to the above address. . . .

There are some English painters here, very rich and stuck up, staying at the big hotel here. One of them came up to me and asked if I would sit for him and he would pay me two francs per hour. He thought I was an ordinary Provencal fisherman. He spoke atrocious French, so I had no difficulty in keeping up the bluff.[4]

Back in London in 1922, after a whirlwind courtship he married Mary Garman, an art student, and sister of Douglas Garman, co-editor with Rickword of the *Calendar of Modern Letters*. Mary Garman's beauty is commented upon by almost all contemporaries who describe her, and the romantic, Bohemian intensity of the Campbells' relationship led Wyndham Lewis, in *Blasting and Bombardiering*, to describe their wedding as typical of postwar literary life. The wedding feast took place in the Harlequin Restaurant in Beak Street, Soho, in characteristically Bohemian fashion. The poet retired with his bride early in the festivities to a room they had hired as a lodging in the same building, but had to return to restore order to the proceedings and rescue Augustus John from the threats of a guest.

Because Campbell was still under age when he married without parental consent, his father was annoyed, and for some time suspended his allowance. Finding it difficult to live in expensive London, the Campbells moved to a remote part of Carnarvonshire, opposite Bardsey Island. There they rented a converted stable extremely cheaply, and lived frugally and happily until 1924. During this period he completed *The Flaming Terrapin,* and his daughter, Teresa, was born. The vitality and independence which

4. Campbell, *Sam Campbell*, pp. 355–56.

the poet celebrates throughout his work are a continual presence in his description in *Broken Record* of his life at Ty Corn:

> We lived at first on about five pounds a month, spending half of it on books, for I had soon the whole country set with traps and springes, and bought a small gun second-hand, which kept us in food. For vegetables I toured the whole district at night.
>
> Over the fire we read Dante, Pope's Homer, Dryden's Virgil, Paradise Lost, Donne, Mickle's Camoens, Cervantes, Rabelais, and the Elizabethans; living for a year under the continual intoxication of poetry. [p. 169]

It was the prospect of the acceptance of *The Flaming Terrapin* which enabled the couple to leave Wales and return to London. Augustus John, who painted Campbell's portrait at about this time, describes his role in its publication: "He had lent me the manuscript of his first long poem, *The Flaming Terrapin*. I thought it a most remarkable work, in spite of its unflagging and, to me, rather exhausting grandiloquence. I showed it to T. E. Lawrence, who, much excited, bore it to Jonathan Cape, with the result of its publication in due course."[5]

Campbell's first work brought him suddenly into the foreground of the literary scene and established a unique reputation among his contemporaries for verbal daring, extravagance, and genuine poetic vision. The reviews of the poem when it first appeared in 1924 show the impact of the young poet's vitality and freshness on a public which was tired of the mild decorum of conventional Georgian poetry. F. L. Lucas's review in the *New Statesman* is typical:

> We wanted air; and here is a south-wester straight from the sea. So, it appears, many have felt in the last few weeks; it is excellent that such a work should win its recognition; but it throws also a strong light on the shabby gentility of modern poetry as a whole, that this book should have been at once so feverishly praised

5. *Chiaroscuro*, p. 77.

and overpraised. Yet it is natural that this should happen; we are so tired of the confessions of second-rate sensitive minds with nothing to confess and no gift for confessing it; with lyrically bleeding hearts on every sleeve, the poor daws can scarcely summon the appetite to go on pecking.[6]

A similar tone characterizes the review by Richard Hughes in the *Spectator:*

Imagine, then, the joy—like a breath of new youth, like a love affair to a lady in her fifties—with which I found myself immediately and flatly deciding that *The Flaming Terrapin* was *poetry*. Whether good or bad poetry was neither here nor there; there can be good or bad poetry as there is good or bad cheese; the point was that I never for a moment imagined it to be chalk.[7]

The energy of the reviews themselves is a striking aspect of the cultural climate in which *The Flaming Terrapin* was written. In passages of serious evaluation the same sensitive urbanity is generally apparent. The long review (almost a whole column) in the *Times Literary Supplement* is much more restrained than those already quoted, but shows a considered understanding of Campbell's strength:

This conception has a primitive simplicity which enables the poet to evoke those broad emotional reactions which are denied to a more sophisticated intelligence. And this perception of a direct relation between impulse and action, which, if an illusion, is peculiarly matched by a similar directness of vision. Vision is the essential of poetic style, for without it imagery degenerates into rhetoric. Rhetoric which enables a poet to sustain his inspiration is not to be despised in itself, and without rhetorical power Mr. Campbell would not have been able to carry through his design on a scale remarkable for so young a poet.

6. *New Statesman* (August 23, 1924), p. 572.
7. *Spectator* (July 19, 1924), p. 98.

But the sincerity of the poetic impulse is attested throughout by the continuously concrete realization of the thought.[8]

The review by Edward Garnett, who gave the young poet a great deal of encouragement as one of the original readers of the poem, is the most perceptive of the contemporary comments, and is again an impressive example of the high standard of the literary journalism of the day. In *The Nation and The Athenaeum* he writes:

> It would be easy for me to pull the poem to pieces, to quote passages inspired by extravagance of manner, and it is true that a cold and correct taste may be repelled by the poetic rhetoric, and by the naive inconsequence of the Argument. But the beauties are so many, the poet's imagination so daring, his descriptive powers so fresh and triumphant, his imagery so strong and often so delicate, that the very immaturity and wildness of his Muse will interest the discerning. . . .
>
> One would need to cite at least a dozen passages to give an adequate idea of the strange stature of the poem, of its reach, its fantasticality, its artistic lapses and shortcomings. It is obvious that it was not planned originally as an ordered whole, but that it is a piecing together of diverse fragments sustained by a loose general Argument. . . . The poet's achievement lies in the leaping fountain of imagination, in its profusion of invention, in its lavish exuberance, and wealth of emotion. Its pictures are so concentrated and its transitions so abrupt that it is not easy to grasp the effect of the whole, even at a second reading. One must add that though there are many reverberations from the seventeenth-century classics, such as Dryden and Milton, and also of Shelley, and even of moderns, the original feeling of the whole transmutes these borrowings, and the poet's youthful, magnificent audacity sweeps all before it.[9]

8. *TLS* (May 29, 1924), p. 337.
9. *The Nation and The Athenaeum* (June 7, 1924), p. 323.

The amorphous quality of *The Flaming Terrapin,* and its occasionally extravagant manner, are accurately assessed by Garnett as unimportant in its total effect. Similar weaknesses are commented upon by the other reviewers, and again are generally dismissed as of little consequence beside the poem's successfully achieved vitality and beauty. The poem virtually establishes its own terms of reference, and Campbell's youthful élan carries it along without any need for an overriding plan or pattern. Nevertheless the lack of organization in the poem indicates a tendency that developed into a real weakness in his later polemical writings in which ardour and lyrical ease are usually missing. For this reason it is remarkable how consistently the most favourable reviewers pointed out an organizational and intellectual weakness in the poem, while at the same time recognizing the unique value of *The Flaming Terrapin,* in which the poet's youth and naivety are used as part of its positive strength.

The poem embodies the young poet's reaction to the violent contrast between the postwar Europe which he encountered in 1919 and the African wildness of his previous eighteen years. It represents the culmination of the experience of his early days in Europe, where his "Zulu" background was as much part of his personality as were the new European attitudes he derived from Oxford literary circles or London Bohemia. In *Broken Record* he describes the pervasive force of his African background while relating the circumstances surrounding the publication of *The Flaming Terrapin:* "Several times when homesick, and more often when hungry, this fantastic Africa of my imagination, blending with the memories of canefires, stampedes, and a great deal of blarney, as in this case, had erupted into paint or speech to save my life or my health. It is as if the muse invoked in the *Terrapin* came to my rescue whenever I was in trouble. The *Terrapin* itself rescued my wife and daughter, Teresa, from starvation. Augustus John had the manuscript, which I had recopied four or five times to give to my friends. Heseltine, Rickword, my father, and my wife's father had the other copies, and they were all enthusiastic about it, but I couldn't get a publisher.

Chatto seemed to think I was playing a joke on them when I sent it to them. John showed his copy to Colonel Lawrence, and the off-shoot was a letter from Cape asking me to lunch" (p. 102).

Desmond MacCarthy was also about to write an article on the poem when it was accepted for publication. Campbell probably omitted his name from the account in *Broken Record* because of the quarrel in 1931 with the London literary world over *The Georgiad*. In 1924, however, that world still had a fascination for the poet. A letter describing his meeting with his publisher captures the excitement he felt at being accepted in the literary milieu he was later to find so distasteful:

My dear Father and Mother,

Mr. Cape invited me to lunch with Edward Garnett and some of the other readers for his firm. They are delighted with the Terrapin. Mr. Cape gave me £10. I get 10 per cent on the first 1000 copies, 15 per cent on the next, and 20 per cent on any others. That does not mean much as the sale won't be very extensive. But as a percentage it is good.

Edward Garnett is very nice. He discovered Conrad, W. N. [*sic*] Hudson, and Doughty, and although he is not a writer, he is supposed to be the most discriminating man of letters in England. He asked Tess and Mary and me to spend Monday at his house. Tess can play with his little grandson who is the same age while we go through the proofs together. He has given me free access to his own library and has taken me to see the Secretary of the British Museum who has given me special privileges in the library there—the biggest library in England. I can go into the print-room whenever I like and sit there as long as I want, without having to order the books I need the day before.[10]

The youthfulness of the letter is all the more engaging when placed against the bold confidence of the regenera-

10. Campbell, *Sam Campbell*, p. 357.

tive moral in *The Flaming Terrapin*. Campbell's sense of awe at being able to go into the print room whenever he likes and sit there as long as he wants provides a delightful biographical background to the celebrator of the "sudden strength that catches up men's souls" and "The Man, clear-cut against the last horizon." Youthfulness itself, and an ability to feel awe are integral to the sense of wonder and delight which he creates in *The Flaming Terrapin*. The explicit moral of the poem, and its plot, loosely organized around a description of the revitalization of the earth after the flood, are less impressive than its local effects. The impact of *The Flaming Terrapin* mainly depends on its energy, which embodies the positive moral value the poet sets out to describe didactically through his mythical plot. To the reader the plot seems in many passages to be only a convenient external framework for the evocation of natural strength and beauty in descriptions of the sea and the elements. But the poet himself regarded his plot as organic to the whole poem. In a letter to his parents he explains an early draft of *The Flaming Terrapin*:

My dear Father and Mother,

You wrote to ask me about the meaning of my poem, or rather its purpose. I am afraid its moral is rather too deeply embedded in the symbolism I have used, to be evident at first sight, if at all. But I hope that the poem in its new form will be more intelligible as I have tried to develop its moral issues in a clearer manner and to get them into direct rhythm with the progress of the poem.

However, I'll try to explain. The whole moral of the poem is contained in Christ's words, "Every tree that bringeth not forth good fruit, is hewn down and cast into the fire," and again in His words, "Ye are the salt of the earth but if that salt shall have lost its savour it shall be scattered abroad and trodden under the feet of men" (I have possibly misquoted it). Christ was one of the first to proclaim the doctrine of heredity and the survival of the fittest. Nietzche *[sic]* was too dull to

understand the aristocratic outlook of Christ, he slangs
Him for inventing a religion for the weak and the
wretched. But in this he was wrong for Christ in his
gospels is continually emphasising how hard it is for
any one to enter into the Kingdom of Heaven, or as we
would say the Kingdom of Man. . . .[11]

Such a fundamental belief in self-reliant, aristocratic
heroism is central to Campbell's outlook from this point
until his death. The often ostentatiously "enlightened"
humanism of *The Flaming Terrapin* in no way affects his
passionate belief in rugged vitality as the solution to the
malaise of a shell-shocked world. This same belief is basic
to the poet's later tributes to the aristocratic, equestrian
world of the pious and self-reliant vaquero who will
"anachronise" the sordid industrial values of modern civilization. The latter views are often couched in an aggressively reactionary tone, or become part of a fervid
Christian mysticism, but they are still based on Campbell's
instinct to identify himself with the vigours of an intuitive,
natural world.

In the letter to his parents he goes on to give formal
expression to the regenerative heroic principle which is
suggested throughout the poem:

However, to continue my explanation: in a world suffering from shell-shock, with most of its finest breeding-stock lost, and the rest rather demoralized, it is
interesting to conjecture whether a certain portion of
the race may not have become sufficiently ennobled
by its sufferings to reinstate and even improve on the
pre-war standard, and in the end to supplant the descendants of those who have become demoralised and
stagnant, like the Russians for instance. I have taken
this more cheerful view, as I would much sooner feel
that I was a Simian in the state of evolution into something higher, than a fallen angel in a state of decline.
So, with the deluge as symbolising the war and its subsequent hopelessness, I have represented in the Noah

11. Ibid., pp. 356–57.

family, the survival of the fittest, and tried to describe the manner in which they won through the terrors of the storm and eventually colonised the earth. The Terrapin is the symbol for masculine energy.

There is an element of insensitivity suggested by the detached tone with which he discusses the loss of the world's "finest breeding-stock," and the possibility of a "certain portion of the race" being able to "improve on the pre-war standard." This suggestion of insensitivity is not part of the poem itself, which is free of sociological theory. Nevertheless, here his serene theoretical discussion in nonhuman terms of race and breed gives an ominous hint of the poet's own predilection in his polemical writings for social theory and abstract social values. His interest in Nietzsche and in the aristocratic outlook of those who may "supplant" the "demoralised and stagnant" gives a further hint of the direction into which his theories were to take him in the thirties. Still, youthful ebullience, and not insensitivity, is the main impression given by the letter.

Just as the poem itself does not embody the regenerative theory in anything like the formulaic clarity which Campbell explains in his letter, so too its "symbolism" is far less consistently developed than would be expected from his explanation to his parents. The flexibility of the use to which he puts the Terrapin alone can be seen in the letter, when, after describing it as "the symbol for masculine energy," he adds in a second postscript: "P.P.S. Throughout China, Japan and India the tortoise is the talisman which represents strength, longevity, endurance and courage. It is also the symbol of the Universe, the dome representing the heavens and the body the earth." "Strength, longevity, endurance and courage" are all qualities suggested by the Terrapin in the poem. The additional explanatory detail—that it also represents the "Universe" —is typical of his tendency to overload the symbolic effects in *The Flaming Terrapin* until they become too general and all-embracing.

The Terrapin itself tows Noah's Ark to safety through the storm that "drowns" the world. Although the plot of the poem depends on the Terrapin's having an existence of its own, it is first introduced as part of a simile, the embodiment of "this sudden strength that catches up men's souls":

> This sudden strength that catches up men's souls
> And rears them up like giants in the sky,
> Giving them fins where the dark ocean rolls,
> And wings of eagles when the whirlwinds fly,
> Stands visible to me in its true self
> (No spiritual essence or wing'd elf
> Like Ariel on the empty winds to spin).
> I see him as a mighty Terrapin,
> Rafting whole islands on his stormy back,
> Built of strong metals molten from the black
> Roots of the inmost earth: a great machine,
> Thoughtless and fearless, governing the clean
> System of active things: the winds and currents
> Are his primeval thoughts: the raging torrents
> Are moods of his, and men who do great deeds
> Are but the germs his awful fancy breeds.
>
> [1, 60]

As a symbol of spiritual and physical vitality, the concrete, massive Terrapin is obviously dearer to Campbell than any "spiritual essence or wing'd elf." Yet it is described in such general terms that at times it loses its own concrete reality. Even the natural elements and the men who do great deeds become projections and facets of the Terrapin itself. The value associated with its "thoughtless and fearless," machine-like quality is related to his idealized view of intuitive reflexes in the natural world, as seen in the graceful vigour of wild animals, or even athletes, when "Action and flesh cohere in one clean fusion / Of force with form" (1, 59). His emphasis in the description is on the active, flawlessly energetic values which the Terrapin represents, and not on any of the mechanical overtones which the words "thoughtless" and "machine" normally carry. It is its capacity for tireless action which is the basis of the Terrapin's regenerative power:

> The Flaming Terrapin that towed the Ark
> Rears up his hump of thunder on the dark,
> And like a mountain, seamed with rocky scars,
> Tufted with forests, barnacled with stars,
> Crinkles white rings, as from its ancient sleep
> Into a foam of life he wakes the Deep.
> His was the crest that from the angry sky
> Tore down the hail: he made the boulders fly
> Like balls of paper, splintered icebergs, hurled
> Lassoes of dismal smoke around the world,
> And like a bunch of crisp and crackling straws,
> Coughed the sharp lightning from his craggy jaws.
>   [1, 61]

Such dazzling descriptions stamp Campbell's personality on the poem. His ability to create so compelling an un-European wildness justifies the praise with which *The Flaming Terrapin* was greeted. There is also an inherent danger in the "foreign" quality of his responses and values. As he grew older, it became increasingly difficult for him to abandon the role of the outsider with a down-to-earth heroic answer to most problems. He had been the "Zulu" from his earliest days in England, and he invokes African muses in *The Flaming Terrapin*. It is a tribute to its poetic vitality that the exuberant evocations of primitive force are convincing, and not quaintly colonial. The poem is exciting and refreshing. Not surprisingly, it is at its best when his vivid imagery supports the basic regenerative moral, and less convincing when he is trying to describe abstract moral qualities.

The vagueness at the core of many of his depictions of moral values can be seen in an early passage describing Samson, roused by the Terrapin to perform heroic feats:

> Tigers he mauled, with tooth and ripping nail
> Rending their straps of fire, and from his track
> Slithering like quicksilver, pouring their black
> And liquid coils before his pounding feet,
> He drove the livid mambas of deceit.
>   [1, 63]

Samson's physical prowess is being described in the first lines, and the tigers he mauls are real. Similarly the description of the snake is a typically vivid picture of an observed detail from Campbell's African background, and the mambas, like the tigers, are still physical opponents. A new element is suddenly introduced in the last line when the snakes are described as "mambas of deceit." The addition of the specific moral concept can only weaken the snaky quality of the preceding lines; from the real tigers and realistic writhing of the snakes we have suddenly moved to snakes which symbolize an abstract quality. The next lines make explicit the shift in focus to a new emphasis on Samson's moral strength:

> Oppression, like a starved hyaena, sneaked
> From his loud steps: Tyranny, vulture-beaked,
> Rose clapping iron wings, . . .
>
> [1, 63]

At least the link between the animal world and the qualities it represents is made explicit here, but the arbitrary cataloguing of two-dimensional aspects of degeneration has a vagueness which the animal descriptions themselves conspicuously avoid. There is a similar vagueness in the description of the degradation which settles on the drowning world:

> Each Nation's banner, like a stinking clout,
> Infecting Earth's four winds, flaunts redly out,
> Dyed with the bloody issues of a war,
> For hordes of cheering victims to adore.
> While old Plutocracy on gouty feet
> Limps like a great splay camel down the street;
> And Patriotism, Satan's angry son,
> Rasps on the trigger of his rusty gun.
>
> [1, 75]

In the best passages there is a brilliant vividness which depends both on suggestions of vastness and on the reality of specific details. The ark is carried along by the flood waters in this way:

On fiery Coloradoes she was hurled,
And where gaunt canyons swallowed up the light,
Down from the blazing daylight of the world,
She plunged into the corridors of night
Through gorges vast, between whose giant ribs
Of shadowing rock, the flood so darkly ran
That glimpses of the sky were feeble squibs
And faint blue powders flashing in the pan
Of that grim barrel, through whose craggy bore
The stream compelled her with explosive roar,
Until one more she burst as from a gun
Into the setting splendour of the sun.

[1, 67-68]

Not only is the violence of the gun image in keeping with the cataclysmic nature of the flood, but also the sense of massive natural force is placed within a setting highlighted by the concrete reality of images like that of the "giant ribs / Of shadowing rock." These well-realized details are particularly sharply outlined against more generally evocative imagery. After picturing the universal splendour of the setting sun, Campbell modulates easily into a beautifully vivid scene from his African past where the earthy, gliding presence of sleeping crocodiles gives a solid basis to the wilder flights of fancy suggested by "unimagined Congoes":

Down unimagined Congoes proudly riding,
Buoyed on whose flow through many a grey lagoon,
The husks of sleepy crocodiles went sliding
Like piles of floating lumber in the moon.

[1, 68]

Campbell's use of nature and sea imagery to suggest emotional and moral attitudes, as well as his actual description of the ark's voyage, are strongly reminiscent of Rimbaud's "Bateau ivre." Earp had led him to French poetry during his Oxford days, and the influence of French culture on the young poet had been profound. He himself has described most of his early verse as "bad Rimbaud," and the resemblance between *The Flaming Terrapin* and "Le Bateu ivre" was noted at once by the reviewer in the *Times Literary Supplement* who wrote that the poem showed "probably the first instance of the direct influence of Rimbaud on English verse."[12] However, neither comment does justice to the originality with which Campbell develops his own mood of intoxication in *The Flaming Terrapin*. The difference is marked between his overt moral purpose in describing the rehabilitation of man through the symbolic Terrapin's journey, and Rimbaud's subjective, fantastic account of the driftings of his drunken boat, which at times is described as only a projection of himself. There is nothing in *The Flaming Terrapin* as subjective as this passage:

> Moi qui tremblais, sentant geindre à cinquante lieues
> Le rut des Béhémots et les Maelstroms épais,
> Fileur éternel des immobilités bleues,
> Je regrette l'Europe aux anciens parapets!
>
> [*Oeuvres*]

The personal note in the longing for the settled pleasures of Europe and its ancient parapets, in spite of all the visionary splendours experienced "dans le Poeme/De la Mer," is quite different from Campbell's external view of the journey of his ark. Nevertheless, in spite of the differences between Campbell's comparatively objective poem and Rimbaud's subjective identification with the visionary voyage of his drunken and passive boat, the moments are similar in each poem when exotic, cosmic experiences are being evoked. The groaning and rutting of the behemoths, and the thick maelstroms in the stanza already quoted are conceived on the same scale as many of Campbell's descriptions in *The Flaming Terrapin*. The abstract quality of a phrase like "fileur éternel des immobilités bleues," however, is an element which Campbell avoids in his evocations of natural forces. His strength does not lie in the surrealist, fantasy-world which Rimbaud creates with such

12. *TLS* (May 29, 1924), p. 337.

compelling suggestion, but in the concreteness and vitality of his imagery:

> Till the stream, casting wide its forest sleeves,
> Heaved out its broad blue chest against the sea,
> And from their leafy bondage they were free.
>
> [1, 68]

A sense of athletic energy in the image of the chest of the river heaving, as against the tape at the end of its race down to the sea, shows his feeling for the tangible in his writing, and is typical of the way his personality informs *The Flaming Terrapin*. When Rimbaud is personal, on the other hand, "Le Bateau ivre" is flooded with the overtones of a private, introverted sensitivity:

> Si je désire une eau d'Europe, c'est la flache
> Noire et froide où vers le crépuscule embaumé
> Un enfant accroupi plein de tristesses, lâche
> Un bateau frêle comme un papillon de mai.

The echoes of Campbell's childhood in *The Flaming Terrapin* are far from being "plein de tristesses." Quite apart from the invocation to the African muse of his past, there are occasional brilliant flashes of childhood experience. The ark is described being washed ashore:

> Dizzy she soared that foaming ridge to skim,
> And as a top, whipped into frantic pain,
> Scribbles the dust, so on the boiling main
> She swirled and eddied.
>
> [1, 83]

The whole scene has a mood of wild childhood frenzy, which is typical of the South African poet's vigour.

In spite of these general differences between *The Flaming Terrapin* and "Le Bateau ivre," there are many similarities, particularly in the broad outline of the respective voyages through an exotic world. The two poems have different themes and describe different incidents, but

Campbell's debt to Rimbaud is clear. Nevertheless, even when under the influence of Rimbaud, his own personality dominates the lines.

That personality continually reveals its African origins. Not only is his imagery consistently and ecstatically tropical, but in the poem he invokes his own African muse to string his "lyre of savage thunder":

> Far be the bookish Muses! Let them find
> Poets more spruce, and with pale fingers wind
> The bays in garlands for their northern kind.
> My task demands a virgin muse to string
> A lyre of savage thunder as I sing.
> You who sit brooding on the crags alone,
> Nourished on sunlight in a world of stone,
> Muse of the Berg, muse of the sounding rocks
> Where old Zambezi shakes his hoary locks,
> And as they tremble to his awful nod,
> Thunder proclaims the presence of a god!
> [1, 77–8]

Such a delight in the savage wildness of the virgin continent is organic to his forthright reaction against the introspective, polished values of Europe. In a letter to his parents after they had read a draft of *The Flaming Terrapin*, he describes his absorption in the African scenery of his childhood. The "sakaboola" about which he reminisces is a brightly coloured, long-tailed bird:

> I remember taking the side of Dr. Loram in an argument against Father when Father was saying that it was quite as possible to immortalise the "sakaboola" as the English nightingale. Father said that a "sakaboola" for him had much the more significance, and I agree with him now. One cannot do away wholly with the surroundings of one's youth.
>
> English scenery to me is like those pictures one sees on chocolate boxes. I would sooner see one sakaboola rising in the wind than have a thousand nightingales sitting on my chimney top and singing for all they were

worth. But it does not make me homesick—I have got everything quite clearly in my mind and I do not need to go back to it.[13]

His need to defend the African sakaboola bird against the European poets' nightingale shows how deep was Campbell's instinctive feeling of being a barbaric outsider. In *The Flaming Terrapin* these feelings of exclusion are completely absorbed into his defiant challenge to shell-shocked Europe. The tropical elements in the poem show no signs of homesickness, but form an integral part of its wildness and beauty:

> All night he watched black water coil and burn,
> And the white wake of phosphorous astern
> Lit up the sails and made the lanterns dim,
> Until it seemed the whole sea burned for him;
> Beside the keel he saw the grey sharks move,
> And the long lines of fire their fins would groove,
> Seemed each a ghost that followed in its sleep
> Those long phantasmal coffins of the deep.
>
> [1, 65]

Campbell's descriptions are often playful. Without weakening his central impression of the vigour of the natural forces around the ark and Terrapin he continually achieves a charming lightness of effect. From a grim picture of the Horn as the brothel of Death he can easily move on in this humorous tone:

> Round the stark Horn, where bleak and stiffly lined,
> Hooked ridges form a cauldron for the wind,
> And droning endless tunes, that gloomy sprite
> Stoops to his dismal cookery all night,
> And with his giant ladle skims the froth,
> Boiling up icebergs in the stormy broth,
> Brewing the spirits that in sinking ships
> Drowned sailors tipple with their clammy lips.
>
> [1, 69–70]

13. Campbell, *Sam Campbell*, p. 356.

A similar control informs the openly satirical moments when he exaggerates the very epic effects on which his poem depends at other points:

> ... On earth again
> Foul Mediocrity begins his reign:
> All day, all night God stares across the curled
> Rim of the vast abyss upon the world:
> All night, all day the world with eyes as dim
> Gazes as fatuously back at him.
>
> [1, 74–5]

A feeling of the poet's own mental alertness, which derives from the variety indicated by these passages, is one of the most appealing features of The Flaming Terrapin. Its changes in mood, together with the extraordinary vividness and colour of so many moments, provide an interest which the poet's overt moral intention does not always realize. As a first poem the work shows the rare quality of demonstrating an originality and distinctly personal style, which Campbell in his twenty-third year could legitimately claim to be his own. At the same time, both the wild delights and the controlled vitality of The Flaming Terrapin give it a permanent value which is not simply that of showing a promising poetic quality.

CHAPTER 2

RETURN TO
SOUTH AFRICA

The favourable reception of *The Flaming Terrapin* co-incided with a reconciliation between Roy and his father, and the already well-known young poet was invited home at his family's expense in the same year, 1924. His letter accepting this invitation illustrates the strength of Campbell's attachment to his wife and shows his basically in-genuous nature, in spite of his new literary eminence:

Dearest Mother,

Mary and I were made very happy by your letter. I am so glad that Mary was liked so much by Colin and Natalie and the Dunnachies. I am awfully pleased that you appreciate and understand how much she is to me; our life together, in spite of its ups and downs, has been almost like a dream. In these days when girls are, as you say, rather selfish and are brought up to keep an eye on their own comfort, she seems all the more won-derful. She was very ambitious about her work, but gave it up altogether, simply to be an ordinary little mother and wife. She looks after Tess wonderfully and in spite of the fact that she has no natural gift for housekeeping has taken great pains to learn everything. I used to think you were very old fashioned when you did not like girls who went to dances or covered their faces with powder. But I realise how right you are now and I have come round.

I was thrilled to get the cable. I will hate leaving my two girls but I think that a trip home will set me up again. Mary will have Tess for company while I am away and she insists on my going. So in spite of the fact that we will feel rather lost without each other, I am looking forward "with a long stretched neck" to seeing you all again. After all Mary and I have years to be together so we will not grudge the few moments that I spend with you.

It is awfully kind of you all to have me out among you. It is so long since I have seen you that I am beginning to feel very shy.

> With love,
> Roy[1]

The tumultuous success of *The Flaming Terrapin* on both sides of the Atlantic meant that he was famous by the time he had returned to Durban. Shortly after his return his wife and daughter joined him in 1925, and the Campbells entered one of the more unhappy periods of their life together. The colonial life which he discovered and rejected was quite unlike that of his early youth, and the intellectual isolation which he experienced during his return visit influenced most of his later attitudes. His antagonism towards his native culture is not an isolated phenomenon. Many writers from Commonwealth countries have reacted similarly after experiencing the richness of European culture, from which their own "colonial" upbringing also partly isolates them. Campbell's reaction against South African people and values was particularly strong, although he remained devoted to the land itself and its untamed

1. Ethel Campbell, *Sam Campbell: A Story of Natal*, p. 357.

animal life. In London his "Zulu" mannerisms had stamped him as a colourful individual in an intellectual group which stressed individualism. In South Africa, Africanness was not only out of place, but also perilously close to the narrow chauvinism which so irritated him. To identify oneself with the vitality of the dark continent is one thing, but to accept smugly that local ways are best is another. Ironically, Campbell found himself the spokesman for European breadth of vision and a staunch opponent of local provincialism. At this time he adopted the persona of the isolated, aloof poet, scorned by the masses because he understands what they do not. The intensity of his feeling of rejection in South Africa gave his writing a bitterness which was as distinctive as its flamboyance. His later feeling of rejection by the British literary world could only add to the bitterness associated with his persona.

After a small amount of lecturing in adult education at the Durban Technical College, he became associated, early in 1925, with the establishment of *Voorslag* ("whiplash"), a projected "magazine of South African life and art." The main force behind the journal was Lewis Reynolds, the son of the sugar magnate, Sir Frank Reynolds. Lewis Reynolds had been at Oxford, and was interested in modern literature. His father's estate, Umdoni Park, at Sezela on the Natal south coast, had a cottage on its extensive grounds which had been used by the artist Edward Roworth, and in which the Campbells were established. There was a guest house in the form of a rondavel close to the main cottage, and in this William Plomer was to live during his co-editorship of *Voorslag*. The business manager of the projected journal was Maurice Webb, a Durban business man. The preliminary work on the journal took some time, and when William Plomer met Campbell in Durban in June 1925, he was asked to help with its production. After the publication of his novel *Turbott Wolfe*, early in 1926, Plomer left his trading station in Zululand and joined the Campbells in May.[2] The first number of *Voorslag* appeared in June 1926.

Turbott Wolfe had been well received in the overseas

2. See William Plomer, "*Voorslag* Days," *London Magazine* (July, 1959), pp. 46–48.

press, but had provoked much patriotic abuse in the local press because of its overt attack on South African colour prejudice. Plomer was thus already regarded as a wild young man before he was associated with *Voorslag*. When the first number appeared, the uneasiness of the public towards a journal in which he played an important role was increased by the forthright tone of much of the writing, which included an energetic defence of *Turbott Wolfe* by Campbell. The second number, published in July, exacerbated a general distaste for the arrogant young men who denounced South African pretensions and foibles. The opening article, Campbell's "Fetish Worship in South Africa," which attacked local prejudices with vigour and confidence, was particularly unlikely to allay public opinion. Lewis Reynolds became alarmed at the unpopularity caused by the journal he was sponsoring and decided to curb its editors. In his introduction to the 1965 edition of *Turbott Wolfe*, Laurens van der Post, who worked as an Afrikaans editor for *Voorslag*, describes the final break between the editors and the sponsors of the journal. Lewis Reynolds, Maurice Webb, and Edward Roworth, the journal's art critic, came down to the cottage at Sezela with the proposal that Webb should become the superior editor, exercising a managerial role. Van der Post writes:

> Campbell, whose sole source of income was *Voorslag*, squatted on his heels in the native South African fashion, a brisk sea-breeze tugging at his beard, while the visitors sat on the sands in front of him. It was all over in a few minutes. I saw Campbell suddenly gesticulate with his hands like a Zulu orator, get up abruptly and walk over to us, while the three others turned away disconsolately. Paler than usual with anger and in a voice still shaken with emotion, Campbell said, "They want to put Webb in over us. I told Lewis straight, 'You yourself confided to me in the beginning that we must take care not to let *Voorslag* develop *Webb*-ed feet, now you want it to have a *Webb*-ed head. You have my resignation here and now.'" [pp. 26–27]

From that moment the connection between the ex-editors and *Voorslag* ceased, although the third number, published in August 1926, after their resignation, did contain the final episode of Plomer's novella "Portraits in the Nude" and the translations of four French poems by Campbell, under the pseudonym Lewis Marston.

The Campbells and Plomer left Umdoni Park at the end of August 1926. Plomer and Laurens van der Post sailed on a trip to Japan shortly afterwards, while the Campbells returned to England early in 1927. The return to South Africa had been a fruitful one for Campbell, in spite of his unhappiness at the anger aroused by *Voorslag* and the constant nervous irritation which South African provincialism and conformity caused him. At least three of his finest poems were written at Sezela, and the constant intellectual interplay between him and Plomer, together with their inexhaustible creative energy at the time, caused both writers to respond with some of their best work. Plomer's description of him at Sezela gives an intimate picture of the writer at a stage when he was totally committed to literature:

> Much of Campbell's time was spent in a recumbent position, which suited him for the production both of his own poetry and of material for *Voorslag*. He worked at night, slept in the morning, and appeared at lunchtime. He ate scantily and at odd moments, took no exercise to speak of, had a great many baths, and was often sucking lemons or smoking cigarettes. He sometimes went fishing, or flew a kite from a fishing rod, and he would sometimes make a bonfire at night on the rocks near the sea, which seemed to me the sort of thing Shelley might have done—not that he took after Shelley. He was much under the influence of Nietzsche and somewhat under that of the French Symbolists, and I do not remember his speaking with warmth of any English poet alive or dead, except Marlowe, Pope, and Robert Nichols. I think English tradition and English life were alien to him, and that he

neither understood nor responded to them: he was a wild Highlander.[3]

Only on Campbell's return to England in 1927 was his problem of responding to English life and tradition to become acute. During his editorship of *Voorslag* he was sharply aware of the gap which separated colonial culture from metropolitan European culture. His attack on South African political values was really only an extension of his attack on South African cultural values. One of the reasons the public viewed *Voorslag* with suspicion was its aggressive championing of modern trends in literature. The young poet's praise of *The Waste Land* in a review in the first number is typical of the uncompromising broadside which *Voorslag* levelled at the unenlightened or complacent:

> More than any other modern artist Mr. Eliot has captured the brooding restlessness of the age: he has captured the gloomy introspection and bitter disillusionment of the youth of Europe.
> . . . One hears the crash of falling ruins, the querulous expostulation of the old ideals and idols against the powers of a new and inscrutable darkness. High over the sleepy self-satisfaction of middle-age one hears again and again the agonised searching question of youth now rising into a hoarse shout and then breaking off into an exasperated hyena-like chuckle— mocking, blasphemous, unanswerable. [pp. 59–60]

It is little wonder that the "sleepy self-satisfaction of middle-age" reacted with distrust towards the "agonised searching question of youth" embodied in *Voorslag*. The closing paragraph of Campbell's review must have appeared archetypally ominous: "To read Mr. Eliot's poems is to realise the necessity for new values in modern life. There must be a great destruction in the human consciousness: we must gibe, sneer and ridicule our venerable reviewers into epileptic fits: we have plenty of muck to clear

3. "*Voorslag* Days," p. 52.

out of the way before we can start the great work of re-construction" (p. 62).

The same verve characterizes his attack on Georgian and Victorian poetry in the second number of *Voorslag*. Writing under the pseudonym Lewis Marston, in " 'Eunuch Arden' and 'Kynoch Arden,' " Campbell draws heavily on *Who Killed Cock Robin?* by Osbert Sitwell, whom he ac-knowledges to be "a useful satirist," and from whom he adapts the title of his article. Of the contemporary writers Wilfred Owen, Siegfried Sassoon, Robert Nichols, and the contributors to the anthology *Wheels* are praised, but the development of English poetry is described in characteris-tically Campbellian terms: "Yet when we come to the end of the romantic period we come to the end of English liter-ature. After the death of Byron we descend almost verti-ginously through the later Wordsworth, Tennyson, Swin-burne, Marris [sic] and Wilde till we land in the puddle of Georgian poetry" (pp. 32–33). While scorning the deca-dence of nineteenth-century English poetry, he praises Baudelaire and Rimbaud, "the father of modern poetry," saying, "Futurism was merely a manoeuvre to get into line with Rimbaud." Once again it is only in the younger gen-eration that he sees much hope for English poetry: "It is doubtful whether, with the exception of D. H. Lawrence and Hardy, there is any English poet who is read on the continent; one can think of very few who would not pale into insignificance beside Paul Valery, Pellerin, Toulet or Marinetti. But the younger generation are coming on, and with such a vigorous forerunner as D. H. Lawrence there should be no fear for the future" (p. 38). Campbell shows an exceptional range of reading and response in an out-burst of this kind, but it is not surprising that there was a reaction against his aggressive flaunting of knowledge and praise of the avant-garde. Quite apart from the unpopu-larity caused by his sweeping literary judgements, how-ever, his scorn for group feelings and group judgements led him to attack South African racism in a way which was bound to cause trouble.

"The Significance of 'Turbott Wolfe' " in the first num-ber of *Voorslag* shows how easily his literary convictions lead him into broad sociological concepts. The review opens with a typical attack on behalf of the young, and shows legitimate scorn for the grounds on which Plomer's novel had been attacked:

> Literary criticism in South Africa is either in its infancy or in its dotage; and the present younger generation who have produced the bulk of that not very bulky growth, South African literature, have had to be patient and forgiving. It seems that political, moral, and theological standpoints are still considered legitimate criteria in reviewing a work of art. Mr. Plomer has probably had to be far more patient and forgiving than anybody else. He has been subjected to the various tests of patriotism, morality and even sportsmanship, and naturally, being a very conscientious artist has failed to pass any of them. [p. 39]

From this insistence on the literary standards by which the book should be judged Campbell himself moves on to sociological theory. Plomer is a serious artist because he thinks for himself, and is not part of a group consciousness:

> We look on politics as a cause when they are merely a result! On politicians as leaders, when they are merely representatives. Political histories are merely the spoor and dropping of those vast inscrutable impulses, the crowd-emotions, and supply the most convenient formula that we have for tracking them back through time. These impulses are not rational they are generated emotionally and instinctively and they are as primitive as the bison-herd or the wolf-pack. [p. 40]

It is his dislike of the bison herd and wolf pack which is at the bottom of almost all Campbell's attacks on South African culture and racial prejudices. In his review of *The Waste Land* in the first number of *Voorslag,* he talks of "the sordid drifting of industrialised herds, the obscenity of the sham ideals of the crowd, the mental non-existence of the man in the street. . . ." The same hatred of conformity is quite clearly the impetus behind "Fetish Worship in South Africa," which again attacks colour prejudice. It is ironic that the identical reaction against mediocrity and conformity should be the basis of his later distrust of urban civilization and left-wing "materialism."

"Fetish Worship in South Africa," published in the second number of *Voorslag*, manifests what could be called a left-wing attitude. Group loyalties, group prejudices, and group prides are all attacked with intelligence and energy, while "priests, politicians, journalists and military commanders" are ridiculed as the "bogey-men or tribal medicine-men" of the conforming community. The South African colour bar is adduced as the central prejudice and taboo in the national herd life, which is as blindly adhered to as beliefs in national superiority. The tone of the article is well illustrated in the following passage addressed to the Reader, who questions the Writer at various points in the argument:

> You people get an ideal like "White South Africa" tied to your noses and then you can't see anything else. You consider White South Africa to be more important than South Africa itself. It is all the fault of that dear old colour-fetish. It is the incarnation of all that is superstitious, uneasy, grudging and dishonest in our natures. Individually taken, we are all very nice people, a little pudding-headed, but that is all. But we are all afraid of our individual decency: we have to submerge it in respectability. The mob consciousness rules everything. It puts the cart before the horse: and worships Mumbo Jumbo in the name of Jesus, and it worships the Colour Bar in the name of White South Africa. [pp. 16–17]

Although Campbell is taking a "progressive" point of view here, writing of this kind is not very different from his later attacks on the Left, and on the conformist principle which he associates with a left-wing belief in the value of material improvements in the human condition. The basis of his attacks on South African conformity in the twenties and left-wing conformity in the thirties and forties can be seen in the opening statement of his thesis in "Fetish Worship": "A prominent German scientist after exhaustive researches recently came to the conclusion that out of every million individuals only one is really conscious. The others are entirely submerged in the mass-consciousness. Now this mass-consciousness as far as the average human being goes is Omnipotence, the True God—*Vox Populi, vox Dei*" (p. 3). When he returned to England in 1927 he came into contact with a different kind of sameness in outlook from that which he had struggled against in South Africa. His violent reaction against Bloomsbury and country-house mores and his withdrawal to France are further episodes in his struggle to remain himself. The fact that the English society in which the poet found so strong a conformist principle was predominantly left wing caused his own distrust of left-wing attitudes to become more and more pronounced after he left England in 1928.

Campbell's long satirical attack on Natal, *The Wayzgoose,* was published in England in 1928 after he had left Africa. Other African poems written between 1924 and 1927 were published in book form in *Adamastor* in 1930. The volume contains poetry written before *The Flaming Terrapin,* poems written during his return to South Africa, and Provençal poems written in Martigues, where the poet was living when *Adamastor* was published. As a result, there is more variety of subject-matter and mood in the collection than is suggested by its well-known anthology pieces, which so often share a similarity of manner and theme. The obsessive nature of these predominant themes was noticed by many of the contemporary reviewers, and, in some cases, assessed as a dangerous weakness in his work as a whole. The warning note struck by C. Henry Warren in *The Bookman* is typical:

> There is still in fact too much venom in the man. It gives his fierce epithets an occasionally fictitious strength. Only when the venom is washed away by an intense sympathy of understanding, leaving the old

power of words and the old stupendous imagery, does he achieve the fine quality of which one now knows him to be capable. . . .

Proof enough is in this book then that Mr. Campbell has "arrived." His note is as individual as anyone's now singing. Purged of some unnecessary rancour, he may one day give us really peerless poetry; for he has an intensity of vision that often reaches white heat.[4]

The fact that the distinctive qualities of Campbell's poetry are often linked with an unsettlingly excessive response to situation is again pointed out in the unsigned review in *The Nation and Athenaeum*:

For the rest there is much that is notable in these pages, and little that does not carry the signature of its authorship in every vivid line. Yet if with familiar virtues, fine language, imaginative range, new and vigorous metaphor, go the familiar vices, an over-intensity, an occasional quite comic inappropriateness . . ., still one's criticism—in itself a tribute to this poet's standing—goes deeper than that. The fact is that Mr. Campbell, as a poet, does protest too much. He urges the superiority of the poet over the blind mob, but not content to live in that superiority he must keep talking about it. . . .

Mr. Campbell has yet to come into his kingdom, but there are half a dozen poems in "Adamastor" which are the clearest warrant we have yet received from him of the poetry he will, we fully believe, ultimately write.[5]

Although *Adamastor* was regarded at the time of its publication as promising, or indicative of the poetry Campbell would be capable of writing in the future, in retrospect it is his best known, and most successful volume. Certainly no original volume of his published after *Adamastor* received as much attention or praise. The reason that the press found his promise unfulfilled in the later volumes lies

4. *The Bookman* (October, 1930), p. 50.
5. *The Nation and Athenaeum* (May 17, 1930), pp. 224-26.

largely in the tendency to violent reaction which the reviewers point to in *Adamastor*. The lack of interest taken
by the press in *Flowering Reeds* is difficult to explain on
any poetic grounds, particularly as the control, which many
reviewers found wanting in the early volumes, is so prominent a feature of the mature and subtle verse of the volume
published in 1933. The lack of engagement in *Flowering
Reeds,* ironically enough, is probably the reason for the
lack of public interest in it when it appeared in the politically turbulent world of the mid-thirties. After *Flowering
Reeds,* however, the violence of Campbell's political reactions did affect the quality of much of his poetry, and,
in addition, the unpopularity of his politics often made his
poems unpopular. Much of his best poetry was written
after *Adamastor,* and shows a significant advance in content and manner. But the excessive anger and acerbity
which the reviewers point to in the "promising" first volume of poems is a severely limiting factor in the volumes
published after *Flowering Reeds.*

The earliest poem in *Adamastor,* "The Theology of
Bongwi, the Baboon," dates from Campbell's Oxford days.
It is the only pre-Terrapin poem in *Adamastor*. "Mazeppa,"
the third poem in the volume, although one of the last to
be written, is the first to announce the central motif of the
collection. The story of the young man who is bound to
a wild horse by the husband he had wronged and yet sur-
vives the ordeal to become a famous Tartar prince is used
to illustrate the painful and isolated position of any exceptional man who is strapped down on "the croup of genius"
in a dull and hostile world. In many of the *Adamastor*
poems similar descriptions of natural energy are linked to
a statement of the isolation and pain suffered by an energetic intellect. Their peculiar intensity is directly derived
from the poet's instinctive identification with the wildness
of his African environment and from the obsessive quality
of his feeling of estrangement from the South African
society in which he was living. The African quality of his
creative instinct during this period is thus all-pervasive,
and the intense struggle of the young South African to
maintain his personal equilibrium in the cultural milieu of

his native land is in many ways as typically African as his
feeling for its natural delights. The final stanza of "Mazeppa" points its moral with a melodramatic flourish:

> Out of his pain, perhaps, some god-like thing,
> Is born. A god has touched him, though with whips:
> We only know that, hooted from our walls,
> He hurtles on his way, he reels, he falls,
> And staggers up to find himself a king
> With truth a silver trumpet at his lips.
>
> [1, 22]

The nature of the "truth" which results from this painful
isolation is partly the artistic truth which creative artists
establish in their work, and partly the insight into the dull
mob which comes with isolation from it.

A sense of isolation, and of being possessed of a firmer
grasp of reality than those around him, were inevitable reactions in what appeared a smug and self-centred colonial
world. Not only had his own interests broadened in Europe,
but also the uninhibited freedom of his almost feudal African childhood was now unattainable in an increasingly
urban environment. The seriousness of his attempt to discuss real issues and values in the face of the contentedly
blinkered ethic of the white colonial ruling class is obvious
from the total commitment which *Voorslag* and the contemporary poems show. William Plomer describes the aims
and attitudes of the *Voorslag* editors:

> Propinquity had brought us together. It is unlikely that
> we should have been mutually attracted at Oxford or
> in London; the differences in our backgrounds, tem-
> peraments, outlooks, ambitions and tastes were great.
> But in South Africa we were isolated, and isolation can
> be a social cement. We were of about the same age,
> and both high-spirited. Each was dedicated to the
> written word, to the recognition and perpetuation of
> the first-rate in literature, and to the art of creative
> writing. We liked the same sort of jokes, and agreed
> that the cultural pretensions of English-speaking South

Africa at that time were mostly absurd. Campbell, instantly recognizable as a poet, began to widen and enrich my understanding of poetry. At the same time, an evident intensity in my feelings about racial conflicts in South Africa, and my open sympathy with Africans, was not without its effect, its temporary effect, upon him. This short period of our close association was in fact remarkably fruitful for both Campbell and myself.[6]

Plomer's dislike of racism and his recognition of the provincial nature of colonial life went hand in hand. In *Turbott Wolfe* the outlandish, uncouth quality of life in "Lembuland" is continually contrasted with the absurdity of the local whites' claim to "White Men's Prestige" and to European culture. The absurdity of white racial prejudice and the oddity of white colonial behaviour are inextricably linked. Campbell's alliance with Plomer inevitably involved a common front against racism. Since the white group mentality was connected to assertions of racial superiority, Campbell's own tastes also made him an opponent of racism. But the bitterness of his feelings towards white South Africans was caused far more by his sense that their cultural taste was an insult to him than by a genuine human interest in black South Africans such as Plomer shows.

In "Poets in Africa" Campbell describes his alliance with Plomer in terms which show both the intensity of his feeling of exclusion and his awareness that the continual insistence on high seriousness brings with it the persona of the angry man:

> We had no time for make-believe
> So early each began
> To wear his liver on his sleeve,
> To snarl, and be an angry man:
> Far in the desert we have been
> Where Nature, still to poets kind,

6. "*Voorslag* Days," pp. 48–49.

Admits no vegetable green
To soften the determined mind,

But with snarled gold and rumbled blue
Must disinfect the sight
Where once the tender maggots grew
Of faith and beauty and delight.
Each with a blister on his tongue,
Each with a crater in his tooth,
Our nerves are fire: we have been stung
By the tarantulas of truth.

[1, 192]

The flaunting of their anger does not affect its intensity, nor does it alter the "truth" of the writer's insight. At another point in the poem they are described as "venomous with truth," and at the same time "true sons of Africa . . . / Though bastardised with culture." This sense of his insight being part of his "indigenous," "wild," and "free" personality is essential to Campbell's concept of his own superior detachment, and one which he elaborates frequently. In "The Making of a Poet," his separation from the herd is described in terms of African wild life:

In every herd there is some restive steer
Who leaps the cows and heads each hot stampede,
Till the old bulls unite in jealous fear
To hunt him from the pastures where they feed.

Lost in the night he hears the jungles crash
And desperately, lest his courage fail,
Across his hollow flanks with sounding lash
Scourges the heavy whipcord of his tail.

[1, 27–8]

His attitude towards the restive steer is surprisingly complex, and shows the real pain underlying his isolation. A sense of despair is as prominent as the sense of the steer's superiority, and the whole poem affords a candid insight into the impetus behind Campbell's satirical attacks of the period.

In "To a Pet Cobra" Campbell again compares himself
to a lonely yet dangerous African creature and again shows
that his hostility arises from fear and "neglect." His fascination with the deadliness of the snake is beautifully vivid.
In his ability to enjoy the experience on "the brink of some
profound abyss," he does embody in the poem a capacity
to pursue experiences which are inaccessible to the mediocre majority of mankind:

> With breath indrawn and every nerve alert,
> As at the brink of some profound abyss,
> I love on my bare arm, capricious flirt,
> To feel the chilly and incisive kiss
> Of your lithe tongue that forks its swift caress
> Between the folded slumber of your fangs,
> And half reveals the nacreous recess
> Where death upon those dainty hinges hangs.
>
> [1, 31]

When he makes the comparison openly between himself
and the cobra, his emphasis is mainly defensive:

> Our lonely lives in every chance agreeing,
> It is no common friendship that you bring,
> It was the desert starved us into being,
> The hate of men that sharpened us to sting:
> Sired by starvation, suckled by neglect,
> Hate was the surly tutor of our youth:
> I too can hiss the hair of men erect
> Because my lips are venomous with truth.
>
> [1, 31]

The extraordinarily violent hostility to the ideas in *Turbott
Wolfe* and *Voorslag* gives a factual basis for Campbell's
claim to hiss the hair of men erect. His well-loved epithet,
"venomous," could easily be applied today by practising
South African politicians to the ideas which he and Plomer
were propagating. The confident assertions in the poem
are balanced by reflective passages which are not assertive,

and the result is not brutal or cruel as C. J. D. Harvey has suggested:[7]

> Dainty one, deadly one, whose folds are panthered
> With stars, my slender Kalihari flower,
> Whose lips with fangs are delicately anthered,
> Whose coils are volted with electric power,
> I love to think how men of my dull nation
> Might spurn your sleep with inadvertent heel
> To kindle up the lithe retaliation
> And caper to the slash of sudden steel.
>
> [1, 32]

In spite of Campbell's obvious delight in the picture of the dull men suddenly being attacked, the attack itself is not gratuitous, but a retaliation against being trod upon by a dull, inadvertent, insentient heel. The fear of being trod upon in a metaphorical sense has informed most of the comparisons between himself and the cobra, whose lithe power does establish a positive beauty and a grace in contrast with the crushing, unthinking tread of a dull nation. His fascination with the precise element in the snake's cruelty, far from being a ghastly secret, is openly part of the poet's reflective honesty.

Campbell's insistent need to express both his loneliness and his scorn for those from whom he felt isolated is a constant feature of the poems written in South Africa. Their success varies. In the best, his personal problem is usually incorporated into a work which captures the elemental strengths and beauties that he associates with *his* Africa. In this way the poet's real affinity for wild life and his ability to describe it with such vivid beauty transform his personal obsessions and yet involve no slackening in

7. After describing as repulsive Campbell's "delight in physical violence and inflicting pain," Harvey quotes a passage from "Estocade" and the final lines from "To a Pet Cobra." He continues to argue that, "although in each case it is the dullness and clumsiness of the victim that is stressed, we cannot simply read the lines as symbolic representations of the fight against dullness and stupidity in general. There is too obviously a real delight in the killing of the bull and the 'capers' of the unfortunate man *[sic]*." ["The Poetry of Roy Campbell," *Standpunte* (October, 1950), p. 54.]

the intensity of his feelings. In "The Albatross" there is no explicit linking of the bird with the poet,[8] but the pain of the bird's collapse when struck by a ship, and its resulting desolation, are elements typical of the openly personal *Adamastor* poems:

> Loose on the gale my shattered wreck was strewn
> And, conquered by the envious winds at last,
> A rag upon the red horns of the moon,
> Was tossed and gored and trampled by the blast.
>
> [1, 33]

The bird's superhuman freedom of movement is implicitly the reason for the "envious" nature of the winds. Its superior vitality and speed are even seen as enabling it to impose its own perspective on the world:

> To the dark ocean I had dealt my laws
> And when the shores rolled by, their speed was mine:
> The ranges moved like long two-handed saws
> Notching the scarlet west with jagged line.
>
> [1, 33]

This concept of the earth as a satellite of the bird's orbit re-appears constantly:

> The globe, revolving like a vast cocoon,
> Unwound its threading leagues at my desire:
> With burning stitches by the sun and moon
> My life was woven like a shawl of fire.
>
> [1, 36]

8. In Baudelaire's poem, "L'Albatros," the poet is likened to the "prince of the clouds" who is an exile and an object of scorn on earth, although capable of rejoicing in the tempest and soaring above the earth which despises him. Baudelaire's last stanza has obvious affinities to Campbell's mood during the *Adamastor* period:

> Le Poëte est semblable au prince des nuées
> Qui hante la tempête et se rit de l'archer;
> Exilé sur le sol au milieu des huées,
> Ses ailes de géant l'empêchent de marcher.
>
> [*Les Fleurs du Mal*]

Throughout the poem the visual brilliance of the imagery is closely connected to the underlying concept of the bird's ecstatic vitality. In the preceding stanza its "sight" and "life" actually enhance the richness of the insentient world:

> Broidering earth's senseless matter with my sight,
> Weaving my life around it like a robe,
> Onward I draw my silken clues of flight.

[1, 36]

The albatross's role of beautification, and its freedom from the dull, mundane life below it, clearly associate the bird with Campbell's own view of himself at the time. But for all the subjective associations between the two, the poem above all evokes the soaring, unrestrained life of a bird.

Campbell identifies himself quite openly with the lonely island in "Tristan da Cunha," but here too the personal element is absorbed into a vivid and controlled evocation of natural force. The poem was written in the period of intense strain during the final crisis over *Voorslag*. William Plomer recalls that it was on July 25, 1926, that Campbell broke with Lewis Reynolds over Maurice Webb's future role in the journal, and that he completed "The Serf" on the night of July 28, and both "The Making of a Poet" and "To a Pet Cobra" on the night of July 31. Plomer goes on to describe the writing of "Tristan da Cunha": "On Thursday, 5th August, I read aloud some passages from a letter addressed to me from Oxford by my schoolfellow, D. R. Gillie. In one of them was a translation of part of Kuhlemann's 'Tristan d'Acunha.' This so enkindled Campbell that he began to write a poem on the same subject. He worked at it all night and brought me the first version just after sunrise. It was not until Saturday, 14th August, that he read me the completed version. He had not in those days the mannered South African accent, and read it so well that I was moved to the verge of tears."[9]

This derivation from Kuhlemann (via an English translation) was sensed at once by T. S. Eliot when the completed

9. "*Voorslag* Days," p. 50. See Appendix for Gillie's translation of Kuhlemann.

poem was published in the *New Statesman* on October 15, 1927. The next week, on October 22, the journal published a letter from him in which he congratulated Campbell on the poem. After praising both the "remarkable" control of metre and the language, which he described as "less flamboyant" than Campbell's earlier work, Eliot pointed to a "curious resemblance—not in detail, but in rhythm and general spirit," to Kuhlemann's little-known poem. He himself, he said, had at one time attempted to translate the poem without success. If Campbell knew German "he might make a very brilliant translation" (p. 44).

The total quality of the creative urge behind "Tristan da Cunha" is obvious from the opening lines, where Campbell's instinctive response to the naturally rugged mingles with echoes of Corbière. The poem is inspired by Kuhlemann and grounded on his own deep feeling of isolation:

> Snore in the foam; the night is vast and blind;
> The blanket of the mist about your shoulders,
> Sleep your old sleep of rock, snore in the wind,
> Snore in the spray! the storm your slumber lulls,
> His wings are folded on your nest of boulders
> As on their eggs the grey wings of your gulls.
>
> [1, 40]

It is to the opening lines of "Au Vieux Roscoff" by Tristan Corbière that Campbell's stanza bears a distinct resemblance. Roscoff is a fishing village in Brittany, and the poem is subtitled "Berceuse en Nord-Ouest mineur," which captures the affectionate tone that is used to describe the sleepy but tough old "nid à corsaires." The first lines show the derivation of Campbell's "Sleep your old sleep of rock":

> Trou de flibustiers, vieux nid
> A corsaires! —dans la tourmente,
> Dors ton bon somme de granit
> Sur tes caves que le flot hante.
>
> [*Les Amours Jaunes*]

The likeness to the opening of "Tristan da Cunha" is even more pronounced in the lines that follow:

> Ronfle à la mer, ronfle à la brise;
> Ta corne dans la brume grise,
> Ton pied marin dans les brisans . . .
> —Dors: tu peux fermer ton oeil borgne
> Ouvert sur le large, et qui lorgne
> Les Anglais, depuis trois cents ans.
> —Dors, vieille coque bien ancrée;
> Les margats et les cormorans,
> Tes grands poètes d'ouragans,
> Viendront chanter à la marée.

These last four lines share only a general mood with Campbell's poem, and there is little in the remainder of "Au Vieux Roscoff" to suggest further links with "Tristan da Cunha."

In spite of Campbell's deliberate identification with the island, the poem is neither introverted nor overassertive. There is enough self-knowledge in the poet's discussion of his alienated state to keep the effect well this side of indulgence:

> Why should you haunt me thus but that I know
> My surly heart is in your own displayed,
> Round whom such leagues in endless circuit flow,
> Whose hours in such a gloomy compass run—
> A dial with its league-long arm of shade
> Slowly revolving to the moon and sun.
>
> [1, 41]

The statement about his isolation is not made as a flamboyant Byronic gesture; his recognition that his heart is "surly" is typical of the self-awareness which continually establishes a sense of proportion. In particular, his own pain is always a part of the comparisons between his situation and that of the island, even when the predominant effects of the verse are to depict a massive tidal struggle:

Exiled like you and severed from my race
By the cold ocean of my own disdain,
Do I not freeze in such a wintry space,
Do I not travel through a storm as vast
And rise at times, victorious from the main,
To fly the sunrise at my shattered mast?

                                                                [1, 42]

The Byronic posture is adopted with assurance, but his
pain and distress are realized with the same rhetorical conviction as his heroic defiance. Unlike Byron, who often
strikes a self-pitying note in passages from *Childe Harold*
where he adopts a similar persona ("and move / In hearts
all rocky now the late remorse of love"), Campbell shows
no desire to be liked by the people he scorns. The estrangement causes him pain, but his self-reliant reaction has an
inexorable self-sufficiency.

When there is no direct comparison between the poet
and an African environment, there is still a remarkably intense, sensuous richness in the African poems. The "delight" Campbell associates with untamed vitality of any
kind is a corollary to his feeling of being trapped and con-
fined by the mediocrity and smugness of the society in
which he found himself. In "The Zebras" he describes a
stallion as an "engine of beauty volted with delight," and
pictures the flawlessly athletic herd in a natural harmony
with the universe beyond them as they "draw the dawn
across the plains." A delight similar to that generated by
both the creatures' rhythmic beauty and their spontaneous
sensuality informs "The Sisters," where two girls on an early
morning ride are shown in harmonious interaction with
their African environment. The reason for the girls' naked
ride is that "after hot loveless nights" they are "Bored with
the foolish things that girls must dream / Because their
beds are empty of delight." Their repressed sensuality
gives the whole poem a sense of illicit excitement. In the
final lines the visual impression of their naked bodies silhouetted against the dawn is fused with the concept of
their organic relation to the universe beyond them, as "The

day burns through their blood / Like a white candle
through a shuttered hand."

The primitive vitality of the native African population
interests Campbell remarkably little in *Adamastor*, and
when he does depict black African sensuousness he creates
much more a sense of threat than one of delight. In "The
Serf" the insulted and outcast status of a black ploughman
is shown to be potentially hazardous in that he "moves the
nearest to the naked earth/And ploughs down palaces, and
thrones, and towers." In "The Zulu Girl" this explicit threat
is made an implicit, menacing undertone, while the predominant effect is of the physical vitality which makes the
serf so latently dangerous. From its opening line the poem
embodies a harsh, unrelieved violence:

> When in the sun the hot red acres smoulder,
> Down where the sweating gang its labour plies,
> A girl flings down her hoe, and from her shoulder
> Unslings her child tormented by the flies.
>
> She takes him to a ring of shadow pooled
> By thorn-trees: purpled with the blood of ticks,
> While her sharp nails, in slow caresses ruled,
> Prowl through his hair with sharp electric clicks.
>
> [1, 30]

Unlike the harmonious interaction of "The Sisters" or "The
Zebras," the relation between human emotions and African environment reflects the smouldering discomfort of
the whole scene, where caresses "prowl." The Zulu girl
herself is peculiarly inscrutable and faceless in her actions,
while the animality of her child is another part of the untamed quality in the lines. The sensuous values of a people
bred in the sun, and living close to the earth are beautifully
suggested in Campbell's description of the relation between mother, child, and setting, but he is viewing them as
distinctly foreign:

> His sleepy mouth plugged by the heavy nipple,
> Tugs like a puppy, grunting as he feeds:

Through his frail nerves her own deep languors ripple
Like a broad river sighing through its reeds.

Yet in that drowsy stream his flesh imbibes
An old unquenched unsmotherable heat—
The curbed ferocity of beaten tribes,
The sullen dignity of their defeat.

Her body looms above him like a hill
Within whose shade a village lies at rest,
Or the first cloud so terrible and still
That bears the coming harvest in its breast.

                                                            [1, 30–31]

A contrast between the peace of the child and the menacing overtones of his mother's "looming body" is typical of
the juxtaposition of violence and tranquillity throughout
the poem, just as the stormy quality of the "harvest" is
profoundly chilling.

The sensuality rippling under the surface of the poem
is a feature of the massive female body of the last stanza,
where the image of the child asleep beneath the woman's
breasts like a village nestling against a hill is derived directly from Baudelaire's poem "La Géante." There it is the
culmination of a sensual fantasy that the poet begins by
saying:

Du temps que la Nature en sa verve puissante
Concevait chaque jour des enfants monstrueux,
J'eusse aimé vivre auprès d'une jeune géante,
Comme aux pieds d'une reine un chat voluptueux.
                                        [Les Fleurs du Mal]

The primitive quality of the giantess is intimately connected to a whole experience of voluptuousness in the
lines, and this mood exactly suits Campbell's poem on a
totally different subject. In Baudelaire's poem it is the
breasts of the giantess which throw the shade. In Campbell's it is the girl's "body," but the fact that she has been
suckling her child shows how totally he has assimilated the
mood of "La Géante":

[J'eusse aimé] Parcourir à loisir ses magnifiques formes;
Ramper sur le versant de ses genoux énormes,
Et parfois en été, quand les soleils malsains,
Lasse, la font s'étendre à travers la campagne,
Dormir nonchalamment à l'ombre de ses seins,
Comme un hameau paisible au pied d'une montagne.

An easy absorption into his poem of the Baudelairean images that suit him is typical of the total quality of his creative reaction at this time. His reading, his experiences, and his writings are all fused in the same process. His stanza describing the killing of the ticks has a similar general resemblance to Rimbaud's "Les Chercheuses de poux," and also has one directly derived image in the description of the electric clicks of the searching nails.

Il entend leurs cils noirs battant sous les silences
Parfumés; et leurs doigts électriques et doux
Font crépiter parmi ses grises indolences
Sous leurs ongles royaux la mort des petits poux.
                                                    [Oeuvres]

Descriptions of instinctive grace or vitality in African wildlife reflect only one side of Campbell's uneasiness in Natal. His scorn for the norms of the society from which he feels excluded, together with his instinct for combat, also lead him to satire. William Plomer describes how total his reaction was against South African society and how it was anything but an artistic pose: "Although high-spirited, he was in a state of constant nervous tension, which he called neurasthenia. He seemed much affected by the death of his father, but much more persistently by his environment. His native land had got on his nerves. 'The whole of this country,' he said one day, 'has an acid smell, and all the white people have khaki faces.' "[10] The intensely subjective feeling of rejection which informs the lyrical poems in *Adamastor* is not, however, so prominent a feature of Campbell's satires on South African life and standards. Of the satirical works the most sustained is *The Wayzgoose*.

10. "*Voorslag* Days," p. 51.

Its lighthearted and good-humoured tone does not deprive it of sting, but its romping quality does, for the most part, eliminate rancour, even though he uses the poem to settle personal scores. It is the personal element which limits its range. The colonial smugness which he despises is well captured in *The Wayzgoose,* but few of the follies which he lampoons are made to transcend their specific place in the description of Banana Land malaise.

The imaginary picnic-meeting of journalists and writers, the Wayzgoose, gives him an opportunity to ridicule the journalists who had attacked him and Plomer. The editor who is most often singled out for ridicule is H. H. Wodson of the *Natal Advertiser.* Laurens van der Post describes Wodson as in many ways an enlightened and competent editor, who strove for high standards of journalism.[11] He had employed van der Post himself, an Afrikaans youth from the backveld, in the face of a near mutiny from his proudly British staff. *Turbott Wolfe* had infuriated Wodson as an example of moral degeneracy (he had given it to van der Post to read as an indication of "what the modern world is coming to"), and he attacked it in his columns. His entrenched opposition to Plomer naturally led to scorn from Campbell, and in his attacks on the editor the poet is often only redressing the balance against a powerful and outspoken enemy. *Voorslag* provides two other objects of attack in *The Wayzgoose*: Edward Roworth, the artist who contributed articles on art to the magazine, and Maurice Webb. Webb's intellectual fads and his Fabianism are easy targets for Campbell, whose resentment was aggravated by Lewis Reynolds's attempt to make Webb managing editor. Webb's editorial experience consisted in having edited a Durban business directory, and in *The Wayzgoose* Campbell has him, as Jubb, winning the Eisteddfod "in honour of the Drowsy God" by surpassing all others in dreariness as he reads from his directory.

The whole ironic praise of dullness in Campbell's poem is obviously derived from *The Dunciad,* just as the Natal

11. Laurens van der Post, *Turbott Wolfe,* Introduction, pp. 16–20.

"Eisteddfod" is imitative of Pope's competition, in book two, of the critics' patience in hearing, without falling asleep, two authors reading their works aloud. These derivations and borrowings, made as openly as they are, in no way affect the quality of *The Wayzgoose*, which is not an attempt at serious satire. The good humour and zest of the poem are the most appealing features of its rollicking exposure of specific colonial fads. The buffoons are clearly buffoons, and their buffooneries obviously absurd and trifling:

> Polybius Jubb, in thy kind self I see
> The anagram of what a man should be,
> So versatile thy Webb-like mind is spun
> Thou jack-of-all-arts, but thou Lord of None!
> See how thy various talents fully blown
> Perform all other functions save their own:
> A Socialist thou art in thought and act,
> And yet thy business flourishes intact:
> A Boss in trade, thou art securely placed,
> And only art a Bolshevik in taste.
>
> [1, 261]

A Webb-like mind is exposed as inconsistent and insincere, and to this extent the general values of commonsense and consistency do inform the passage. Its lightness of touch, however, and obviously personal motivation are the predominant impressions.

The same kind of glee is used to capture the ponderousness of one of General Smuts's philosophic statements, that "behind the button there is a great story which Science has not yet discovered."[12] As the propounder of the philosophic theory of Holism, Smuts offered a target for one of Campbell's most famous puns:

> Full high in anticlimax he could soar
> And probe "behind the button" Nature's lore!
> Forgive me, Statesman, that I have purloined
> This deathless phrase by thine own genius coined,

12. *Voorslag*, no. 1 (June, 1926), p. 15.

Seek on, "Behind the BUTTON," in the Void—
Until you come upon the works of Freud!
Statesman-philosopher! I shake thy hand—
All tailors envy thee throughout the land
Whose BUTTON-HOLISM, without reverse,
Undoes the Trousers of the Universe!
Long be thy wisdom honoured, and thy race
Renowned for flinging smuts in "Beauty's" face!

[1, 257]

All his energies are channelled into playfulness of this sort
in *The Wayzgoose.* A controlled commonsense, which
underlies the fast-moving and lighthearted flow of the lam-
pooning, is responsible for the tone of amused superiority
which he consistently maintains. The stronger the sense of
detachment, the more witty are the sallies, and the urbane
understanding which the poet can achieve is at its best
when used to highlight the oddity of colonial standards.
Provincial earnestness is the butt of much of his humour:

Colonial grace on all her motions hung
And wit colonial tittered on her tongue—
She seemed, as there She tossed her wanton curls,
The prototype of all colonial girls,
For like a V upturned, stork-like and thin,
Her long straight legs forked downward from her chin;
Had there been room for one to intervene,
Her body like a goitre would have been—
But what of that? Colonial poets tell
That beauty only in the Soul can dwell.

[1, 263]

Because he attacks provincial stolidity so consistently,
Campbell is most effective when he is least assertive or
earnest himself. Passages in which intellectual dullness is
contrasted with "wit the irreverent, wit, the profane," or in
which the poet asserts his own international status ("My
words, O Durban, round the world are blown/Where I,
alone, of all your sons am known") are typical of his forthright poetic manner, but are not damning as satire. In contrast, lines which do not reveal the fierceness of the poet's

indignation can often present colonial folly with devastating poise, as in this passage from "A Veld Eclogue: The Pioneers":

> For all our scenery's in grander style
> And there are far more furlongs to the mile
> In Africa than Europe—though, no doubt
> None but colonials have found this out.
> For though our Drakensberg's most lofty scalps
> Would scarcely reach the waist-line of the Alps,
> Though Winterberg, beside the Pyrenees,
> Would scarcely reach on tip-toe to their knees,
> Nobody can deny that our hills rise
> Far more majestically—for their size!
> I mean that there is something grander, yes,
> About the veld, than I can well express,
> Something more vast—perhaps I don't mean that—
> Something more round, and square, and steep, and
>   flat—
> No, well perhaps it's not quite that I mean
> But something, rather, half-way in between,
> Something more "nameless"—That's the very word!
>   [1, 25]

At moments like this Campbell has digested the whole experience of his clash with South African standards, and the urbanity of his reaction here is an element in the work of this period which is easily overlooked. The better-known poems of isolation and disgust are more strident and more intense, but he can absorb his feelings of claustrophobia, and ridicule South African foibles with consummate unconcern.

Indignation itself is used effectively, but not in his satires. When he is not trying to force his own superiority on the reader, his disgust can be a convincing part of an intensely personal reaction. "In the Town Square" is such a poem, in which he describes the insidiously crippling effect of the local malaise as he contemplates Durban's main square with its cenotaph in blue and white marble, where the "blue-burnished angels settle/Like flies upon a slab of tripe":

> The Town slept on. So cheaply fine
> Its walls embalmed its festered soul—
> But far along the sky's red line
> There seemed a quiet mist to roll,
>
> The soul of Africa, the grey
> Hushed emanation of her hills,
> The drowsy poison of her day,
> The hand that fondles while it kills,
>
> The subtle anaesthetic breath,
> The vengeful sting that gives no pain
> But deals around it worse than death
> The palsied soul, the mildewed brain.
>   [1 ,188]

The cold-blooded tone with which the condemnation is made gives it a conviction which is totally damning. Not only does the poem convincingly suggest the civic vulgarity of a provincial city. It gives remarkably vivid expression to Campbell's peculiarly intense reaction against the town of his birth and the inertia for which it is well known.[13] His old affection is still a part of the horror of his new attitude, and the African aura "fondles while it kills."

The conflict of emotions caused by his return to South Africa led to one of the most creative periods of Campbell's life and confirmed him in a role of outsider. Any danger of his persona's becoming stultifying was still only a theoretic possibility, however, while his lyrical poems were unquestionably impressive. His symbolic farewell, "Rounding the Cape," illustrates the strength which derives from a combination of his rhetorical skill and intense emotional reactions. The poem crystallizes the complexities in his decision to leave Africa by describing its grim splendour together with his own distaste at the thoughtlessness which he associates with southern Africa.

> The low sun whitens on the flying squalls,
> Against the cliffs the long grey surge is rolled

13. "Natal fever" is a term used in South Africa to describe laziness induced by the subtropical climate.

> Where Adamastor from his marble halls
> Threatens the sons of Lusus as of old.
>
> [1, 27]

Adamastor is the visionary Spirit of the Cape who appears to Vasco da Gama and his sons of Lusus, The Lusiades or descendants of the mythical founder of Portugal, in canto five of *The Lusiads* by Luís de Camões. In the epic, Adamastor, the embodiment of the craggy Cape of Storms, warns Vasco da Gama of the dangers awaiting the future violators of his territory and seas. This warning to the future conquistadores is, of course, so similar to Campbell's own attitude towards the colonials of his day that it is implied in the title of his volume. In the closing stanzas of "Rounding the Cape" the Spirit of the Cape and its physical embodiment in the promontory itself are fused:

> Farewell, terrific shade! though I go free
> Still of the powers of darkness art thou Lord:
> I watch the phantom sinking in the sea
> Of all that I have hated or adored.
>
> [1, 27]

The insistence of the central theme in the *Adamastor* poems, the insight deriving from isolation and hardship, tends to conceal the wit and urbanity of many poems included in the volume. Although the recurrent themes are seldom repetitious in any one poem, they do lead to a suggestion of sameness in the collection as a whole. When the similarity of theme is coupled with a repetition of imagery in different poems, the hint of an obsessive recurrence of mood and content is strengthened. This general defect in the early poems is slight, however, in contrast with the poetic strength which the collection shows. Campbell's feeling of rejection can lead him into occasionally empty posturing. The creative drive which results from his intense struggle to find emotional equilibrium is, on the other hand, the impetus behind his most famous lyrical poems. In them the intensity of the poet's problem is transmuted into a lyrical intensity that shows his poetic gift at its most distinctively personal and its most compelling.

CHAPTER 3

GEORGIAN INTERLUDE

The Campbells did not have much money when they returned to England in 1927. After living for short periods in cottages lent to them by other writers, they were invited to stay in a bungalow owned by Sir Harold Nicolson and his wife, Victoria Sackville-West, at Long Barn in Kent. Campbell's attack in *The Georgiad* on literary society grows directly out of his unhappiness in Kent, where he felt his own manly virtues threatened by the decorum of a literary coterie which tacitly accepted coterie values. Once again he found himself an alien, but this time the prospects of finding a group in which he would not be an outsider were becoming more remote.

During this period he was writing regularly for the *New Statesman*. Many of the poems later published in *Adamastor* appeared in that journal between 1927 and 1930, and several reviews by him appeared during the same period. Prominent among the reviews he wrote for the *New Statesman* were those on *Time and Western Man* by Wyndham

Lewis and *Paleface* by the same author. It is clear that Campbell's friendship with Lewis and his affinity for Lewis's views qualified him as the *New Statesman* "Wyndham Lewis man," and it is probably for this reason he was given *The Apes of God* to review in 1930. The anger with which he reacted to the rejection of the review led to his first public clash with the Left (in the form of the *New Statesman*), and it is significant that Wyndham Lewis figured prominently in the clash. Lewis's insistence in *The Art of Being Ruled* (1926) and *Time and Western Man* (1927) on the conformism and herd instinct of contemporary life delighted Campbell, who had expressed similar views in *Voorslag*. Lewis's analyses of prejudice in political and artistic attitudes had a lasting influence on the young poet, and the two writers constantly supported each other. Campbell's "Albatross," which had first appeared in *Voorslag* (no. 1), reappeared in Wyndham Lewis's pamphlet, *The Enemy* (no. 3, 1929), a journal with surprisingly similar aims to those of the equally aggressive *Voorslag*.

Campbell's sojourn in Kent was not to his taste, and in 1928 he left England to settle with his family at Martigues in Bouches-du-Rhône in Provence. In the same year his salvo against South African culture was fired when *The Wayzgoose* was published in England. His next volumes appeared while he was still living at Martigues. Both *Adamastor* and the less well-known *Poems* were published in 1930. *Adamastor* received an enthusiastic reception, and although *Poems* is not well remembered now, Campbell's reputation was such that the volume was fully subscribed before its publication by Nancy Cunard from her Hours Press in Paris. In the same year his quarrel with the *New Statesman* over the rejection of his review burst into the open with the publication of Wyndham Lewis's pamphlet, *Satire and Fiction*. Campbell had been asked by Clifford Sharp to review *The Apes of God*, but when the review was submitted, the new literary editor, R. Ellis Roberts, rejected it with a lengthy letter of explanation, saying, "I find you take a far more serious view of its merits than I can, & indeed take Mr. Lewis altogether more seriously than I think is justifiable. I might wink at this from so vehement a contributor as you, but. . . ." After explaining that his "serious complaint against the notice" is that Campbell ignores Lewis's "obvious lack of composition," Ellis Roberts concludes, "I cannot reconcile it with my sense of what is [sic] an editor's duties to insert anything which gravely controverts my own views on literature."[1] True to his "Zulu" image, Campbell reacted hotly; he told Ellis Roberts to go to hell. Quite apart from the merits of The Apes of God, a feature which makes Ellis Roberts's rejection all the more whimsical is the fact that he himself reviewed the book favourably in the New Statesman of August 16, 1930, saying, "The Apes of God is not only a novel; it is, in spite of some lapses in proportion, a brilliant novel" (pp. 597–98).[2] Campbell wrote to Lewis explaining that his review had been rejected and that he intended publishing a pamphlet on the subject under the title "A Rejected Review." Lewis asked him to join in the publication of Satire and Fiction, which Lewis published himself through his own "Arthur Press": it included Campbell's letter to Lewis as well as Ellis Roberts's letter, the review itself, and a "Reviewer's Preface" by Campbell.

The tension caused by Satire and Fiction in 1930 was not allayed when, in the following year, Campbell eventually published his satire, The Georgiad. His attack on coterie values and morals in the literary world owes much to The Apes of God, although deriving from his experience in Kent. After its publication Campbell was no longer regarded as an acceptable topic. The New Statesman, which had published long and enthusiastic reviews of The Flaming Terrapin and Adamastor, only mentioned The Georgiad in its column, "Brevities on Books," on November 14, 1931. The entire notice, which is quoted here, embodies English

1. Wyndham Lewis, Satire and Fiction, pp. 10–12.
2. The favourable quality of this review prompted Augustus John to write to Lewis: "I read Ellis Roberts' review of The Apes in the N.S. Like most of your press, it was almost completely eulogistic and I think Roy Campbell's flurry rather unnecessary . . . just imagine our cumbersome and overcharged poet in the BULL RING! (at Nimes) farting a volley of epithets as he vaults to safety. Quelle blague!" Lewis replied, "It was a good thing that I had a pugnacious matador (a credit to the Camargue) to take up the banderillo for me! Vive le Roy!" [Lewis, Letters, p. 194]

pique at its most absurdly dignified: "The omelette of satire cannot be made without breaking eggs; but Mr. Campbell is mistaken in thinking that it is enough to throw rather ancient eggs at distant objects, and then tease them a little. The result is that dismal dish, cold scrambled eggs" (p. 620). As the reviewer in the *Times Literary Supplement* was to comment in 1950, when speaking of *The Georgiad* in *Collected Poems* (vol. 1), "It was unpardonable; but it was also undeniably funny. And what was the immediate response? From the public, laughter, mingled with some indignation: from the victims, a conspiracy of silence, a stiffening of the upper literary lip. On behalf of literary gaiety one could wish that it had been otherwise—that some merciless, retaliating pen had found some appropriate theme to embroider: the screaming inferiority-complex of the 'Colonial,' perhaps."[3]

One of the "victims" did reply. In the *New Statesman* of June 27, 1931, Humbert Wolfe published his own satirical poem, "The Ranciad," which, although not in the same class as *The Georgiad,* did make pertinent jibes at Campbell's style:

> ... Have I not also strayed
> by the Pierian spring, disgusting Maid,
> and spat into the waters to ensure,
> whatever else they are, they shan't be pure?
> Am I not willing with the rest to sneer
> at what in secret I respect and fear?
> Ready with the sycophantic awe to flinch
> at anything that's written by the French,
> particularly if it apes the stutter
> of a dead rat decaying in the gutter?
> . . . .
> or like the comic juggler of the Halls
> toss in the air my vision's coloured balls,
> and, when they crash, anticipate with vigour
> the crowd by teaching them myself to snigger.
> Or call upon me in a reckless hurry
> to do the utmost violence to Murray,

3. *TLS* (March 24, 1950), p. 184.

> and you shall find in me (I swear) the man to
> invent a new gorilla Esperanto,
> which, scorning English, with a jungle sound
> salts, as it causes, reason's hopeless wound.
> Nor will I stop at that. My Muse shall curb
> the native insolence of noun and verb,
> seeking that happiest of all conditions
> when verse is one long string of prepositions.

Victoria Sackville-West, who was treated most savagely in *The Georgiad,* made an oblique reply in *Life and Letters,* April 1931, when she published a curious essay called "The Poet." In it she describes meeting a romantic and exotic young poet with wild eyes. The poet claims that, "He never read poetry nowadays, . . . for fear of being influenced, though, of course, he had read through the whole of English literature in his early youth" (p. 262). He dies of consumption, and on going through his papers, the writer finds that he has written nothing but copies and imitations of famous English poems.

In attacking well-known literary figures, Campbell was not delivering a new challenge. Since the end of the First World War there had been constant tribal skirmishing among "progressive" and "conservative" poets. *The Georgiad* was a latecomer on the field. In 1919 Harold Monro launched his new periodical, *The Chapbook,* with a series of parties above the Poetry Bookshop, at which, according to Douglas Goldring, "warfare between the Left Wing literary rebels and the 'stuffed shirts' of the Establishment, who had formed themselves into a racket and controlled most of the post-war reviewing was carried on with enormous gusto."[4] The "warfare" was conducted mainly between the allies and opponents of the anthology *Georgian Poetry.* *Georgian Poetry* had been founded by Edward Marsh in 1912 to give to poetry a publicity and standing which seemed to be denied it at the time. The editor used his anthology to present serious work which might otherwise have remained inaccessible. He and his supporters were hostile to Victorian and Edwardian sentimentality. Their

4. Douglas Goldring, *The Nineteen Twenties,* p. 153.

emphasis on detachment and on the real was part of the
revolt against late nineteenth-century taste, which modernist writers such as Hulme, Pound, and Wyndham Lewis
were also conducting at much the same time. With the
war, however, the change in values and sensibilities began
to leave *Georgian Poetry* in limbo. Edward Marsh's own
distrust of experimentation and his hatred of "obscurity"
made him appear increasingly conservative in a world in
which old orders and codes were toppling. As early as
1918 T. S. Eliot attacked the poetry in the third volume as
"inbred" and said it had "developed a technique and a set
of emotions all of its own."[5] Even the reviewer in the *Times
Literary Supplement* pointed out that in *Georgian Poetry*
III, "there is nothing in the poetry of our young writers to
alarm or distress the most conservative. Not only youth,
but example and, more than either, new conditions of life
might offer them the excuse for impatient rejection of the
established and for the playing of all sorts of pranks. . . .
And what they are found for the most part to be doing is
pouring their new wine into the old bottles."[6] By the time
the fourth volume appeared in 1919, hostility was wide-
spread, and Middleton Murry, in the *Athenaeum,* began
a series of damaging articles about its standards.[7] Marsh's

5. *Egoist* V (March, 1918), p. 43. The review is signed "Apteryx,"
Eliot's pseudonym.

6. *TLS* (December 27, 1917), p. 646.

7. Murry's best-known comments on *Georgian Poetry* came in a
review of both *Georgian Poetry 1918–1919* (fourth volume) and *Wheels*
Fourth Cycle. First published in the *Athenaeum* in December, 1919, the
review was reprinted in 1920 as "The Present Condition of English
Poetry" in Murry's *Aspects of Literature.* "*Georgian Poetry,*" he writes, "is
like the Coalition Government; *Wheels* is like the Radical opposition.
Out of the one there issues an indefinable odour of complacent sanctity, an unctuous redolence of *union sacrée*; out of the other some acid-
ulation of perversity." He identifies "the corporate flavour" of the
coalition as "false simplicity" (while excepting "absolutely" Walter de la
Mare, W. H. Davies and D. H. Lawrence), and characterizes the "corporate flavour" of the opposition as "false sophistication." He concludes
with a tribute to Wilfred Owen's "Strange Meeting," which had been
published in *Wheels*: "You will find in 'Strange Meeting' an awe, an im-
mensity, an adequacy to that which has been most profound in the
experience of a generation. You will, finally, have the standard that
has been lost, and the losing of which makes the confusion of a book
like *Georgian Poetry* possible, restored to you" (pp. 139–49).

taste as compiler of the anthology was as much under fire
as was the verse of the poets who appeared in it. In his prefatory note to the final volume, *Georgian Poetry 1920–
1922*, he defended his critical principles with an open
challenge to the "modern":

> I may add one word bearing on my aim in selection.
> Much admired modern work seems to me, in its lack
> of inspiration and its disregard of form, like gravy imi-
> tating lava. Its upholders may retort that much of the
> work which I prefer seems to them, in its lack of in-
> spiration and its comparative finish, like tapioca imitat-
> ing pearls. Either view—possibly both—may be right.
> I will only say that with an occasional exception for
> some piece of rebelliousness or even levity which may
> have taken my fancy, I have tried to choose no verse
> but such as in Wordsworth's phrase
>
> > The high and tender Muses shall accept
> > With gracious smile, deliberately pleased.

Experimental poets had been forming coteries of their
own during this period. In 1916 Edith Sitwell launched her
anthology, *Wheels,* in which members of her family and
other young poets displayed their avant-garde talents.
Wheels set out to shock the complacent and conventional
with a flippant, glossy parade. Work by its contributors
also appeared in *Art and Letters,* of which Osbert Sitwell
became editor in 1919. The Oxford journal, *Coterie,* which
ran from May 1919 to winter 1920–21, also included poetry
by the *Wheels* group, and was, as a result, a target for conservative criticism. It was with the poetic standards and
ideas of *Wheels* that Campbell instinctively allied himself
after going up to Oxford in 1919. Work by T. W. Earp
appeared in *Coterie,* and five poems by Campbell appeared in the same journal. These poems have not been
anthologized. There were two ("Gigue Macabre" and
"Bongwi the Baboon") in the fourth number published in
Easter 1920, and three ("Canal," "The Head," and "The
Sleepers") in the final "Xmas Double Number," 1920–21.

In a letter from Oxford to his father, Campbell describes his attitude towards *Wheels:*

> Art is not developed by a lot of long-haired fools in velvet jackets. It develops itself and pulls these fools wherever it wants them to go. It reacts more thoroughly and easily than the most sensitive artist in the world. . . .
>
> The Georgians, those who in the reign of George V (in the age of machinery, and probably one of the most important stages in the history of our evolution) persist in groping amongst the dust of ancient folios for what they write. They are treading the same ground that was trodden by the Elizabethans, 400 years ago—and they are not treading it half so well. What is their importance? If a man wants to read that style of work he will surely read Ben Jonson or Marlowe. So it is pretty certain that our Georgian friends will fizzle out pretty soon.
>
> The last school is that of very young people like Rickword and myself. We have had the shell broken for us by futurism. We accept *Wheels* as a very necessary but badly written hypothesis on which to work our theorems. We apply our work closely to the life that goes on around us.[8]

As late as 1926, while lecturing on "Modern Poetry and Contemporary History" in South Africa, Campbell mentions *Wheels* as the journal which every young poet should read. His early alliance with Rickword, Earp, the Sitwells, and Wyndham Lewis placed him naturally in the avant-garde, and therefore in a camp hostile to the group of writer/critics who upheld the values of *Georgian Poetry* IV and V. J. C. Squire was the main target. One of the most influential critics of the period, he had begun his career in journalism as the literary editor of the *New Statesman,* and after the war had founded the conservative *London Mercury.* In its columns he attacked the *Wheels* group consistently and vigorously, while at the same time champion-

8. Ethel Campbell, *Sam Campbell: A Story of Natal,* p. 355.

ing those writers who appeared in the last volumes of *Georgian Poetry*. His own verse was first included in the third volume of 1917.[9] In his capacity as editor, critic, and poet, he gathered about him a following of poets and reviewers against whom many younger writers reacted. By its extensive influence over what was said in reviews, the cluster was seen as a threat to public acceptance of new work by other writers. Osbert Sitwell had attacked the Squirearchy in 1921 in his pamphlet, *Who Killed Cock Robin?* And Campbell incorporated many of those ideas into his own criticisms of Georgian poetry in *Voorslag*. In September 1922 Osbert Sitwell's next blow fell when *The Chapbook* published his "Mime-Drama, with copious notes by the Author: The Jolly Old Squire or Way-Down in Georgia." And once again many of his stage-props[10] reappear in a similar attack by Campbell—this time in *The Georgiad*.

In *The Georgiad* he does not merely carry on an old battle against Georgian poets and reviewers, however. His assault on Bloomsbury vices belongs to a newer squabble. The cult of youth, and the sexual perversions of polite literary society (which are ridiculed in the poem) had been exhaustively exposed by Wyndham Lewis in *The Apes of God*. Campbell's satire on Georgian literary society is far less extensive than Lewis's demolition of the preciosity and perversion which he saw in the literary establishment around him. The scorn for "social" literary groups and their artistic chitchat informs both Lewis's and Campbell's work, as does the underlying fear that literary or social cliques

9. Robert H. Ross, in his detailed study of *Georgian Poetry*, argues convincingly that the third volume represents a turning point in the history of the anthology. Once the work of Squire, W. J. Turner, and John Freeman had been included, the influence of the "Neo-Georgians" became increasingly dominant: "In leading *Georgian Poetry* down the path of the moonlit, exotic jungle the Neo-Georgians were beginning to force the anthology into a cul de sac. Already by late 1917 their misty escape poetry was an anachronism, but within the next five years it was to become even more obviously out of step with the age it lived in." [*The Georgian Revolt 1910–1922: Rise and Fall of a Poetic Ideal*, p. 165.]

10. Sitwell ridicules the Squirearchy "Press-Gang," lists "A Goddess: Mediocrity" among his dramatis personae, singles out Squire's "The Rugger-Match," and sneers at the Hawthornden Prize.

lead to uniformity and mediocrity. Campbell's boisterous sallies against Bloomsbury cults, however, are not based on the carefully observed analysis of attitudes, mannerisms, and beliefs which informs Wyndham Lewis's encyclopaedic discussion in *The Apes*. Similarly Campbell does not attempt the ideological discussion of artistic malaise which Lewis presents through the mouthpiece of Pierpoint in his novel. Campbell's satire is directed against only a part of the Georgian literary world: the writers and reviewers of poetry, and the literary hostess and her circle with whom Campbell makes it clear he was personally familiar.

The writers whom Campbell attacks as representative of late Georgian values are Squire himself and Humbert Wolfe, poet, lampoonist, reviewer for the *Saturday Review*, and author of numerous critical essays. Wolfe's work during the war in the Ministry of Munitions and his prominent role in the civil service after the war gave his status as a writer a tinge of that middle-class amateurism which is the butt of so much of the scorn of Lewis and Campbell. Desmond MacCarthy is mentioned in the poem as a typical reviewer, and his own journal, *Life and Letters,* appears in Campbell's parody as *Love and Letters,* although Campbell begrudgingly admits he is "not a bad old fellow in the end." Other reviewers who come under Campbell's lash are Arnold Bennett, who wrote for the *Evening Standard*, and Harold Nicolson, who joined the staff of the *Evening Standard* in 1930, after retiring from the diplomatic service. Later he became a reviewer on the *Daily Express,* and had praised *Adamastor,* declaring of Campbell, "I like him and admire him immensely." Nicolson and his wife, Victoria Sackville-West, were friendly with many literary figures in the fashionable Bloomsbury world. While living at Long Barn, Victoria Sackville-West had published her volume of "British Georgics," *The Land,* which won the Hawthornden Prize in 1927. The title of "Georgiana," which Campbell bestows on her, plays upon the "georgic" associations of her prize-winning poem, and in addition suggests that she is the epitome of the literary/social Georgian hostess.

The Nicolsons had been hosts to the Campbells in 1927, when the poet and his family lived in the bungalow on

their property in Kent. By setting *The Georgiad* for the most
part in "Georgiana's Summer School of Love," he makes
his satire a personal and intimate attack on attitudes and
values which he could claim to know from the inside. The
poem is loosely shaped around the visit of the hermaphro-
ditic hero, Androgyno, to Georgiana's "hostel." There
Georgiana herself is violently attracted to him, but is unable to cope with his amorous exuberance, which horrifies
the whole Georgian household. The opening description
of the hostel shows the pointed nature of Campbell's
attack, and at the same time the comic gaiety which is his
own distinctive satiric gift:

> But now the knives and forks are cleared away
> My wanton muse, continuing the day,
> Summons, from Venus' grove, a moulted dove
> To Georgiana's Summer School of Love.
> Like some Y.M. and W.C.A.
> It welcomes waifs whom love has cast away—
> A sort of Hostel where we seem to feel
> The earnest pulsing of some high ideal—
> "Be your own Shakespeare. Step it with the fashion.
> Broadcast your love and Pelmanise your Passion.
> Our short-cut to the Passions and the Arts—
> A correspondence course in seven parts—
> Try it! We sterilise our Cupid's darts.
> Up-to-date methods: breezy situation:
> And only twenty minutes from the station."
>
> [1, 207–8]

Victoria Sackville-West's poem, which is itself typical
of what Campbell dislikes in Georgian poetry, is ridiculed
by him with much the same vigour. The opening lines of
The Land clearly suggest the exaltation of the ordinary
which is so distasteful to him:

> I sing the cycle of my country's year,
> I sing the tillage, and the reaping sing,
> Classic monotony . . .
>
> · · · · · · · · · · · · · · · ·

> I sing once more
> The mild continuous epic of the soil,
> Haysel and harvest, tilth and husbandry:
> I tell of marl and dung, and of the means
> That break the unkindly spirit of the clay;
> I tell the things I know, the things I knew
> Before I knew them, immemorially;
> And as the fieldsman of unhurrying tread
> Trudges with steady and unchanging gait,
> Being born to clays that in the winter hold,
> So my pedestrian measure gravely plods,
> Telling a loutish life.

Such an author's attitude embodies the upper-middle-class, county sense of decorum and false modesty that he attacks as leading in life to uniformity and a lack of any distinction. This "tweedy" quality in the easy, prosaic flow of *The Land* could not but irritate a poet of Campbell's incisive and colourful talent, and his sneers at the poem are made with accuracy and wit:

> Sing but of country joys and you shall rise,
> Praised by the world, from prize to golden prize:
> Now to the soil address your bumpkin Muse,
> To some old rick declaim your billets-doux:
> Or drive, slow trudging down some boggy road
> Your Clydesdale Pegasus with creaking load.
>
> [1, 229]

Robert Graves and Laura Riding, the couple whose co-operation in critical writing is attacked at the opening of *The Georgiad*, do not fit into the world which Campbell satirizes. The two critical works which they had written together before the publication of *The Georgiad* were *A Survey of Modernist Poetry*, published in 1927, and *A Pamphlet Against Anthologies*, published in 1928. The seriousness of their views and the intelligence of their attempt to explain both the rationale and the aesthetic history behind contemporary poetic techniques would normally exclude them from the ranks of the pseudocritics whom Campbell dislikes. Although his own poems had appeared in *Georgian Poetry* and he was friendly with Edward Marsh, Graves dissociated himself from the late Georgian cult of the twenties. In *A Survey of Modernist Poetry,* Georgianism is described as a "dead movement contemporary with Imagism." Its period of "great vogue" is placed in the past, between the years 1912 and 1918. The recommendations of the movement are described as the "discarding of archaistic diction," the avoiding of either "improving themes" in the Victorian manner, or "wicked café table themes" in the manner of the nineties, and an attempt to be English, pantheistic, and simple. "This was all to the good, perhaps," write Graves and Riding, "but such counsels resulted in a poetry that could rather be praised for what it was not than for what it was. Eventually Georgianism became principally concerned with Nature and love and leisure and old age and childhood and animals and sleep and other uncontroversial subjects" (pp. 118–19). One of the writers whom Graves and Riding attack in their "text-books" is Campbell's own bête noire, Humbert Wolfe. In *A Pamphlet Against Anthologies* their assessment of his poem, "Morning," from *Kensington Gardens,* has a tone similar to that of *The Georgiad,* and their dislike is based on the same grounds: "But perhaps what Mr. Wolfe really means is that if you let sixty seconds run, among the perambulators, where the brain softens, some early morning at Kensington, when spring is in the Gardens, you are likely to achieve a perfect modern lyric" (pp. 114–15). Again the tone and values in this passage from *A Survey of Modernist Poetry* are similar to Campbell's: "Never, indeed, has it been possible for a poet to remain unknown with so little discredit and dishonour as at the present time. The prima donna reputation acquired by Mr. Humbert Wolfe with work of the most crudely histrionic and imitative brilliance (his original comma-effects in *Kensington Gardens* began it) should not only comfort the obscure poet but drive him further into obscurity" (p. 222).

The main reason for Campbell's reaction against Graves and Riding is his feeling that their succession of serious critical writings was an attempt to dominate critical fashion, and constituted an exclusive combination of critical intelligences. This feeling of being dictated to underlies the lines:

> Shall we allow this double child of Bashan
> To Yankify our unresisting nation
> And, all unrivalled, play its sounding parts
> As heavy Pop-and-Momma to the arts.
>
> [1, 201–2]

The "heavy" quality of the "Pop-and-Momma" attitude to the arts is a legitimate target of attack. For all its intelligence, there are many parts of *A Survey of Modernist Poetry* which have a heavy-handed, dogmatic tone, while the authors tend to generalize about "the Modernist poet" in an irritating way.

Although many of its attitudes were held by several young writers of the period, the strength and gaiety of *The Georgiad* are clearly Campbell's own. The hot-blooded quality of his frontal attack is typical of a poet who demands a lyre of savage thunder, and the ribaldry with which he pokes fun at his enemies is also characteristic of his earthy humour. His ability to produce a concise, epigrammatic jest is his greatest gift as a writer of satire, and one which he uses well in the best parts of *The Georgiad*. But the work as a whole shows the difficulty he has in disciplining and controlling his satiric talents in an extended poem. The poem is too long for the limited nature of its subject, and he tends to hammer away insensitively at the same point. Its organization around the farcical visit of Androgyno to Georgiana's summer hostel is too loose to be effective. Although Campbell assumes a Byronic unconcern at the interruptions in his narrative, the change from narrative to digression is hardly controlled at all, unlike the subtle variations of direction and mood with which Byron organizes a poem as long as *Don Juan*.

The confusion in organization manifests itself in two ways: Androgyno himself disappears so soon after being introduced that his function in the poem is not clear until the closing section of part two, and it is not clear where

Campbell wishes Androgyno to be placed in the framework of Georgian values. When he is first presented,
Androgyno appears to be a typical Bloomsbury poet: her-
maphroditic, self-approving, and frowsy. It is true that
Campbell makes his sexual prowess appear to be infinitely
more varied than that of commonplace "modern homos,"
but in spite of Androgyno's "fifty horsepower apparatus,"
the whole function of the boisterous presentation of the
"new Orlando" is to push what Campbell regards as common Bloomsbury traits to an absurd extreme.[11] At one
stage his "apparatus" is explicitly described as one that

> . . . beggared Bloomsbury of half its trade,
> While Chelsea swelled the ranks of unemployed
> And many a reputation was destroyed
> Behind the mystic editorial veils.
>
> [1, 205]

Androgyno "prevails" over Bloomsbury, Chelsea, and the
world of journalism, but at these moments he is shown to
be the logical superman once Bloomsbury values have
been accepted. In the middle of this opening description,
however, Campbell attacks Bloomsbury values through
Androgyno, by showing the hero's independence from the
stifling emotional and moral preoccupations of the typical
Georgian intellectual, who is "Wasting his life, poor
startled fugitive / From life, to find a reason why we live"
(1, 223). Androgyno, on the other hand, is described as
having a life and vitality of his own:

> Even his misdemeanours, the most sooty,
> Were more of a diversion than a duty:
> He was not even member of some Church-
> Society for sexual research,
> Like Bertrand Russell or the wise MacCarthy—
> For frowsiness his disrespect was hearty:

11. In Virginia Woolf's *Orlando*, the hero turns into a woman in the
middle of the novel. The fact that *Orlando* is dedicated to V. Sackville-
West, and for the most part set at Knole, her family home, makes
Campbell's reference to the "new Orlando" an intimate part of the
attack on Georgiana's hospitality.

> He read no text-books: took himself for granted
> And often did precisely what he wanted:
> Taking his pleasures in and out of season,
> He gave for his perversity no reason,
> But leaped alive (as you have seen) in rhyme
> And forged ahead to have a happy time.
>
> [1, 204]

In these lines the contrast between him and other Georgians is marked. The whole point of the passage is to show the restricted values of other writers in comparison with Androgyno's instinctive participation in life. An even more obvious discrepancy is the statement that, "For frowsiness his desrespect was hearty," when fifty-five lines earlier Androgyno meets his own approval in the glass," with "the hair-pins falling from his frowsy hair." In the earlier passage he is explicitly a 1930 model, with a Bloomsbury accent.

The same confusion about Androgyno's status in Georgia occurs at the end of the poem. After his riotous night the hero is excommunicated by Freud and Jung, the law-givers to Bloomsbury, at a mass meeting of "indignant boarders." His alienation from Georgiana's circle could not be more complete, and the hero explicitly curses the hostel as a sham. His vitality and independence dissociate him from the imitative and circumscribed world which he has shocked. In the next lines, however, his future is described in terms of the normal Georgian success story:

> But having cursed the hostel for a sham,
> Punched the hostess, and kicked the poor proprietor,
> Went back to London feeling somewhat quieter.
> Where now he's editing a posh review—
> For solid industry has pulled him through,
> Where in the subtle strife of heads or tails
> The later, as by magic, still prevails.
>
> [1, 204]

The confusion resulting from his being at times typical of Bloomsbury attitudes and at times directly opposed to those attitudes leaves the reader uncertain what function the hero has in the poem as a whole. His farcical adventures do bind the parts loosely together, but the poet uses him indiscriminately as a vehicle for his satiric outbursts.

A similar sense of indirection underlies a more serious flaw in *The Georgiad*, when the values informing Campbell's *indignatio* become obscure. At times he ridicules follies and pretensions with wit and precision, but often the aim of his attack is lost, and the poet adopts a nose-thumbing pose in order to sneer at personal enemies or dislikes. As in the *Adamastor* satires, his own presence in the poem becomes forced when he insists on his superiority to those he is attacking. The poem loses the external tone which is prevalent in both the obviously absurd Androgyno incidents and the passages which ridicule the observable follies of recognizable characters. The boasting in the following lines is unsatisfying:

> Let any now of "arrogance" accuse me
> Or my true share of modesty refuse me,
> As to his ears my soft complaint I coo
> In whom the whole commercial tribe I woo—
> Each knight and pundit of the weekly scrawl
> From him to Bennett (weekliest of all)
> From those who've praised me higher than the skies
> To those, more rare and fifty times more wise,
> Who had the caution first to damn my eyes—
> For if one scribbles in the cause of Cash
> To praise a satirist is wildly rash.
>
> [1, 216–17]

Campbell has just described himself as "cowering" beside "the humblest of them all," Humbert, to whose side he has crawled. The object of his opening satirical attack is quite clearly the ultimately dehumanizing effect of an insistence on Bloomsbury niceties, such as standard-issue humility. As the passage continues, however, the reasons for his assault become confused. Is he attacking the reviewers because they are journalists, or because they have praised him, or because they are paid for reviewing? It

seems that he expects the reader to find all these activities
equally distasteful. Later, it is true, he censures the inconsistency of critics who praised his earlier satire, but disliked
the later work in which their own values were criticized.
This dislike of inconsistency, however, and the feeling that
the critics' "somersaults" are undignified do not inform
the lines under discussion here. His personal dislike of
journalist-reviewers is being unconsciously presented as a
valid reason for the reader to dislike them. A sense of
pique underlying this assumption is one of the most unsettling elements in the lines and turns into braggadocio:

> And all you Nicolsons and Arnold Bennetts
> Be circumspect with Satire, even when it's
> To show you have the taste (which you have not)
> To know true poetry from Tommy Rot:
> For thus your tails before my boot to stick—
> It's hardly worth the pleasure of a kick,
> It makes me hesitate, and spoils my fun,
> Who love to take my victims on the run.
>
> [1, 217]

Even the attempt to base the attack on general standards
of taste depends on the weak and undemonstrated claim
that the critics do not know true poetry from tommy rot,
while the momentum in the lines really comes from the
delight surrounding boots, tails, and kicks.

When Campbell keeps his own presence out of the
satire, his satiric intention is clear, as are the standards on
which his attack is based:

> Here the blood racehorse with the useful dray
> Stands tugging from the selfsame shock of hay
> And lifts no hoof to spurn it from his way:
> On gouty feet here limps the slow gazelle,
> And though all night the nightingale may swell
> Her silver stream, the bullfrog bears the bell:
> Here the blue phosphor of the lowly snail
> Outshines the splendour of the comet's tail
> For o'er the high the humble still prevail—

All creatures here the laws of God forswear—
The wistful lion, and the bleating bear;
But dearest to the Deity, her throne
Encircling with a motley human zone
And nearest to the centre of the Pit,
First in humility if last in wit,
A thousand poets shank it on all fours.

[1, 216]

The reason for his dislike of the cult of humility and polite self-effacement is that it leads to mediocrity, the quality to which the mock-epic invocation in part two is addressed. The absurd creatures described in these lines are under the sway of the "sacred throne of Modesty." At the same time as it illustrates a positive feeling for aristocratic and elevated forms of life, the passage embodies an ominous imperviousness to cruelty which is to intrude more obviously into Campbell's later polemical writing on the good life. The contrast is pointedly disparaging between the "useful"-ness of the dray and the "blood" breeding of the racehorse. The poet's heart is clearly behind the aristocratic hoof which, in different circumstances, would "spurn" the humble labourer "from his way."

Polite Bloomsbury values are again shown to be exclusive and boring in the delightfully nonchalant description of Androgyno's Bloomsbury voice:

It was a voice of 1930 model
And in a Bloomsbury accent it could yodel
Between its tonsils drawling out long O's
Along its draughty, supercilious nose:
Or coo in satire gentle and polite
To fill the soul of Humbert with delight.

[1, 203]

Campbell grounds his attack accurately on specific attitudes and values. In his collection of critical essays, *Dialogues and Monologues,* published in 1928, Humbert Wolfe writes: "Barton was not merely an Oxford man in Bradford. He was not, that is to say, merely vowed to, and

a part of, all the things that the warehouses sullenly repu-
diated. He had not merely won the Newdigate Verse Prize
for a poem in heroic couplets on *Gibraltar*. He did not
merely pronounce his 'a's' and 'o's' long, in a world where,
in order to save time and therefore money, they were
savagely abbreviated. But he was actually a writer of articles in *The Saturday Review* . . ." (pp. 257–58). Although
Humbert Wolfe's cooing with delight in this passage is
coloured by a wistfully amused attitude towards the
naivety of youth, the knowing clubbiness of its tone is
sickening. Even the quasi-sociological explanation of the
Bradford accent is no more than a cliquish innuendo, "and
we all know about Bradford, don't we?"

   Many of the jibes in *The Georgiad* are closely derived
from specific lines and poems by Georgian writers. Squire's
poem, "To A Bulldog," is cleverly ridiculed in a general
attack on Georgian sentimentality and tastelessness, while
his poem, "The Rugger Match," is parodied in a passage
which illustrates Campbell's own intellectual agility and
lightness of touch at the same time as it exposes the absurdly ponderous attitudes of the original:[12]

   Nor at his football match is Squire more gay—
   Heart-rending verse describes funereal play;
   While swarming adjectives in idle ranks,
   As dumb spectators, load the groaning planks,
   See the fat nouns, like porky forwards, sprawl
   Into a scrum that never heels the ball—
   A mass of moving bottoms like a sea,
   All fatter than his head, if that could be;
   While still attentive at their clumsy calves
   The adverbs pine away, dejected halves,
   The verbs hang useless by, like unfed threes
   With trousers idly flapping in the breeze,
   And while they strike their arm-pits for some heat
   Or idly stamp their splayed trochaic feet,
   The two full-backs of alternating rhyme
   Walk sadly up and down to kill the time.

                                                    [1, 212]

12. See J. C. Squire, *Poems in One Volume,* p. 176.

The flexibility of style which Campbell shows in ridiculing the work of Georgian poets is not sustained throughout the poem. He attempts variations in tone and manner, but in many passages the changes in mood give the effect of being contrived. When the poet's own feelings are involved, the force of his personal animus gives bite to consciously mannered passages like those describing Georgiana's country joys:

> Seek some old farm (the image of your mind)
> Where in some farmer's ledger you may find
> Fodder to please the ruminative mind,
> Which, thrice-digested, into cud refined,
> May clatter down in cantos from behind.
> [1, 229]

Here the sense of leisured, georgic ease is skilfully combined with bucolic details and the poet's own ribald scorn at what Georgiana's songs of the land amount to. The conciously epic passages, however, lack the conviction which his contempt gives to other stylized parts of the poem. His feeling for language, and his ability to play with words, which give the zest to his best satire, are both missing. Passages reminiscent of Pope show the rigidity of Campbell's imitations of this sort:

> While truth in terror from the slaughter flies
> And probability in anguish dies.
> [1, 234]

The abstractions are not integrated into the writing, but are superimposed onto the colloquial description of a literary dinner that precedes the lines. In another passage clearly derived from Pope, wordiness, which is a normal stylistic fault of Campbell's, is elevated by him into a style of its own, with the lifeless play on the word "bore" in the description of a "wordy tempest":

> Loud and more loud the wordy tempest roared
> And crashing bores by others were out-bored,

> Till one by one, with leaden maces floored,
> The minor crashers were constrained to yield
> And super-bores alone contend the field.
>
> [1, 234]

Again the poetry does not ring false, but the epic overtones in the description are not enough to give epic proportions to the sense of overpowering boredom which it is Campbell's aim to create. He does use epic rhythms and gestures with great effect in *The Georgiad,* but usually they are then supported by some typically irreverent or coarse jest, as in the following passage. Here his ability to incorporate fads or common experiences from contemporary life into his poetry gives a boisterous vitality to the description:

> As down the table-length, in optic morse,
> His amorous glances wing their sprightly course,
> And Mr. Georgiana in reply
> Sits dot-dash-dotting with his great, glad eye.
> But Georgiana, watching, writhes with pain
> And mournful sonnets flicker through her brain,
> Upon her tongue dries up the very spittle
> All green with envy of her own good wittol.
>
> [1, 235]

Throughout the poem his instinctive feeling for an earthy joke is implicitly used to suggest his own vigorous freedom from the restrictive decorum of Georgia. Usually he is successful in suggesting his own healthy recognition of the earth-bound element in man's condition which Georgians attempt to forget. But often he becomes involved in his bathroom humour for its own sake, as in the lengthy description of Androgyno's "apparatus," or of his faunlike sexual prowess at the summer hostel. At these points the coarseness becomes boring. At their most effective the earthy overtones reinforce Campbell's pose of Byronic unconcern and superiority. The pose is well under control in the outrageously crude gesture with which he dismisses the possible complaint that he has wasted his time "daubing simpletons with Stephen's ink":

Remember how King David spent his leisure,
Between his deep devotions and his pleasure,
Leaving at times both muse and concubines
To hack the foreskins off the philistines—
An innocent and pleasing hobby, such
As to his fame supplies a human touch,
Endearing him as do the anecdotes
Of Alfred's cakes and Shelley's paper boats—
Such intimate and unimportant details
As Plutarch in his lives of heroes retails,
Opining as he does so that such facts
Endear as much as high, heroic acts:
And so in David's case, and so in mine—
Though foreskin-snipping was not his chief line,
Such foibles served to pass his idler hours
Without diminishing his lyric powers.

[1, 239–40]

His attitude of bored, man-of-the-world condescension sets off the casual obscenity with a fine Byronic ease. The length of the passage indicates that he shares with Byron the inability to condense the effect of offhand unconcern.

The poem as a whole is an important part of Campbell's work, and certainly his best long satirical venture. The values underlying his attack on Georgia are those which inform most of his later work, and its stylistic faults and virtues are both typical of the author. His dislike of literary cliques and his impatience with drawing-room intellectual chatter are attitudes which were to make him consciously isolate himself from established literary circles throughout the thirties. Although he usually makes clear in *The Georgiad* what elements of literary Georgia he despises, the tendency in later years to ridicule "MacSpaunday" as the literary establishment which succeeded the Squirearchy, is often only an attempt at a blanket condemnation of any English clique which excludes Campbell himself. Similarly the fear of mediocrity and of the levelling off of any aristocratic or vital forms of life, which he explains clearly in his attitude towards drawing-room socialism in Georgia,

> They hatch Utopias from their dusty brains
> Which are but Hells, where endless boredom reigns—
> Middle-class Hells, built on a cheap, clean plan,
> Edens of abnegation, dread to scan,
> Founded upon a universal ban
>
> [1, 223]

becomes a fear of social change itself in his later life, where the idea of social progress makes the poet instinctively suspicious. In style the poem does show at times Campbell's dangerous tendency to prolixity and to boasting. But the dominant effect of *The Georgiad* is of a boisterous, critical vitality which justly ridicules a mediocre and exclusive world for follies and failings which the poet has accurately diagnosed. It is not surprising, however, that the members of that world should have reacted by closing their ranks against the wild outsider who had been funny at their expense.

CHAPTER 4

THE PROVENÇAL POEMS

After leaving England in 1928, Campbell lived at Martigues in maritime Provence until 1933. Since his first visit to France with Earp in 1920, he had been enthralled with French culture and literature, and now he began to live a Provençal life. The French influence on his writing, which had been apparent since the publication of *The Flaming Terrapin*, becomes more and more important in the Provençal poems. It reaches its climax in *Flowering Reeds*, published in 1933, the year he left France to settle in Spain. Although he had removed himself from the English scene, he felt less isolated living a relaxed, outdoor life in a "foreign" country. As a result, the feeling of estrangement, which is so dominant in the South African poems, dies away in the *Adamastor* poems written in Provence. In the Provençal poems recurrent descriptions of isolation and hardship are linked to a general concept of the wisdom and strength growing out of suffering. The Provençal environment has a wild splendour similar to that of Africa, but does not offer the same constant irritant which Durban society provided. As a result, Campbell's feeling for the wild and lonely does not become part of a retaliatory gesture in these later poems, but is related to a classical world of heroic independence and energy.

In "Horses on the Camargue" Provençal culture and scenery are both subsumed into one of his best known paeans to Mediterranean vitality. The poem is a free adaptation of a passage from Frédéric Mistral's Provençal epic *Mirèio*,[1] and yet is typical of Campbell's own response to the wildness of his new home. He describes the horses' ecstatic freedom of movement and action side by side with the deserted quality of the coast, in which they thrive:

> In the grey wastes of dread,
> The haunt of shattered gulls where nothing moves
> But in a shroud of silence like the dead,
> I heard a sudden harmony of hooves,
> And, turning, saw afar
> A hundred snowy horses unconfined,
> The silver runaways of Neptune's car
> Racing, spray-curled, like waves before the wind.
> Sons of the Mistral, fleet
> As him with whose strong gusts they love to flee,
> Who shod the flying thunders on their feet
> And plumed them with the snortings of the sea.
>
> [1, 47]

The mythological atmosphere surrounding the "silver run-

1. Campbell himself says in the introduction to Paul Koston's 1950 edition of *Adamastor* that "Horses on the Camargue" was " 'lifted' from the great Provençal poet Mistral who has had a powerful influence on my later work published after *Adamastor*." The passage in the fourth canto of *Mirèio* describes the wild horses of Veran, the *gardien*, who comes as one of the three suitors for the hand of the heroine, *Mirèio*. The most obvious likenesses lie in the description of the enslaved horse from the Camargue racing back to his native land to "breathe the foam" again after years of absence. Both poems share the story, while Mistral's line, "Respira de la mar lou libre salabrum," reappears in Campbell's poem, "Will never rest until he breathes the foam." The Provençal stanzas linking the horses with their "elemen," the sea, and describing their happiness at the height of a storm have further obvious similarities to "Horses on the Camargue."

aways of Neptune's car" is part of his newly found absorption in the supernatural Mediterranean past, an interest which is to lead to the involved Mithraic symbolism of "Mithraic Frieze." Here, the classical echoes are easily absorbed into the heroic moral of the close, which reflects his lifelong admiration for an animal life that blends naturally into its environment:

> Still out of hardship bred,
> Spirits of power and beauty and delight
> Have ever on such frugal pastures fed
> And loved to course with tempest through the night.
>
> [1, 48]

There is a similar blending of French influences and Campbell's own values in "The Palm." A picture of the isolated, despairing poet recurs in "The Palm," but its moral of restraint and forbearance is characteristic of the poems written in Provence rather than those written in Natal. The palm appears to the poet in a desert landscape, and contrasts its indomitable resourcefulness with his listlessness:

> The roots are my anchor struck fast in the hill,
> The higher I hanker, the deeper they drill,
> Through the red mortar their claws interlock
> To ferret the water through warrens of rock.
> Each inch of my glory was wrenched with a groan,
> Corroded with fire from the base of my throne
> And drawn like a wire from the heart of a stone.
>
> [1, 50]

It is the conceit of the palm's whole existence being a tug of war between the sky to which it aspires and the earth from which it springs which gives life to the stoical moral. A similar intelligence informs the typically heroic lines:

> Your spirit that grieves like the wind in my leaves
> Shall be robbed of its care, by those whispering thieves
> To study my patience and hear, the day long,

The soft foliations of sand into song—
For bitter and cold though it rasp to my root,
Each atom of gold is the chance of a fruit.

[1, 50]

The heroic mood and moral of "The Palm" are so characteristic of Campbell, and so distinctly his, that it is surprising how close "The Palm" is to its acknowledged
source, Valéry's "Palme." It is an angel who appears to the
poet in the French poem and discusses the lesson to be
learnt from the palm:

—Calme, calme, reste calme!
Connais le poids d'une palme
Portant sa profusion![2]

Although the speaker is not holding himself up as an example, the didactic tone is similar to that in Campbell's
poem, and the description which follows of the paradoxical relation between the palm, the earth, and the firmament is obviously the origin of Campbell's metaphysics:

Admire comme elle vibre,
Et comme une lente fibre
Qui divise le moment,
Départage sans mystère
L'attirance de la terre
Et le poids du firmament!

The rooted, tied quality of the tree is as important to
Valéry as it is to Campbell. At one stage even the tree's fruit
is described as its "bonds" ("Ses fruits lourds sont ses
liens"). The limitation implied in this fixed situation is related to an ultimately fruitful search in which the roots
themselves provide more nourishment the deeper they
drill, and the more barren their environment:

Ces jours qui te semble vides
Et perdus pour l'univers

2. Valéry, Oeuvres (Paris: Gallimard, 1957), pp. 154–55.

Ont des racines avides
Qui travaillent les déserts.
La substance chevelue
Par les ténèbres élue
Ne peut s'arrêter jamais,
Jusqu'aux entrailles du monde,
De poursuivre l'eau profonde
Que demandent les sommets.

Patience, patience,
Patience dans l'azur!
Chaque atome de silence
Est la chance d'un fruit mûr!

The ability of the palm to thrive in the desert and of the Camargue horses to "course with tempests through the night" is presented with the firm moral assent that is characteristic of Campbell's directness of vision and judgement. This theme of "beauty and delight" growing from hardship and strife is essentially similar to the regenerative moral embodied in *The Flaming Terrapin*, and not very different from the sacrificial element stressed in his later Christian poetry. The religious resurrection he was later to extol is anticipated in the resurgence, in spite of stress and difficulty, of the natural life celebrated in *Adamastor*. The resurrection theme appears in the poem of that name, and is suggested in "Autumn," where the strict technical control which informs the later *Flowering Reeds* is becoming more pronounced. A classical feeling for "clear anatomy" and "purity" of outline shows a marked change from the sensuous revelling of his early work:

I love to see, when leaves depart,
The clear anatomy arrive,
Winter, the paragon of art,
That kills all forms of life and feeling
Save what is pure and will survive.
                              [1, 52]

There are no explicitly Christian poems among the

early Provençal works. "Mass at Dawn," describing the poet's quasi-sacramental breakfast after a night's fishing, is an elusive poem in which the Christian overtones are never really explained. A similar ambiguity hangs over the witty and urbane "St. Peter of the Three Canals." Part of the elusiveness of "Mass at Dawn" lies in the uncommitted tone of the poet towards the sacramental elements in the scene he describes. Similarly in "St. Peter of the Three Canals" the irony with which Campbell describes the "old green idol" and the faith it fosters leaves his final Christian prayer within the central irony of the poem as a whole. The first description establishes a tone of Olympian understanding towards the multitude of beliefs which the statue of Saint Peter represents to the fishermen who use the harbour of Martigues:

> High stranded on the Rock of Ages,
> Of all the ocean-gods and mages
> The last surviving Robinson—
> Saint Peter-Neptune fronts the wind,
> In whose Protean rôle combined
> All deities and creeds are One.
>
> [1, 182]

From the outset the fishermen's belief is explicitly idolatrous. A mind that can conceive the Saint Peter-Neptune-Robinson is not unambiguously devout. Similarly, the irony with which conventional Christian dogma is shown to be stretched by the idol's worshippers would verge on the blasphemous but for the fact that the narrator maintains a bland neutrality:

> For when the Three-in-One grow thrifty,
> Saint Peter, he is One in Fifty,
> Saint Peter, he is All in All!
>
> [1, 182]

This matter-of-fact tone with which the inversions of Christian belief are described is part of the consummate wit of the poem. Campbell can spin out the saintly metaphor indefinitely, linking Christianity, mythology, and old wives' tales with the same raconteur's absorption. He describes Saint Peter "walking the waves" to aid drowning fishermen with as light a tread as "Mother Carey's chicken / Foot-webbed with Mercy and with Faith." The bells in the tower are "By faith and ivy kept from falling / When the night-long mistral rolls." Such a merging of the miraculous and the ordinary does not destroy the possibility of miracles taking place, but rather gives an insight into an ancient and simple outlook in which the distinction between the real and the supernatural is not clearly defined. The worldly wisdom of combining ivy with faith to keep the bells from falling is part of the whole civilized mood of the poem in which fanaticism of any kind is ruled out, and sectarian interests are easily absorbed. The irony of this accommo-dating attitude is never presented with a heavy hand. Even the most basic details of the saint's appearance are given with the outwardly straight-faced reverence befitting a token of seraphic love:

Deep in his bosom nest the doves
In token of seraphic loves,
To keep his garments—white as snow.
[1, 183]

At the end of "St. Peter of the Three Canals" the tone appears to lose its irony in the direct Fisher's Prayer, which appeals to the fisherman in Saint Peter and describes the hardships of a fisherman's life. After reminding the saint of the night in Galilee when he "floundered in the sea / Because your faith was in your flesh," the narrator seems to be making an unambiguously Christian plea for help amid the dangers of the Bouches-du-Rhône:

Be with me, then, when nights are lone
And from the pampas of the Rhone,
Thrilling with sleet, the great guns blow:
When the black mistral roars avenging
Increase the horse-power of my engine,
Hallow my petrol ere I go!
[1, 185]

This final request completely upsets the balance of the preceding lines. We are back again in the ambiguities of the bland creed, and the poet's own belief is tactfully hidden.

Flowering Reeds shows a continuation of both the metaphysical ingenuity and the movement towards greater restraint which began to appear in the Provençal poems of *Adamastor*. The tranquillity of Campbell's life at the time is reflected in the tranquillity of the poems, which show none of the stress so characteristic of his earlier and later volumes. Apart from love poetry, the subject matter of *Flowering Reeds* derives mainly from the Mediterranean setting in which he had made his home, and from a discussion of the ideas of permanence and change, which form a natural part of love poetry and nature poetry. At first the similarity of theme and technique in the *Flowering Reeds* poems seems to indicate a sameness about the volume, but the depth of experience in so many of them and the remarkable technical control give even the short lyrics a distinct identity and seriousness. At the same time, Campbell's fault of repetition appears again in this volume as it did in *Adamastor*. Images are repeated, as are favourite words like "refulgent" and "azure." Similarly the clever clinching of the ideas of a central image or conceit tends to become a stylistic mannerism in many of the octosyllabic sonnets. In most cases each individual poem in this genre is free of obtrusive mannerism and is neatly rounded by the precision of the closing. But when so many of the short pieces are crowned by a decisive closing line or couplet, the technique itself becomes repetitious in a series of individually successful works. The pyrotechnics of *The Flaming Terrapin* and *Adamastor* are mainly lacking in *Flowering Reeds*, but the intellectual, emotional, and technical control in its poems embodies a real and original achievement for which the popular image of Campbell as a flamboyant "lord of language" gives little credit.

He experiments with symbolic imagery throughout the volume. At its best his symbolic technique gives an impressive cohesion and clarity to the short works, such as the title poem itself. In "The Flowering Reed" he sees a

reed reflected in the Rhône. The way its fragile image
seems to "resist" the "passing leagues of gloom, / Torren-
tial in their strength and speed," makes him aware that it
requires infinite passing and dying to liberate an ephemer-
al element that will not die:

> It held a candle to the eye
> To show how much must pass and die
> To set such scatheless phantoms free,
> Or feather with one reed of rhyme
> The boulder-rolling Rhone of time,
> That rafts our ruin to the sea.
>
> [1, 95]

Because the final idea of poetic creation surviving the ruin
of mortality is so completely grounded in the original experience of seeing the flowering reed reflected in the dark
river, the early description of the Rhône, the sunshine, and
the reeds is redolent of the symbolic associations which
the final lines make explicit. At any stage in the opening
lines the Rhône can stand for time, and its flow for the
destruction which time brings.

"The Flowering Reed" depends on a complete interaction of thought and imagery. The degree to which Campbell achieves this interaction is not consistent in the volume. At times he links attitudes to actions with delicate
simplicity, as in the opening lines of "Reflection":

> My thought has learned the lucid art
> By which the willows lave their limbs,
> Whose form upon the water swims
> Though in the air they rise apart.
>
> [1, 107]

In this case the link is provided by the pun on the reflection
which both the poet's thought and the willows share. In
"Rejoneador" the fusion of symbols is less subtle and depends on a blunt equating of ideas:

> His horns the moon, his hue the night,
> The dying embers of his sight
> Across their bloody film may view

> The star of morning rise in fire,
> Projectile of the same desire
> Whose pride is animate in you.
>
> [1, 106]

Not only is the linking of the dying bull's horns and colour with the moon and the night too direct to be really evocative, but also the ideas themselves gain little by the arbitrary link. The confusion of the picture which follows is directly attributable to the arbitrary quality of the imagery. Almost invariably Campbell's symbolic technique is most effective when the imagery accurately captures real sights, sounds, or movements at the same time as it suggests emotions or concepts. As a result it is not surprising that when he turns from the conceptual emphasis of some of the shorter poems in *Flowering Reeds* to a more direct description of the physical world, the imagery has strength without a hint of preciosity. In "The Road to Arles" a picture of windswept trees along the moonlit road merges into the myth of Actaeon and his petulant Moon Goddess. In the myth, Artemis' indignation results in Actaeon's being turned into a stag to be hunted by his own dogs. In the poem, the bare trees appear to be stags' antlers, and in the wind of a clear night they appear to be chased by the moon:

> Along the cold grey torrent of the sky
> Where branch the fatal trophies of his brows,
> Actaeon, antlered in the wintry boughs,
> Rears to the stars his mastiff-throttled cry.
>
> [1, 99]

By the time the tortured Actaeon tree "rears to the stars his mastiff-throttled cry," the pain, the sound, the image of the trees against the sky, and their movement are all united in the description of the myth's tortured ending. Thought and image are flawlessly interwoven.

The two Olive Tree poems are similarly built around a central conceit and investigate the sculptured effects of twisted trees. In "The Olive Tree II," the conceit of the squat and contorted tree, silhouetted against moon or sun, resembling the bent and tense statue of the discus thrower, is the experience of the poem:

> Curbed athlete hopeless of the palm,
> If in the rising moon he hold,
> Discobolos, a qoit of gold
> Caught in his gusty sweep of arm,
> Or if he loom against the dawn,
> The circle where he takes his run
> To hurl the discus of the sun
> Is by his own dark shadow drawn:
> The strict arena of his game
> Whose endless effort is denied
> More room for victory or pride
> Than what he covers with his shame.
>   [1, 109]

The visual image on which the comparison is based and the mood of impotent and endless effort are inseparable. Each is a part of the other, and their interdependence gives the little poem its life.

The many love poems in *Flowering Reeds* and the poems deriving from natural scenes all show the effects of Campbell's careful blending of imagery and thought in a way that is not common in English poetry. It is only the metaphysical poets who use a similar technique and who develop their conceits with as much rigour, while Blake's symbolic imagery in poems like "The Sunflower," "The Sick Rose," and "London" has an even greater effect of simple yet universal suggestion than Campbell's symbols. His interest in conceits and symbols is not derived from the metaphysical poets alone, however. French poets such as Baudelaire, Rimbaud, Apollinaire, and Valéry are, by his own account, the central influence on his technique.[3] This

3. In *Broken Record* Campbell writes, "It was Earp who really taught me the most: through him I learned about French poetry which I had hitherto ignored, but which has had more influence on my work than anything else" (p. 36). He repeats these comments in almost identical terms in *Light on a Dark Horse:* "Earp's unofficial tuition saved me years of trial and error: and it was through him that I found the French symbolists who have since influenced me most—if we discount my own basic self-immersion in the English Elizabethans and metaphysical poets" (p. 183).

influence on *Flowering Reeds* is marked. In "Overtime,"
sonorous French tones blend with English wit in an original
reworking of two poems by Baudelaire.

"Overtime" opens on an oppressive note, with the
poet in an idle mood looking at dull text books. The tone
changes to one of macabre revelling as the central conceit
is introduced in the form of a "carnival" of anatomical
illustrations:

> Amongst the ponderous tomes of learning,
> Dull texts of medicine and law,
> With idle thumb the pages turning
> In sudden carnival, I saw,
> Revelling forth into the day
> In scarlet liveries, nine or ten
> Survivors of their own decay—
> The flayed anatomies of men:
> And marked how well the scalpel's care
> Was aided by the painter's tones
> To liven with a jaunty air
> Their crazy trellises of bones.
>
> [1, 113]

The conceit is elaborated with great skill, and the tone
remains unconcerned:

> In regimental stripes and bands
> Each emphasised the cause he serves—
> Here was a grenadier of glands
> And here a gay hussar of nerves:
> And one his skin peeled off, as though
> A workman's coat, with surly shrug
> The flexion of the thews to show,
> Treading a shovel, grimly dug.
>
> [1, 113]

A sense of grimness in the illustrations is made explicit for
the first time in the picture of the "surly" shrug of the
"grimly" digging figure. The painful elements in the situation now become the centre of interest as the poet aban-

dons his mask of disinterest to make the concluding moral comment:

> Dour sexton, working overtime,
> With gristly toes he hooked his spade
> To trench the very marl and slime
> In which he should have long been laid.
> The lucky many of the dead—
> Their suit of darkness fits them tight,
> Buttoned with stars from foot to head
> They wear the uniform of Night;
> But some for extra shift are due
> Who, slaves for any fool to blame,
> With a flayed sole the ages through
> Must push the shovel of their fame.
>
> [1, 113]

"Overtime" is an original work, and yet derives much of its imagery and mood from "Le Squelette Laboureur" and "Une Gravure Fantastique." Campbell's poem has a wider range of mood than either Baudelaire poem and draws on elements from each to make its own point; nevertheless it incorporates a great deal of Baudelairean material. The anatomical text-book imagery and the digging figure clearly derive from "Le Squelette Laboureur," as does the sullen mood of the labourer and the idea of eternal toil replacing "le sommeil promis." Typical of the way Campbell both retains and changes an image is the addition of a new element to the painful

> Et pousser une lourde bêche
> Sous notre pied sanglant et nu?

by the use of his pun, "with a flayed sole." In his poem the "extra shift" of the digging figure, eternally serving as an illustration of muscular contraction, is not used as a vague existential warning. It is pointedly related to the overtime served by men of fame and reputation as objects of idle praise or blame after death.

The macabre gaiety of Campbell's "sudden carnival"

has affinities to the grotesque mood of "Une Gravure Fantastique," where the frightful crown of the "spectre singulier" is "sentant le carnaval":

> Ce spectre singulier n'a pour toute toilette,
> Grotesquement campé sur son front de squelette,
> Qu'un diadème affreux sentant le carnaval.
>> [*Les Fleurs du Mal*]

At the same time, the idea of the phantom horseman crushing nameless crowds in Baudelaire's poem, and of the huge, cold cemetery containing all the peoples of ancient and modern history, has overtones of the insentient uniformity Campbell attributes to "the lucky many of the dead." The main difference between these poems and "Overtime" is that Campbell controls a variety of tones, while Baudelaire has a more uniform tone in each poem. Campbell's tonal control is part of the wit which informs "Overtime," and combines with the verbal play to make a coherent, telling point about fame and reputation. There is no verbal playfulness in "Le Squelette" to compare with "their suit of darkness fits them tight," "a grenadier of glands," a "gay hussar of nerves," or "buttoned with stars from foot to head." The wit with which the elements of pain and crazy carnival are combined, to relate to both the text-book figures and the similar, puppet-like carnival of reputation, embodies an English urbanity with its feet planted firmly on earth, wryly commenting on the human situation. The almost surrealist gloom of "Le Squelette" is quite different and gives the French poem its metaphysical glamour. Its sonorous questioning, tone of controlled disillusion, and use of abstract ideas (destin, le Néant, la Mort) all contrast sharply with the more specific and pointed English wit:

> Voulez-vous (d'un destin trop dur
> Épouvantable et clair emblème!)
> Montrer que dans la fosse même
> Le sommeil promis n'est pas sûr;

Qu'envers nous le Néant est traître:
Que tout, même la Mort, nous ment,
Et que sempiternellement,
Hélas! il nous faudra peut-être

Dans quelque pays inconnu
Écorcher la terre revêche
Et pousser une lourde bêche
Sous notre pied sanglant et nu?
                    [*Les Fleurs du Mal*]

There is nothing in "Le Squelette" corresponding to
the jaunty, maniacal mood of the revelling survivors in
scarlet livery, or to the pointedly clinical detachment with
which Campbell marks the "scalpel's care," "aided" by
the painter to "liven" the pictures. In comparison Baudelaire treats the drawings without irony, but with a sombre
insistence on their beauty (a concept quite lacking from
Campbell's Swiftian poker face), in spite of the sadness of
the subject:

Dessins auxquels la gravité
Et le savoir d'un vieil artiste,
Bien que le sujet en soit triste,
Ont communiqué la Beauté.

The difference between Baudelaire's sense of the unknown
and Campbell's deliberately casual explicitness is marked
in places where the poems are outwardly similar. Campbell's figure is digging, "the flexion of the thews to show,"
while Baudelaire's figure "rend plus complètes, / Ces mys-
térieuses horreurs." Campbell's figure is a dour sexton,
while in "Le Squelette" the suggestions of grave digging
are much more general and abstract in the phrase, "manants résignés et funèbres." In the same way the explicitness of trenching "the *very* marl and slime / In which he
should have long been laid" (italics mine) is quite different
from the uneasy, puzzled questioning of Baudelaire:

De ce terrain que vous fouillez,
Manants résignés et funèbres,
De tout l'effort de vos vertèbres,
Ou de vos muscles dépouillés,

Dites, quelle moisson étrange,
Forçats arrachés au charnier,
Tirez-vous, et de quel fermier
Avez-vous à remplir la grange?

The whole theme of clothes, uniform, and skin is Campbell's alone. It links the metaphysical concept of the skinned figures being worked overtime after death (Baudelaire's idea) with that of reputation and fame providing a stimulus for eternal anatomizing and flaying of famous men by any "idle fool" (an original idea of Campbell's). In spite of the obvious similarities among "Overtime," "Une Gravure Fantastique," and "Le Squelette Laboureur," Campbell has made an original poem, with a different theme from those of the poems whose ideas he takes over. In this case the peculiarly English quality of his wit and wry commonsense changes his Gallic material in much the same way as Chaucer changes borrowings from Romance poetry.

He is as original in handling borrowings from Paul Valéry. "The Gum Trees" is an example of a genuinely new poem growing from the stimulus of Valéry's "Cantique des Colonnes." In "The Gum Trees" the picture of a plantation of trees blowing in the wind, and silhouetted against the light of evening, night, and dawn, is investigated in detail. The visual illusion, that the geometrically planted trees are moving as the wind blows them, is described in terms which present a paradox of flight and the static, action and passivity. The paradoxical elements in "The Gum Trees" are not superimposed intellectually on the scene, but are intrinsic to the situation itself. The trees are rooted to the ground and yet do move about violently in the wind. The parallel lines in which the trees are planted appear to meet on the horizon without in fact doing so, and when light plays across its massed symmetrical lines, the background of stationary trees appears to move. These rather dull, commonsense facts are transformed by the poet into a vivid picture of restlessness in which are united the visual mirages, the sounds, and the sense of captivity in the trees' rooted movement.

The first stanza shows the interaction of sound and movement caused by the trees rustling in the wind:

> Half-hid by leaves, in lofty shoots,
> The long lit files of stems arise,
> An orchestra of silver flutes
> That sing with movement to the eyes.
>
> [1, 110]

Both the interaction of the impressions of sound and movement and the vigorously active nature of the trees' arising and singing are part of a straightforward description of the scene, but lead inevitably to the succeeding paradoxes:

> Each interval between their feet
> A dryad's stride, as they recede
> In immobility more fleet
> Than in the whizzing wind of speed.
>
> [1, 110]

Sound and movement are still linked here, but the idea of the speed of the trees' immobility is a new element in the scene. The intellectual and verbal play is of virtuoso quality when the poet elaborates on this timeless element in the trees' race, and adds another synaesthetic image of sound and movement:

> Along the red-lit rim of space
> In lofty cadences they rhyme,
> Their march is one victorious race
> Of immobility with time.
>
> [1, 111]

Again the trees have all the active qualities in the stanza: they march, they rhyme, and they race. This inversion of

normally active and passive roles underlies much of the
effect of paradox in the poem. Optical illusions become
charged with feelings of delight or depression, and the
lines of trees are described in terms which challenge our
ideas of flight and motion. The unity of the poem is remarkable because it grows organically out of one, simple,
observable scene.

The geometric lines in which Campbell's gum trees
are planted recall the regular pattern of the pillars, the
"égales radieuses," of Valéry's "Cantique des Colonnes."
Their paradoxically combined associations of sound and
brightness, stillness and growth, have distinct similarities to
the paradoxes of "The Gum Trees." The influence of "Cantique des Colonnes" on "The Gum Trees" is seen in the
situation which the poems share, and in many similar
points in the poetic descriptions themselves. At the same
time, the tone and mood with which each poet presents
human thoughts and emotions as an inextricable part of
the description of trees or pillars show a resemblance between the fundamental poetic intentions of Campbell and
Valéry. Nevertheless, the difference between the two poets
is marked, and in spite of local similarities to "Cantique
des Colonnes," "The Gum Trees" shows its author's originality even in the passages where the likenesses are obvious. Campbell again alters the images he borrows, and
the changes he makes embody his own poetic virtues of
clarity and forthrightness, even if the original stimulus has
in many cases come from the more elusive impressions in
the French original.

The opening stanzas of "Cantique des Colonnes" indicate Valéry's approach to the world of the columns:

> Douces colonnes, aux
> Chapeaux garnis de jour,
> Ornés de vrais oiseaux
> Qui marchent sur le tour,
>
> Douces colonnes, ô
> L'orchestre de fuseaux!

Chacun immole son
Silence à l'unisson.[4]

The phrase, "Chapeaux garnis de jour," plays on the
French word for a capital, "chapiteau," and, as well as
suggesting a personal aura around the pillars with their
"hats" edged or trimmed with the daylight behind them,
does capture a specific visual effect. In the next line the
birds are explicitly described as real, "vrais." Campbell
never has to insist on the physical reality of an image as
distinct from its conceptual reality. Even though the force
of "vrais" in the stanza under discussion derives from the
last image of the previous line (instead of artificial birds on
their "hats" the columns have real birds), this does not
alter the fact that Valéry is going out of his way to insist on
the reality of the birds on the symbolic, conceptual hats.
The mood created by Valéry's description is central to the
impact of the opening stanzas, and the soft femininity
suggested by "douces" is enlarged by the sense of feminine caprice which surrounds "chapeaux" bedecked and
betrimmed with the daylight. This mood, of a delicate and
womanly presence, is the unifying force behind the stanza.
The shift from describing the pillars as figures topped with
hats, to picturing them as an orchestra of slender shapes,
can be made so simply in Valéry's poem because the real,
physical scene is not his only interest. That interest includes the mood and qualities which the poet associates
with the soft gentleness of his columns. In contrast, Campbell's opening is based on the real scene. Although he experiences the same sensuous illusions from his lines of
trees as Valéry does from his lines of pillars, Campbell is
above all describing real trees.

When the two poets suggest that it is the number of
the trees or pillars which creates the varied effects, the
differences between the two poems can be clearly demon-
strated. Campbell is typically direct. The visual and the
intellectual elements exist side by side:

4. Valéry, *Oeuvres* (Paris: Gallimard, 1957), p. 116.

Softly as a breeze that slumbers
They glide across the tufted floor,
For their motion is in numbers
And the shadows are their spoor.
[1, 111]

Apart from the somnambulatory quality of the breeze,
which is an effect calculated mainly to create mood, the
real scene is being presented right down to the "tufted"
texture of the ground. The statement that "their motion is
in numbers" is true, in that the appearance of movement
is created by the numbers in each line of trees, and grows
quite naturally from the description. Valéry, on the other
hand, uses the conceit of intricacy growing from numbers
to elaborate the sense of female subtlety and attraction
suggested by his "douces colonnes":

Nos antiques jeunesses,
Chair mate et belles ombres,
Sont fières des finesses
Qui naissent par les nombres![5]

Campbell's trees are seen against the background of
evening, night, and morning. The changes in mood in "The
Gum Trees" are an intricate part of the changes of light
and wind in a real setting. The cyclic quality of their race
and struggle is as natural and inevitable as the cycle of
dusk to dawn through which the poem has moved:

The dusty winds begin to sweep,
The distance stretched before them lies,
Antaeus-like from caves of sleep
Their old antagonists arise.
[1, 112]

Valéry, in contrast, uses a deliberately vague closing to
"Cantique des Colonnes":

5. Ibid., p. 117.

Nous marchons dans le temps
Et nos corps éclatants
Ont des pas ineffables
Qui marquent dans les fables.[6]

The pillars have a real existence—they "walk" in a normal
time-world—but their personal qualities, their "steps" are
indescribable, unutterable, and connected with the imaginative, symbolic world of fiction and fable.

The two poems are distinctly different in mood and
tone. What distinguishes the poems most clearly is the
use to which Campbell and Valéry put their conceptual
and metaphysical imagery. Valéry creates in dialogue a subjective poetic experience in which a complex and subtle
suggestiveness is the predominant effect. Campbell describes a real scene and reflects in it complexities of emotion and thought. Once again his technique is more
English, more down-to-earth than that of the French poet.

Valéry's poem, "Au Platane," also has images similar
to those in "The Gum Trees," but the similarities are only
local. The impression of the trees wrestling with the winds
as antagonists is only a small part of Campbell's poem, but
one which is created in some detail by Valéry in "Au
Platane":

Haute profusion de feuilles, trouble fier
    Quand l'âpre tramontane
Sonne, au comble de l'or, l'azur du jeune hiver
    Sur tes harpes, Platane,

Ose gémir! . . . Il faut, ô souple chair du bois,
    Te tordre, te détordre,
Te plaindre, sans te rompre, et rendre aux vents la voix
    Qu'ils cherchent en désordre![7]

The feminine attraction of the tree scene in "Au Platane"

6. Ibid., p. 118.
7. Ibid., p. 115.

strongly suggests the sweet attractions of Campbell's pine in another poem, "Choosing a Mast." Here he recreates the sensuous beauty of the forest world, and at the same time returns to a familiar theme: the delight which derives from an instinctive participation in a natural life shared with the wind, the sun, and the seasons. The idea of the nymphs of the tree, river, and mountainside is the symbolic embodiment from an earlier culture of the qualities associated with the world of forest and mountain. It is a tribute to the freshness of his poem that he can endow the idea of oread and naiad with new life. Instead of suggesting a dead pastoral tradition, he recreates in human terms the feeling which the old myths embody of the private world of the tree, the river, and the mountain. Campbell captures the wonder of the Provençal outdoors, and at the same time suggests his personal code of values by embodying in the pine's history qualities which he represents as having positive value in any form of life. The trees, mountains, forests, and human values all interact and mingle without a hint of preciousness and coyness. The vitality of the tree merges into a complex picture of the sights and sounds of its windswept habitat:

> I chose her for her eagerness of flight
> Where she stood tiptoe on the rocky height
> Lifted by her own perfume to the sun,
> While through her rustling plumes with eager sound
> Her eagle spirit, with the gale at one,
> Spreading wide pinions, would have spurned the
>   ground
> And her own sleeping shadow, had they not
> With thymy fragrance charmed her to the spot.
>
> [1, 104]

These disparate sense impressions exist separately in the reader's mind, although shown to be only aspects of the organic beauty, vitality, and peacefulness of the tree. In the next stanza, however, Campbell maintains the lyric

excitement of his description with well-controlled synaesthetic images:

> . . . for there she loved to sing
> Through a long noon's repose of wave and wing,
> The fluvial swirling of her scented hair
> Sole rill of song in all that windless air,
> And her slim form the naiad of the stream,
> Afloat upon the languor of its theme.
>
> [1, 104]

The heady, sensuous quality of the writing does not lead
to vagueness in an impressionistic sense. Each image is
based on accurate, observable details. The generally lan-
guorous, drifting effect of the stanza grows out of the
overlapping of specific sense stimuli, and not out of an inability of the poet's to create anything but a vague mood
of drowsiness.

It is the delightful vivacity of Campbell's mast which
distinguishes it from Valéry's plane tree in "Au Platane."
There is little sexuality associated with the pine tree, and
her girlish charms are either explicitly young and pure or
nunlike. The heavy sexual feeling in "Au Platane," on the
other hand, is essential to its total effect. After the poet has
"chosen" the plane tree, he indulges in erotic fantasy:

> O qu'amoureusement des Dryades rival,
>   Le seul poète puisse
> Flatter ton corps poli comme il fait du Cheval
>   L'ambitieuse cuisse![8]

Campbell does write unrestrained erotic poetry like this,
but not in "Choosing a Mast." The arbitrary effect of "am-
bitieuse" is typical of Valéry's attempt to involve the tree,
the horse, and their physical attractions in an inward emotive pattern which does not depend on the observable.
Valéry's languid mood is different from Campbell's vigour,
but the likeness of imagery in the two poems is consistent

8. Valéry, *Oeuvres* (Paris: Gallimard, 1957), p. 114.

enough to cause an unwary reader to suspect Campbell's originality.[9] The real originality with which he transforms borrowings in imagery, subject matter, and poetic technique is, however, apparent throughout any close comparison of his work with that of Valéry. The precision and clarity which the English poet achieves in *Flowering Reeds* are quite different in effect from the deliberately indefinite, but highly suggestive moods created by Valéry. And the fact that both poets use similarly symbolic imagery shows how far Campbell can develop and change the elements he admired in the work of another poet.

Both the influence and the change can be seen in the closing of the short sonnet, "The Secret Muse." In it Campbell describes his inspiration in ideal terms, yet even that idealized picture is perfectly precise:

> Though veiled to me that face of faces
> And still that form eludes my art,
> Yet all the gifts my faith has brought
> Along the secret stair of thought
> Have come to me on those hushed paces
> Whose footfall is my beating heart.
>   [1, 105]

The conceit is rigorously sustained; the link between the steps we can imagine, and the metaphysical coming of inspiration is made through the beating heart, which unites

9. The third stanza of "Choosing a Mast" clearly derives much of its imagery from the following stanzas of "Au Platane":

Ombre retentissante en qui le même azur
        Qui t'emporte, s'apaise,
La noire mère astreint ce pied natal et pur
        A qui la fange pèse.

De ton front voyageur les vents ne veulent pas;
        La terre tendre et sombre,
O Platane, jamais ne laissera d'un pas
        S'émerveiller ton ombre!

Ce front n'aura d'accès qu'aux degrés lumineux
        Où la sève l'exalte;
Tu peux grandir, candeur, mais non rempre les noeuds
        De l'éternelle halte!
                [*Oeuvres* (Paris: Gallimard, 1957), pp. 113–14]

suggestions of feeling and living with the regular sound of steps. The last image is taken directly from Valéry's poem "Les Pas," which also discusses inspiration:

Si, de tes lèvres avancées,
Tu prépares pour l'apaiser,
A l'habitant de mes pensées
La nourriture d'un baiser,

Ne hâte pas cet acte tendre,
Douceur d'être et de n'être pas,
Car j'ai vécu de vous attendre,
Et mon coeur n'était que vos pas.[10]

These seductive female qualities of Valéry's muse are quite absent from Campbell's poem which presents an intellectual account of an emotional experience. "Les Pas" recreates the emotions and the mood. Again the English poem depends on greater clarity than "Les Pas," and on making a statement about an inward experience which it is the aim of Valéry to recreate.

In *Flowering Reeds* the number of short poems built around a central conceit illustrates Campbell's deep concern for technical restraint. Although all the short poems stand on their own as original works, the fact that the volume contains so many suggests how strenuously the poet was striving for control in many short pieces which are almost exercises in precision. His repeated turning to French sources and models shows too how far his interest was from current English trends or issues. The timeless quality of *Flowering Reeds* is remarkable for a poet in whose three previously published volumes are included *The Georgiad* and *The Wayzgoose*. Although he continued to experiment with symbols and images after 1933, he never recaptured the extended mood of lyric ease which is embodied in the volume he published that year.

10. Valéry, *Oeuvres* (Paris: Gallimard, 1957), pp. 120–21.

CHAPTER 5

"FOR EACH VAQUERO
IS A STAR"

Not only was Campbell's popularity in England on the
wane after the publication of *The Georgiad,* but also a new
poetic trend was catching the public interest after the
appearance in 1930 of Auden's *Poems.* Once Campbell
had left England in 1928, he himself turned away from
English life and became totally immersed in the Provençal
life at Martigues. His pastimes included water-jousting,
fishing, and bullfighting in the Provençal style by snatching
the prize *cocardes* from the horns of young bulls. He was
by all accounts popular, and was later to be honoured in
both Arles and Toulon as an illustrious Provençal figure.
The Mediterranean suited Campbell's mood after his
clashes with Anglo-Saxon culture. The outdoor existence
which he enjoyed there both gave scope to his athletic
interests and provided him with a milieu in which athletic
and imaginative values had been combined since Roman
times. As a result, he became fascinated by local history
and culture, particularly by the old Provençal cult of Mithraism.

Several prominent English personalities lived for varying periods in and around Martigues in the early thirties, including his friends Augustus John and T. W. Earp. Wyndham Lewis paid a visit to the Campbells in 1932 to discuss a draft of his novel, *Snooty Baronet,* in which the poet himself is the model for one of the characters, Rob McPhail. McPhail, in a chapter entitled "A Lord of Language and His Boat," is introduced as "one of the few authentic poets now writing in English," living with his wife, sister- and brother-in-law (an ex-French marine) in Faujas de Saint Riom, "an ideal spot for a poet who is tired of Capitalism." McPhail is described as wanting to "catch fish quietly in a big windy pond," and "gossip with rough fellows (but not too rough) and polish a lovely verse, or pack with guncotton and poisoned epithets another one, that will knock a man down with its well-timed percussion."[1] In the story the enigmatic, misty-eyed McPhail is killed in a local bullfight, affording the central character, Snooty, an opportunity for exhibiting his typical unconcern. The whole affair is made to appear pointless and absurd, and the gratuitous killing off of McPhail obviously caused Lewis some embarrassment. On his return to London he wrote to Campbell explaining that this was not to be taken as an insult.

Wyndham Lewis's influence provides a consistent undertone to Campbell's two prose works, *Taurine Provence,* published in 1932, and *Broken Record,* published in 1934. In *Taurine Provence* he celebrates the bullfighting, ancient culture of Provence, and in praising its equestrian and vital element, gives free rein to his scorn for conforming, joyless, urban, and therefore pedestrian, masses. Here is an example of equestrian theory from the book: "The Camargue is surely unique in Europe. It is sparsely-populated, but *well*-populated by hereditary aristocrats. . . . They have still the sense of elegance and style—utility, hustle, and efficiency are only their batmen, not their commanders. Aristocracy, culture and wealth have always been associated with equestrianism" (p. 48). Campbell's feeling for the aristocratic is instinctive and part of his whole emotional background. His hatred of conformity, together with

1. Wyndham Lewis, *Snooty Baronet,* p. 169.

his love of the athletic and the untamed, were powerful stimuli to theorize on the advantages of the equestrian life of the Provençal herdsmen with whom he was mixing in the early thirties and among whom he at last felt at ease. His own unhappiness in 1927, when living among a conforming literary group, strengthened his sense of the value of isolation, while the timidity and femininity he associated with that group confirmed him in his aggressively masculine persona. The influence of Wyndham Lewis was to consolidate these attitudes. Lewis's consistent attacks, during the twenties, on the mediocrity and conformism of contemporary culture are more subtle and varied than Campbell's emotional reaction against a society he dislikes. But Lewis dislikes the same things that Campbell dislikes. Feminism, the abdication of the male through inversion, and homosexuality are seen by Lewis in *The Art of Being Ruled* as part of the "Sex War" which elevates "youth," the "Peter Pan," in order to render man impotent. Campbell incorporates this scorn for the "Peter Pan" into *Broken Record,* and praises Hitler in a way which suggests that he is taking at face value Lewis's tribute to the efficiency of the monolithic fascist structure in achieving reform without interference from the mob. Similarly Campbell uses Charlie Chaplin, the "Charlie," as his symbol of the degraded, pedestrian, shopkeeping values of urban civilization, when Wyndham Lewis has a chapter in *Time and Western Man* on the secret of the success of Charlie Chaplin, whom he sees as a symbol of the contemporary wish for the small to defeat the great, or for the infant to give Dad a wallop.

Campbell's insistence on the superiority of his equestrian values, and his scorn for "pedestrian" civilization can become disturbing in the polemical passages in *Broken Record:*

> I see the new time coming for us. The knight of la Mancha lifts his lance, and on it, like a pinned cockroach, dangles the figure of Charlie Chaplin in the regulation uniform of Mr. Quennell's compulsory pedestrian "business man," with his made-up bow and

dirty shirt-front, sissying, shuffling, giggling and wag-
gling his moustaches. . . . The Boer War showed that
numbers are nothing, that machinery is nothing, that
money is nothing, that cynicism is nothing, that men
are everything, that chivalry is supreme, that loyalty
and courage wins. [pp. 207–8]

Flamboyance of this kind is an integral part of his effer-
vescent challenge to sober British ways. For all its passion,
the plea for a return to chivalric values in a degraded world
is unremarkable enough. However, the tone quickly
changes. After writing, "men are everything, chivalry is
supreme, that loyalty and courage wins," Campbell continues: "there is no harm in tent-pegging any dirty little
pedestrian civilian or shoving his 'civilisation' away, where-
ever we find it refusing to roll away of its own accord like
an automatic carpet." Much of the swashbuckling manner
is assumed deliberately to shock an obtusely fair-minded
Anglo-Saxon audience, but the "tent-pegging" of the
"little" and "dirty" pedestrian betrays an element of really
sadistic delight.

In 1933 the Campbells moved to Spain, accompanied
by the South-African poet, Uys Krige, who had joined them
in Martigues and acted as a tutor to their daughters, Tess
and Anna. They spent a few months in a pension in Barcelona, moved to Alicante for a short stay, and then settled
at Altea near Alicante. In 1935 the family moved to Toledo.
In 1934 the Campbells had been received into the Roman
Catholic Church, and it was as a Catholic and conservative
that the poet began his residence in Toledo in 1935. The
beautiful old cathedral city deeply affected him and became for him a symbol of the traditional, pious, Catholic
life which he celebrates in his poetry of the period.
Throughout their stay in Toledo they were particularly
friendly with the Carmelite monks of the city, and pursued
their religious interests with complete disregard for the
danger in which this could involve them at a time when the
forces of the far Left were more than ready to settle old
scores with the established Church.

Campbell's conservatism and dislike of the British left-wing intelligentsia had been fanned by the fact that the popular writers in Britain at the time were mainly left-wingers and represented a new and powerful coterie. Coupled with the fact that his own popularity as a writer was on the wane, his total and instinctive dislike of literary groups made his aversion to the Auden group violent.[2] The fact that in Spain he was continually coming up against political extremism of all kinds, where the communists represented the centre rather than the left-wing of the political Left, must inevitably have contributed to the un-usual violence of his antileftist sentiments. In the same way the extreme nature of his own right-wing attitude can also be partly attributed to the Spanish instinct for extremes in the politics on which he began to express opinions. When anti-clerical feeling was running high before the outbreak of hostilities in the civil war, and shortly after hostilities began, he openly maintained his Christian loyalty and pro-tected the Carmelite archives in his house. The fighting in Toledo was severe after the right-wing rising by its military garrison in July 1936, and the Campbells were evacuated to England. In the same year *Mithraic Emblems* was pub-lished, the second volume of Campbell's to receive scant attention. The book contains most of his Spanish poetry, and embodies a development of both his equestrian-vaquero ideals and his antimaterialist, antisocialist attitude.

The poems in *Mithraic Emblems* show a change in technique and content from Campbell's earlier work. The change in technique is a development towards a personal symbolism, necessitated by the need to give original ex-pression to the religious content of so many of the poems. Symbols in *Flowering Reeds* are used as an organic part of the scene or mood which the poet is describing. Those in *Mithraic Emblems* are imported into the poem from his

2. His attitude could not have been mollified by comments such as those of Stephen Spender, who, in reviewing Wyndham Lewis's *Men Without Art* in the *Spectator* of October 19, 1934, wrote: "It would be easiest to assume that Mr. Lewis has no good opinion of any other living writer, but unfortunately there is one high light in this book which does little credit to his taste: 'Mr. Roy Campbell, in his *Georgiad* has pro-duced a masterpiece of the satiric art, which may be placed beside the eighteenth-century pieces without its suffering by that proximity' " (p. 576).

own concept of the Mithraic element in Christianity. They combine associations of Christian and Mithraic symbolism, both of which have a validity outside the poems themselves. The result is that *Mithraic Emblems* illustrates a major attempt at development in poetic manner, but also contains much that is obscure and confused. Because the new symbolism is personal and freely formulated into a symbolic system, its significance in the poetry is often arbitrary and contrasts sharply with the integrated symbolic imagery in *Flowering Reeds*. The change in content in *Mithraic Emblems* is more significant. Those political and sociological views which Campbell had been expressing in prose in *Taurine Provence* and *Broken Record* appear in his poetry for the first time in *Mithraic Emblems*. From that time he continued to write political poems. He had included political comments in his earlier work, but always as part of a more general discussion. *The Georgiad* is his first published work to attack openly the cliquish, mediocre idealism of drawing-room left-wing attitudes. Nevertheless, in *The Georgiad* his dislike of Georgian decorum as a whole is the informing impulse of the poem, and political attitudes form only a part of the code to which that literary world conforms. Similarly his attacks on colonial smugness and narrowness of outlook in *Adamastor* are only a part of a "violent claustrophobiac struggle to keep my individual being." In each case the poems are essentially subjective. Once he begins to express openly political views, however, there is usually an objective, external truth against which his remarks can be assessed. In *Mithraic Emblems* many of the better poems do not claim to present objective truths about society, but embody the poet's personal reaction to the conflict between forces of reaction and forces of revolution. It is when he tries to pass judgement on the struggle, and to give objective statements about which side is right and which side is to be admired, that his poems go awry. The taking of sides involves an oversimplification of issues and often a distortion of facts.

Campbell's Christian fervour is the impetus behind some fine rhetoric in *Mithraic Emblems*, and is the raison d'être of the complex short-sonnet sequence which gives

the volume its title. At the same time his scorn for those
who complain about social conditions and material discomfort recurs continually. This scorn for social reformers
and the critics of poverty is the logical counterpart of both
the poet's own fervid take-no-care-for-the-morrow brand
of Christianity, and his belief in the heroic values of a
world where men are men, and rely on themselves rather
than on welfare planning and centralized assistance. Although his vindictive attitude towards political opponents
does appear from time to time, and he reveals an increasing fascination with the idea of a messianic purge by
sword, as a whole the collection shows a controlled contempt for the materialist values he saw in socialist movements and what he interpreted as their conformist principle. Beyond the crusading urge there is little excessive in
Mithraic Emblems. But the attitudes Campbell shows here
are those which lead to the heartless views in the Spanish
poems published later, and his Spanish period as a whole
can best be understood through the values he discusses in
Mithraic Emblems. The highly personal Christian vision in
its opening "Mithraic Frieze" demonstrates how his consistently heroic outlook becomes part of a formulaic religious attitude which can easily be identified in the poet's
mind with the spirit of old Spain, and which is by implication opposed to any attempt at social revolution or reform.

The "Mithraic Frieze" sequence begins with a quotation from Mistral which describes a typical frieze scene in
a Mithraic shrine. Campbell himself translates the Provençal in this way: "In the middle is a bull which a scorpion is
about to sting in the belly: a dog also bites it: and a snake
undulates at its feet. The bull, stronger than all, has held
its own, till a man in a cape, a proud young man, crested
with the bonnet of liberty, seizes it by the muzzle and
stabs it. Above the dying beast a frightful raven flies. Let
him divine the mystery who can!" (1, 115) The frieze described in the quotation depicts the central adventure in
the Mithras legend, which was the capturing and slaying
of the sacred bull by Mithras himself. Mithras, ancient god
of light, caught and sacrificed the bull on the order of the
sun, who had sent the raven as his messenger. From the

blood of the dying animal sprang the life of the earth, although Ahriman, the prince of evil, tried to prevent it. The soul of the bull ascended into the heavens and became the guardian of herds and flocks, while Mithras, who by his action had become the creator of life, was taken by the sun in his chariot to the dwelling of the immortals. The relief represents Mithras, the young man, slaying the bull as a sacrifice to bring about terrestial life. The scorpion attacking the bull's genitals has probably been sent by Ahriman to thwart the sacrifice; the dog, leaping at the wound in the bull's side, is usually identified as Mithras' companion. He, like the serpent (who symbolizes the earth), drinks the sacrificial blood and becomes fertile.[3] The raven is the herald of the sun god who has given instructions for the sacrifice. In some friezes the same connection between the sun and Mithras is represented by one ray of the seven-rayed halo around the sun god being directed at Mithras himself.

In Roman times Mithraism had been firmly established along the Rhône valley. Campbell saw a continuation of the tradition in the heroic piety which he associated with the sun-loving, bullfighting values of the people of Spain and Provence. The vigour and colour of a cult associated with the sun god naturally appealed to his own interests, and the heroic athleticism reflected in the cult was a part of his own world of water-jousting, steer-throwing, and cocarde-snatching at Martigues. After the poet's conversion to Roman Catholicism, the sacrificial element in the legend could be associated with his own religious beliefs. By this stage, the cult as a whole can be seen to offer a synthesis of the pagan, sun-worshipping delights of his youth and the formal redemptive urge of his religious conversion. Campbell does not attempt a scholarly investigation of the ideas and practices of Mithraism, but incorporates the central features of the legend freely into his own system of values, where they give a formal ring to beliefs

3. This virtual paraphrase of the article in the *Encyclopaedia Britannica* gives a simple statement of the interpretation advanced more fully by Cumont in *The Mysteries of Mithra*, particularly in pp. 135–40. For a slightly different account see Vermaseren, *Mithras, The Secret God.*

that were already instinctive to him. The facts that Mithraism had been popular in Provence, where he lived himself, and that the bull-slaying, herd-guarding elements in the myth were an essential part of his own environment, are enough to give him his interest in Mithraic values, and his identification with them. When *his* pastoral world seemed threatened by industrial or urban socialist forces, his response incorporated much of the Mithraic pattern which had become a part of his outlook. A legend built around a sacrificial slaying, with new life springing from the victim's blood, has many affinities with the political movement with which the poet was in sympathy, advocating a purging blood bath and military rebellion to restore old, heroic, Catholic Spain. For these reasons his Mithraism is easily assimilated into a total personal outlook, and in the poetry is always part of a typically Campbellian response.

It is the life-giving quality of the sacrifice in either Christian or Mithraic belief which he suggests continually in the sequence, without adhering strictly to a consistent pattern from which to overlap associations from either cult. This flexible approach results in the bull's representing either the self-hood and earthbound interests whose sacrifice leads to newer, brighter life on a spiritual plane, or the sacrificial victim to the sun whose blood represents the possibility of regeneration. Because the similarities between the two sets of symbols are so strong that Campbell can freely represent either Mithraic or Christian values at any given point, the sequence shows both a wide range of reference and a dangerous lack of control over the poet's favourite hunting grounds for pyrotechnic effects.

A successful fusion of Christian and Mithraic interests, such as that which occurs in "The Solar Enemy," does reveal an originality and freshness. In the poem the solar figure is represented as the enemy of the poet's "inward night." The "bestial signs" of his fallen human condition become identified with the bull, which is itself slain by the toreadoring Mithraic deity. The fusion of Mithras and Christ as the forces of light opposed to the darkness of the earthbound condition is neatly and consistently presented,

while the opposition of the physical values of the bull and
the intellectual values of the divine light gives an added
coherence to the symbolic pattern. Because the argument
and the symbols which express it are welded so tightly, the
verbal extravagances are not cloying. They are themselves
organic to the theme:

> Enemy of my inward night
> and victor of its bestial Signs
> whose arm against the Bull designs
> the red veronicas of light.
>
> [1, 116]

The progression is easily made from the idea of the poet's
spiritual darkness being conquered by divine light to that
of the bull being subdued by the passes of the toreador of
light. The ornate imagery with which he goes on to describe the matador's cape of the god of light is within the
bounds of decorum because of its relevance to both the
ornate splendour of a real cape and the picture of a divine
revelation of light:

> your cape a roaring gale of gold
> in furious auroras swirled,
> the scarlet of its outward fold
> is of a dawn beyond the world—
> a sky of intellectual fire
> through which the stricken beast may view
> its final agony aspire
> to sun the broad aeolian blue—
> my own lit heart, its rays of fire,
> the seven swords that run it through.
>
> [1, 116]

The last two lines of "The Solar Enemy" introduce the
concept of the seven swords, or rays of fire, that pierce the
poet's heart. In the central section of "Mithraic Frieze"
Campbell describes the seven swords of vision in poems
which embody the extremely personal significance of his
religion. It is the mingling of broad Christian imagery with

intensely personal views which gives these central poems their peculiar complexity and obscurity. The complexity shows that Campbell's religious preoccupation in the sequence is only part of a total personal response. In many cases the religious framework can be used by him to express values that are not explicitly Christian. The general mood of each poem grows out of its prevalent colour, although the distinction between some "hues" is less obvious than the poet may have liked. A vagueness in the seven sword poems as a group arises from his attempt to create a mood in each rather than investigate a concept. The arbitrary nature of the values represented by each mood further diminishes the coherence of the group. So does the fatal fascination that the colourfully emotive image has for him, a fascination which is given free reign by his overt concern to evoke atmosphere through colour.

The idea of the seven swords which pierce the poet's heart is partly suggested by the seven rays of the sun in some Mithraic representations, and is more directly derived from the section entitled "Les Sept Épées" in Apollinaire's poem, "La Chanson du Mal-Aimé." "Les Sept Épées" is a notoriously obscure description of the seven stages of Apollinaire's unhappy love, in which he coins names and symbols to describe the intimate details of a relationship too painful for him to present directly. Personal symbolism is thus part of a deliberate pattern of camouflage in the French poem. Although Campbell has no conscious wish to conceal the reality of the seven stages of his vision, their private nature can to some extent be attributed to the example of his source. He does not follow the French poem at all closely, but does take over two images almost in their entirety, and borrows the central conceit of each sword's being symbolized by a colour and embodying the mood of one stage in a relationship. The difference is obvious between Campbell's own lit heart being transfixed with rays of fire and Apollinaire's heavy heart being pierced with melancholy:

Sept épées de mélancolie
Sans morfil ô claires douleurs

Sont dans mon coeur et la folie
Veut raisonner pour mon malheur
Comment voulez-vous que j'oublie.[4]
[*Oeuvres Poétiques*]

At the same time, "Vulcan in forging it grew old," is clearly derived from "Vulcain mourut en la forgeant," while Campbell's version of

C'est un cyprès sur un tombeau
Où les quatre vents s'agenouillent
Et chaque nuit c'est un Flambeau.

is:

by day a cypress on a tomb,
but in the night it is a flame.
[1, 120]

There are many passages in *Mithraic Emblems* where Campbell's old heroic values are effectively incorporated into his new religious vision. In the seven sword poems, however, the fusion is arbitrary. In "The First Sword," with old war-horse adjectives making a flaccid reappearance, a capacity for sexual passion, a love of beauty, and an ability to fight heroically for life, all become part of a vision of God. The imagery is as ornate as anything in the whole "Mithraic Frieze," and the resulting confusion is like a parody of his style:

The first of lunar crystal hewn,
a woman's beauty, through whose snows
the volted ecstacy outglows
a dolphin[5] dying in the noon.

[1, 118]

4. This stanza is the last in the section immediately preceding "Les Sept Épées."

5. A passage from *Light on a Dark Horse* clarifies the allusion to the dolphin, but still does not justify the comparison in the poem: "I have seen that famous fish which sailors correctly call the 'dolphin' . . . dying on the deck of the *Inkonka* and the gorgeous colours swirling in humming-bird tornasols, through its greenish-silver body as if a thousand rainbows were chasing each other across the sky" (p. 297).

Even more private and visionary are the second and third
sword poems, which suggest the peace deriving from a
union with God, and the gap between human understanding and revelations of divinity. In "The Fifth Sword," funereal descriptions of grief and shame are given a personal
significance by the subtitle published in *Mithraic Emblems*
in 1936, "In memory of my Father." A subtitle is not printed
in *Collected Poems,* and without it the particularly pointed
significance of the poet's lasting grief remains inaccessible.

In comparison, the sixth sword is linked to identifiable
experiences and attitudes. Its colour, "clear lightning with a
sheath of gold," resembles the picture of Christ as
"Orange, flaring bold with scourges" in the last poem of
the sequence, "To the Sun." In that concluding poem
Campbell addresses a Mithraic sun as the "mirror and the
shield" of Christ. He then relates the seven colours that
make up the solar white of the sun's rays to seven aspects
of Christ's life. The relevance of Christ's scourging powers
to the Spanish Nationalist crusade against allegedly decadent democracy is made explicit in the closing lines of
"The Sixth Sword":[6]

> the sixth salutes the last Crusade
> and her, by all the world betrayed,
> who reared its red and golden streamer
> upon the ramparts of Castile—
> of the mad West the sole redeemer
> and rainbow of the Storms of Steel.
>
> [1, 120]

The "red and golden streamer" is the monarchist flag

6. The political closing to "The Sixth Sword" is an alteration to the
original version, and appears for the first time in *Collected Poems.* The
original version, written long before the outbreak of hostilities in Spain,
first published in the *New Statesman* on August 26, 1933, and republished in *Mithraic Emblems* in 1936, ends with these lines:

> forged only of the living rays
> of whom its lustre is the praise,
> the sixth salutes with lifted blade
> the passing oriflammes of days
> to whose white-mounted cavalcade
> the red blood drums the Marseillaise.

adopted by the Nationalist rebels. Its colours are hinted at in the sword of anger, the fourth sword, which also resembles Christ "flaring bold with scourges." Although the sixth sword is thus connected with an accessible public event, its significance in the sequence is still obscure. The sonnet shows how easily Mithraic and political views can merge, but does little to clarify the relevance of successive aspects of the poet's vision. In the final sword poem there is no resolution of the problem. God's love of his creatures is described in terms of both Cupid's physical love for Psyche and the divine possession of the Pythoness, the priestess of Apollo, at Delphi. In the central image of the "sworded flame" caught in "pale ice," erotic overtones mingle with a suggestion of the divine fire immanent in the cold products of creation:

> As arctic crystals that would shun,
> but each become, the living sun,
> where best his image may be sought.
>   [1, 121]

Here, the identification of the "living sun" with a divine figure leads back to the main Mithraic theme. It repeats the connection between the solar deity and the creatures made in his image, which was suggested in the opening description of the seven swords of vision. The seven stages of the poet's vision arise from his original impetus to aspire to the "dawn beyond the world" by exposing his heart to the rays of fire of the solar deity. To this extent the seven sword poems form a progressive link between the opening sonnets of the sequence and those which investigate the significance of the raven and other symbols depicted in the prefatory quotation. Nevertheless, the private nature of so much of the seven visionary poems shows Campbell's religious preoccupations at their most obscure.

The closing section of the sequence has a wider range of reference. "The Sixth Sword" allied his political and religious attitudes clearly enough, and the concluding sonnets make explicit the divine role of the carefree vaquero, who appears so frequently in later poems as the symbol of

the naturally pious man who will redeem the rotten industrial world, often with a sacrificial bloodbath. Before con-
centrating on his beloved equestrian world, Campbell
elaborates the redemptive element in his Mithraic pattern.
In "The Raven II" the desiccated twigs with which the
bird's nest has been made suggest both the worthlessness
of the products of time and the withering of forms of life
that were once vital. This leads to a suggestion of the eternal regeneration that is attendant on the total sacrifice of
temporal values. The redemptive associations of the con-
suming agency of fire gain force through their association
with the order, submitted by the fiery sun god through his
messenger the raven, for the regenerative sacrifice of the
bull:

> and steeper yet he stacks the pyre
> to tempt the forked, cremating fire
> to strike, to kindle, and consume:
> till answering beacons shall attest
> that fire is in the Raven's nest
> and resurrection in the tomb.
> $\qquad$ [1, 122]

An eagerness for the "cremating fire" in both "The Raven
II" and "The Raven's Nest" is typical of Campbell's total
commitment to a redemptive religion. In "The Raven's
Nest" there is a picture of the twigs lifting up their claws
"in imprecation" for the fire as "a bride." This religious
impetus is translated, in a political situation, into the poet's
repeated longing for a destructive force, either rust or the
sword, to purge away the dross of the industrial world and
materialist values. In "The Dawn" the same redemptive
eagerness informs the picture of the snake, the scorpion,
and the dog, feeding on the dying body of the bull whose
death is about to produce the possibility of new life:

> Tug, monsters, at the badgered meat
> out of whose needs yourselves were born;
> into the east you tug the morn
> whose victory is your defeat;

> drink, thirsty swords, the central star—
> your cup of blood; your kiss of steel
> shall blaze the rising orb afar
> of which you twinkle in the wheel.
>
> [1, 124]

"Thirsty swords" and a "kiss of steel" are in place here as part of the visionary ecstasy. When they reappear in later Spanish poems as the scourging solution to social malaise, they give a sickening note to Campbell's all-embracing belief in the redemptive sacrifice.

In the concluding sonnets the general religious significance of the sequence modulates into a specific view of the superior spiritual virtues of the cowboy:

> "Sing, Cowboy! string your strong guitar!
> For each Vaquero is a star
> and Abel's sons the line will cross,
> under the stretched, terrific wings,
> the outspread arms (our soaring King's)—
> the man they made an Albatross!"
>
> [1, 126]

Christ's sacrifice provides the permanent possibility of redemption, the crossing of the line of death, for each pious Christian. It is typical of Campbell's outlook that the vaquero is singled out for protection under the outspread arms of Christ, that he is associated with the sons of Abel (himself a pious herdsman, slain by his discontented brother), and opposed to the vague forces of destruction, the "they" who crucified the Christian Son of God. The implied comparison between pious peasants and the anticlerical forces of the social revolution is strongly suggested.

Christian fervour, the sun-worshipping vigour of the legend, and the belief in sacrificial regeneration, which form the content of "Mithraic Frieze," are as natural to Campbell's religious as to his political outlook. An occasional fusion of politics and religion in the sequence shows how inseparable are the elements of his total response to situation. The personal note can be a real source of

strength when it is part of the religious, eternal commitment, and not part of an earthly, temporal loyalty. "Death
of the Bull" combines the feeling of personal conviction
with an intricate welding of Mithraic and Christian symbolism to make a compact statement of the central religious theme of the sequence. It shows the strength
Campbell gains by uniting his own religious certainty with
the symbols of the Mithraic cult. The real sacrifice it is to
give up worldly standards is suggested while the Mithraic
sacrifice is being described. But the main impact is to
suggest the life-giving powers of the sacrificial blood:

> out of a Wound that never heals
> rills forth the lily-scented blood,
> the snow-fed wine of scarlet stain,
> that widens, flowering through the plains,
> and from the Wound its anguish drains—
> as you may hear from one who drank,
> down on his knees beside the bank,
> and lost the memory of pain.
>
> [1, 123]

A suggestion of the regenerative quality of Mithraic blood
merges with the overtones of Christian redemption in the
picture of the poet drinking the blood in a kneeling position. Being anointed with the blood of the sacrificed bull
was as essential to the practice of the Mithraic cult as the
symbolic drinking of Christ's blood in the communion is to
Christian worship.

   "Mithraic Frieze" represents a significant attempt at
an extended statement of Campbell's religious position.
The mingling it shows of his old heroic and athletic values
with a new commitment to the Christian sacrifice is the
most important element in his political stand in Spain.
Nevertheless, it is the more accessible poems in *Mithraic
Emblems* to which a reader must turn for a clearer understanding of the mingling of Campbell's general values and
political attitudes. These general values become incorporated into a semipolitical statement in "The Sling." In it his
belief in the pleasures of an instinctive participation in

life is coupled with an idealized picture of his childhood in the open, to make a contrast with the life-denying conformity of urban values and complaints. His control over his material varies at different points in the poem, which is convincing when the positive values of his vital individuality are embodied in the poetry, and strained when he makes a general condemnation of those who do not share his views. The varying quality of the poetic experience in "The Sling" is in this way typical of all the Spanish poems, although it contains comparatively little direct political comment. The change in tone is marked when the poet turns from his own pastoral delights to the despicable qualities from which they save him. At first there is fine restraint in a picture of timeless bucolic ease:

> Guarding the cattle on my native hill
> This was my talisman. Its charm was known
> High in the blue and aquiline ozone,
> And by my tireless armourer, the rill,
> Smoothing his pellets to my hand or eye:
> And how its meteors sang into the sky
> The eagles of the Berg remember still.
>
> [1, 127]

An interaction of human activities and the natural world is a simple part of the description, and yet one which gives an inevitability to the moral value which Campbell attributes in later stanzas to a natural enjoyment of the world as it is. Even the war between the eagles and the young herdsman carries no suggestion of pain and death, but is part of the stylized lyricism of the pastoral scene. The limited range of pastoral values does not affect the validity of his evocation of natural delights, but seriously restricts any attempt to apply these values in toto to the complex modern world, as if it can be discussed in terms of an idealized bucolic concept. The dangers inherent in his retreat into an imaginary and uncomplicated world can be seen even in a poem where the poet still manages to create a sense of the real strength in his pastoral position.

When he turns to describe the symbolic value of the sling, the tone is still well controlled:

> I wore this herdsman's bracelet all day long:
> To me it meant "To-morrow" and "Perhaps,"
> The insults of Goliath, his collapse,
> Much fighting, and (who knows?) a life of song.
> So fine a jewel at his wrist to swing
> (For it was Chance) has seldom graced a king—
> As I have dangled on a rawhide thong.
>
> [1, 127]

His reflective note and the ruminative pauses are in perfect keeping with the deliberately vague aura of a world governed by the unperturbed attitude of "To-morrow" and "Perhaps." Campbell's attitudes are convincing as part of a total, personal reaction to life. It is the specific nature of his own outlook which the poet sets out to capture, and succeeds in embodying in the poetry. His carefree values are credible as part of his own pastoral world, and the exceptional nature of both the world and the values is the element in the poem which he takes most pains to establish. His attempt in later poems to impose these views on the world in general is, as a result, bound to be unconvincing because in effect it entails the logical contradiction of his saying: "I am one of the few who still lead an aristocratic, distinguished existence in a mediocre, undistinguished world. Everyone should be aristocratic and exceptional like me." A wish to have his cake and eat it underlies much of the poet's simultaneous boasting about the uniqueness of his values and his forcing them on the world at large. In "The Sling" he does no proselytizing, but the weak parts of the poem are those in which the uniformity of the rest of the world is sneered at:

> Where none break ranks though down the whole race
>   treks,
> It taught me how to separate, and choose;
> The uniform they ordered, to refuse—
> The hornrimmed eyes, the ringworm round their
>   necks;

And, when the Prince of herdsmen rode on high,
To rope those hikers with that bolshie tie,
To save my scruff, and see without the specs.

[1, 129]

The racy language is in itself a sign that the content of the
stanza is too extravagant to be expressed within the decorum of the opening stanzas. As the insults recur the tone
degenerates inside the stanza itself. Campbell is not describing his own world so much as pointing out its superiority, and when he turns directly to criticizing "them," the
inarticulate nature of his scorn is manifest in the childish
values which underlie the attack and the schoolboy language in which it is couched.

In the next stanza the poetry recaptures the unhurried,
carefree ease of the pastoral setting. Campbell is not only
stating that he prefers a detached and self-contained existence. He is being detached at this point:

Choosing my pebbles (to distinguish, free)
I had dispensed with numbers; finding how,
Since Space was always Here as Time was Now,
Extent of either means a Fig to me;
To the whole field I can prefer a flower
And know that States are foundered by an hour
While centuries may groan to fell a tree.

[1, 129]

This rejection of quantitative, mass-produced values is
typical of the sanity which he can demonstrate. A belief in
commonsense emerges clearly, as well as a hatred of any
emphasis on the theoretic at the expense of the real. He
goes on to give convincing expression of the content to be
derived from an immediate enjoyment of the world as it is:

Slung at his wrist will hang the phantom stress
Of David's stone—to weigh that all is right;
Even to daunt him should the weak unite
In one Goliath, he'll accept and bless,
Whose home's the Earth, and Everywhere his bed

> A sheepskin saddle to his seat or head,
> And Here and Now his permanent address.
>
> [1, 130]

The idea of the weak uniting in one Goliath is part of Campbell's outlook towards socialist movements or "collective bargaining." The sturdy self-reliance celebrated in "The Sling" is the attitude he advocates continually in preference to the, to him, despicable, self-pitying complaints about injustice made by groups of those who have no power as individuals. Stated baldly in these terms, as social comment, his views are cruelly reactionary. But when the positive values of his belief in self-reliance are the centre of interest, as in this stanza, the sheer perversity of the poet's dismissal of the need for the underprivileged to wrest privileges from the privileged is absent. An easy acceptance of life as it is, and the real freedom and stature which such an attitude confers, are the dominant impressions of the closing stanza and round off well the heroic and pastoral mood of the poem.

In *Mithraic Emblems,* Christian simplicity and a heroic, equestrian world become closely associated with "sacred" Toledo and its surrounding plains. Campbell's close identification with the area and its life is part of his feeling of belonging at last, as was his vigorous defence of Provençal life. In "After the Horse-fair" his very personal view of an inclusive Christian piety is used to create a series of sketches of the simple life in the countryside around Toledo. His belief in unself-conscious faith and comradeship emerges without a trace of either the strident or smug assertiveness which creeps into other poems on the same subject. Each stanza in the opening section captures the carefree mood of one scene, after the horse fair on the Castilian plateau. In his ideal world of friendly gypsies, cheerful Civil Guards, and innocuous thieves, there is a total, natural harmony:

> Two figtrees on a whitewashed wall
> Were playing chess; a lamp was queen:
> Beneath the civil guard were seen

With tricorned hats—a game of cards:
One bottle was between them all,
Good health, and kind regards.

A stable with an open door
And in the yard a dying hound:
Out on the dunes a broken spoor
Converging into twenty more—
When torches had been flashed around
Was all they could restore.

[1, 137]

The Civil Guards are completely egalitarian with their
shared bottle, and their unconcerned pleasures result in
the theft which is described in deliberately unperturbed
Castilian terms. A shrug of the shoulders is almost part of
the poetry. There is nothing sinister in the scene of the
policemen or that of the theft, and the commonplace sins,
pleasures, and virtues reflected in the picture are made
explicitly part of a Christian concern for all aspects of life
in the concluding section. There, the whole plateau scene
becomes a "mirage of wonder" to the solitary rider as
Toledo's bells are heard in the distance:

Till with a faint adoring thunder,
Their lances raised to Christ the King,
Through all the leagues he had to go—
An army chanting smooth and low,
Across the long mirage of wonder
He heard the steeples sing.

[1, 137–38]

The visionary ecstasy of the picture is modulated into the
matter-of-fact tone of the preceding stanzas, with the result that the resplendent glory of the army of steeples
appears as only another part of the inclusive, pastoral
world of cathedrals, thieves, gypsies, and "lonesome car-
bineers." Because the presentation of life is deliberately
two dimensional, without any attempt by the poet to
create an impression of depth in his series of tableaux, the

essentially idealistic nature of his description does not affect its credibility. As a convincing evocation of the old Spain to whose values he was so passionately committed, "After the Horse-fair" clearly illustrates how the subjective, suggestive picture of these values can carry a sense of conviction which eludes an objective or polemical statement of them.

Campbell's obsession with the opposition he saw between his own heroic values and those of the forces bent on what he interpreted as the wholly materialist, quantitative standards of social revolution, is as subjective as his visionary feeling for what is vital and distinguished in life. In the poems of this period the obsessive recurrence of symbols which he associates with the redeeming qualities of his simple faith is in itself an indication of the self-enclosed nature of his passionate reaction against social complaint or attempts at social reform. The fact that he himself and his way of life appear to be threatened by reform is the reason for his insistence on the River Tagus or Toledo as symbols of the Christian regenerative principle, and of his own circle of horsemen and villagers as symbols of the carefree piety of the ideal Christian. When he describes these values in the world from which they derive, the presence in the poetry of Campbell's beloved Toledo and Castilian cowboys is a natural part of the environment itself. The effect is strained, however, when he turns to describe the corresponding spiritual decay in the camp of the social reformers, and still attempts to use isolated references to Toledo or the vaquero as symbols of spiritual health and sanity. In many poems in *Mithraic Emblems* he sets out to attack what he sees as the mechanist principle and materialist values of the opponents of old, heroic Spain. Although there is often a glimpse in these poems of the natural energies and beauties denied by the forces of social change, his central intention is to expose what he interprets as the antihuman premise of their position. His negative impulse is not limited to exposing attitudes, but includes a wish to destroy the mechanical world which threatens pastoral values, and to purge society of mechanist views. His crusading vigour and inquisitorial zeal are

not limited to rusting away the machine world. He repeatedly hints at the holy quality of the swords that will purge
the world of meaner men. Campbell's insensitivity towards
violence is often only partly submerged in his earlier
poems, but in his Spanish poems it can come to the surface with frightening unconcern.

The ruthlessness of his vision of a return to the past can
be seen in "Vaquero to his Wife":

> Since from his charred mechanic Hells
> Now to his native form restored,
> The azure soul of Steel rebels
> Refulgent in a single Sword
> Whose edge of Famine, honed with ire,
> Flames forth his threat to all the lands
> Where wheels and furnaces conspire
> To rob the skill from human hands,
> From human hearts the solar fire.
>
> [1, 142]

A wish, which might at first sight seem reminiscent of
Blake, to describe the horror of the "charred mechanic
Hells" is secondary to the main intention in the lines,
which is to evoke the spirit of the reforming sword. The
poet's approval is quite clearly behind the threat to all the
lands where wheels and furnaces dominate, and he uses
his well-loved epithet "refulgent" with almost messianic
overtones. The result is that the values are curiously mixed
in the lines. A suggestion of the horrors of mass industrialism, which is present in the "charred mechanic Hells,"
forms a natural part of a humane reaction to the suffering
resulting from industrial exploitation. However, it is a very
private and extreme reaction to postulate the desruction
of industrialism as the solution to these horrors. Campbell's intense involvement in the political situation continually forces him into similarly extreme positions from
an originally understandable response to the denial of
human values. His fascination with the "azure," "steel" of
the cleansing yet death-dealing sword is just as inhuman
as the gross materialism of the charred mechanic hells.

There is no sense of the poet's feeling any distress that the refulgent sword should be allied with famine and anger.

At times he describes a destructive spirit as part of the materialist world itself from which he remains detached. Normally he cannot remain aloof, however, and he uses rust and locust imagery to depict a divine gift of purgation in "To the Survivors":

> The rust that paints their cities red
> And makes their cast-iron idols reel:
> The russet locust-swarm that's spread
> Upon their wilting crops of steel:—
>
> This gift of our protecting Sire,
> The Solar Christ, to purge the lands—
> Is like the good Promethean fire
> At which to warm our scatheless hands.
> [1, 135]

The partisan mood is most intense when the picture of decay and disuse becomes something worthy of worship, and is directly equated with the divine purpose. So too the sense of personal gain to be derived from the decay emerges when he describes the comfortable warming of "our" hands at the fires which purge the world of steel. The certainty that the purge itself will leave "us" "scathe-less" would in itself do credit to the Comintern agents who saw to the purity of political faith in Catalonia in 1937, and for whom Campbell's scorn was justifiably boundless. His old heroic values appear with the addition of a strange new callousness when the solar qualities of the Promethean fire set the poet off on a well-worn track:

> By it the human heart relumed,
> Shall blaze once more with ruby light—
> The strong shall seize it unconsumed,
> The rest will crumble at its sight.
>
> The brave from out its grudging crust
> Will pull the treasure that it keeps—

Within the red sheath of the rust,
The white Excalibur that sleeps.
                                                                    [1, 136]

The militarist dream of the salvation of the world by the
strong, and the disintegration of the worthless weak is
combined with attitudes that have always characterized
Campbell's outlook:[7] a belief in the blazing light of the
heart and in the treasure that awaits those who struggle
with a "grudging crust." These attitudes become stock
responses when, as in "The Sling," he has to resort to
jargon in order to articulate his contempt for the puny,
urbanized pedestrian in comparison with the equestrian
commando:

Then, like Niagara set free,
Ride on, you fine Commando: vain
Were looking back, for all you'd see
Were "Charlies" running for their train!
                                                                    [1, 136]

Campbell is too automatically committed to his equestrian
world, which will "anachronise" the train, to realize how
ineffectual the taunt is. There is more reality to the most
despicable Charlie running for his train than to any "fine
commando" riding on like Niagara set free. The lack of
control over the verse itself is apparent in the arbitrary
nature of the simile and the wordy slackness of the epithet
"fine," which might well have been found in the idle ranks
of spectator adjectives at Squire's rugger match.

The most sustained attack in *Mithraic Emblems* on the
industrial, urban world is made in "Junction of Rails: Voice
of the Steel." Even here the poetic skill with which its

7. Campbell's belief in the ruthless cutting away of what he sees
as corruption and decay is very similar to a common Nationalist attitude. Hugh Thomas describes in this way the speech of General Millán
Astray at the University of Salamanca on October 12, 1936: "After the
opening formalities, Millán Astray made a violent attack on Catalonia
and the Basque provinces describing them as 'cancers in the body of
the nation. Fascism, which is Spain's health-giver, will know how to
exterminate both, cutting into the live healthy flesh like a resolute
surgeon free from false sentimentality.' " [*The Spanish Civil War*, p. 354]

metallic values are described exists side by side with a furious messianic impulse. The wit of the poem's opening shows all Campbell's skill at working an extensive argument through a succession of conceits. Then the political commitment proves too strong, and the poet resorts to his doctrinaire solution: a storm of steel, associated with Christ and the cowboy, which "brings not peace, but fury of delight," and reaps and cuts among the "pylons prostrate in the dust." The forces which are to bring this Christian and pastoral relief to the industrial world are not investigated with clarity in the poem, but are arbitrarily associated with the stock values and symbols of his heroic paradise. The change in depth and significance is marked between the sections where he uses all his poetic powers to describe the bleak values on which urban industrialism is based, and those where he suggests a solution: holy destruction. In the best passages the insistent energy of the rhythm provides a well-modulated undertone of constant uneasiness which is in perfect keeping with the picture of an inhuman machine-world and its imminent decay:

> Though they have taught the lightning how to lie
> And made their wisdom to misread the sky
> I hold their pulses: through my ringing loom
> Their trains with flying shuttles weave a doom
> I am too sure a prophet to defy.
>
> [1, 150]

In contrast, the closing vision of the tidings of relief relies on assertions that have their basis outside the poem:

> And I have often thought by lonely sidings—
> What shepherd or what cowboy in his ridings
> Forges the Sword so terrible and bright
> That brings not peace, but fury of delight,
> And of whose coming I have had the tidings.
>
> [1, 152]

The introduction of the shepherd or cowboy has to be made arbitrarily as a "thought," because they have no part in the poem. The doom and decay which the rails have sensed are integral to the inhuman world which they describe, whereas this quasi-messianic "coming" has to be taken on faith. In the next stanza the "tidings" are described as "the tidings of a world's relief," but the form they take is left unexplained. Terror is quite clearly part of the bright sword's mission, yet one of the reasons that there is no sense in the lines of the terror of a purgation by sword is that the author is never seen as a victim. He is always a heroic associate of the avengers themselves, the shepherd and the cowboy.

Campbell's formula for regeneration is quite unnecessary in the best sections of the poem which clearly set up the standards by which the industrial world is found inadequate. It is the sense that the decay is internal and inevitable which gives force to the picture of an industrial wasteland. The poet has no need to resort to the scourging cowboy to make his point. The values he describes are self-destructive:

> I tentacle the news: relay the mails:
> And sense the restive anger that prevails
> Wherever shafts descend or girders rise:
> And day and night their steel-to-steel replies
> Hum in my bolts and tingle in my rails.
>
> [1, 151]

The flabbiness of his stock responses at the end of the poem is all the more apparent in contrast with the success of his early evocation of the self-destructive code of an inhuman mode of life. His closing rhetorical flourish makes a typical contrast with the stanza just quoted, not only because the presence of death, valour, swords, and holiness is not realized in any way, but also because the assertion that there is an external solution to be found in crusading Death is as inhuman as the steel world which the poet has described:

> A sword is singing and a scythe is reaping
> In those great pylons prostrate in the dust,

Death has a sword of valour in his keeping
To arm our souls towards the future leaping:
And holy holy holy is the rust
Wherein the blue Excaliburs are sleeping!
[1, 152]

Typical of the vagueness of the whole emotional gesture of the stanza is the clumsiness of "To arm our souls towards the future leaping." The intelligence with which the malaise was described has disintegrated under the appeal of a wholehearted commitment to a death-dealing purge.

CHAPTER 6

"THE DEVIL-ROUTING
LORD OF THE ABYSS"

Even when Campbell turns to the Spanish civil war itself, his poetry can embody a convincing, subjective response to the events. His own fear during the terror in Toledo, his sympathy for the Carmelite martyrs, and his pride at military heroism as epitomized in the defence of the Alcazar can be expressed in his poetry without any distortion of fact. So too his general cynicism at English gullibility and what he regards as the romantic delusions of left-wing sympathizers is often made into a convincing poetic statement of a personal scepticism and independence. More often, however, the later Spanish poems set out to establish the sanctity of the Nationalist cause, and the corruption and cruelty of the Nationalists' opponents. The propagandist intention in so much of the poetry is twofold. On the general issue Campbell continually asserts the superiority of the Catholic and authoritarian mystique of the rebels over what he interprets as either the wholly materialist, communist ethic of his opponents, or the decadent democratic spirit of their allies. At the same time he is often intent on proving specific points about the war; in particular, the superiority of the Nationalist armed forces in the face of overwhelming odds, and the atrocities committed by the undisciplined and rabid mob who opposed them. While he points out the viciousness of the Republicans, he explains away reports of Nationalist cruelty. Many of these propagandist techniques are mutually contradictory. If the Nationalist rebellion was a "great popular National Uprising" and an "extraordinary awakening of a national consciousness," the odds against the rebels could not have been so large. To postulate that the rebellion is both popular, supported by the majority, and that it succeeded in the face of overwhelming odds against an enemy who held the greater part of the country is, to say the least, confusing. In the same way Campbell's intention to describe the heroism and valour of the Nationalists is adversely affected by his simultaneous attempts to describe the fleeing cowardice of their opponents against whom little heroism would seem necessary. Contradictions of this kind are a direct result of the propagandist intention in the war poems in which the sense of distortion is obvious. One side can do no wrong and the other can do no right, while Campbell repeatedly insists on his own superiority of insight in being able to see the truth which eludes all other English intellectuals. The feeling of strain and illegitimacy in the propaganda poems is caused by their obviously biased tone and manner which are apparent to a reader without any specialized knowledge of the events. At the same time, the very fact that poems like *Flowering Rifle* and "A Letter from the San Mateo Front" set out to describe political events and to pass judgement on them leads a reader to the facts themselves, as they exist, independently of the poem. The values of the politics are an inseparable part of the political poems. One's reaction to the facts of the Spanish situation is inextricably linked to one's reaction to a poem which sets out to describe those facts.

In the political poems Campbell's conservative instinct and his wish to eliminate the scourge of socialism are both naturally allied to the cause of the Nationalist rebels, and the poet's scorn for communists can become the hatred for a dangerous military enemy. What makes the propaganda poems different from the prewar poems is that in the former he accepts without question the attitudes of the military rebels with whom his own personal conservatism had much in common, and describes all political opponents of the military rebellion as despicable revolutionaries. The change in the poems is from the expression of a subjective conservatism to an objective statement of the values of Spanish military dictatorship and the futility of both democracy and the whole range of social reform movements opposed to that militarism.

Campbell's religious conviction is inseparable from his political convictions, and leads him into some of his most passionate political statements. Most of the accounts of Christian martyrdom which he relates are true. The persecution of the Church by the revolutionaries who opposed the military rebels was bloody and persistent in the early months of the war. Nevertheless, the way he describes that persecution gives a distorted impression of the motives behind it. Unjustifiable and savage as the suppression undoubtedly was, the reason for the hatred of the Church by the revolutionaries was the political role which the Church itself played in Spain, and its consistent support of conservative interests and the landowning classes. As an example of the way the Church exerted a political influence on its members and represented intransigent reaction to so many Spaniards, Gerald Brenan quotes from the complete Church catechism, republished in 1927. Its opening question, Brenan points out, establishes what "Liberalism" teaches, namely, that "the State is independent of the Church." After arguing that the state has to be subject to the Church, it lists as "heretical" the "false liberties of Liberalism": liberty of conscience, education, propaganda, and meeting. The catechism continues:

> "What kind of sin is Liberalism?"—"It is a most grievous sin against faith."

"Why?"—"Because it consists in a collection of heresies condemned by the Church."

"Is it a sin for a Catholic to read a Liberal newspaper?" He may read the Stock Exchange News.

"What sin is committed by him who votes for a Liberal candidate?"—"Generally a mortal sin."[1]

Campbell's horror at the reign of terror which was unleashed against the Church is a perfectly understandable and inevitable reaction.[2] But the political deductions he makes about the reign of terror do not take into account the political realities of the situation. Similarly his picture of the Nationalist rebels as the defenders of religion is misleading in that he omits to mention the fact that there was no religious freedom in Nationalist Spain itself, and that there was condemnation and persecution even of Catholics who did not support the Nationalist aims. In the Basque provinces, which remained loyal to the Republic and at the same time preserved a middle-class social order, there was virtually no persecution of the Church. The Basque Catholic clergy remained with their parishes, and supported the preservation of the status quo. In a pastoral letter broadcast on August 6, 1936, the Bishops of Vitoria and Pamplona condemned this attitude of the Basque Catholics. After the capture of northern Spain by the Nationalists, a campaign of persecution was begun against Basque Catholics. Monks and priests were imprisoned or deported, while sixteen were executed. These included a Carmelite monk. "There is a far cry from ill-treating or even killing a man, though a priest, for political reasons to a systematic persecution and wholesale murder of priests *qua* priests;"[3] nevertheless the point Koestler makes in *Spanish Testament* seems irrefutable: "Franco does not represent the interests of believers as against the forces that threaten religion. He represents the interests of that section of the Catholic population which is Catholic *and* reactionary. Catholics with Republican sympathies are persecuted

1. Gerald Brenan, *The Spanish Labyrinth*, pp. 51–52.
2. Protestant churches were not attacked, and remained open.
3. Salvador de Madariaga, *Spain*, pp. 376–77.

by him with the same ruthlessness as are Republicans who profess no religion."[4] Gabriel Jackson's description of the public pronouncements of Cardinal Goma captures the tone of the political involvement of the Spanish Church militant:

> His first public pronouncement of the war was a radio address from Pamplona on September 28, 1936, celebrating the relief of the Alcazar. He explained that the Nationalists were fighting against the Anti-Spain, the "bastard soul of the sons of Moscow," the Jews and Masons who had poisoned the ingenuous *pueblo* with Tartar and Mongol ideas, and who were erecting a system manipulated by the Semitic International. In December, in his first wartime pastoral, entitled *The Case of Spain,* he repeated similar charges, and attributed Spain's sufferings also to the servile imitation of foreign ways, the farce of parliamentarism, the falsehood of universal suffrage, and the insensate liberties of university teaching and the press. On January 10, 1937, he published an open letter to President Aguirre of the Basque government, in which, while he deplored the executions of the Basque priests he deplored equally the "aberration" which had led to the regretted incidents. He asked the Basques how it was that they could unite with the Marxist hordes to fight against brother Catholics because of a "nuance of political forms."[5]

The legitimacy of the rebels' cause and the "Red" nature of their opponents' regime are points which Campbell takes for granted in his political writing, and yet they require further explanation. The military rebellion which occurred in Spain in July 1936 began the civil war which lasted until 1939. It was carried out by military leaders, most of the Civil Guard, and supported by right-wing elements throughout the country, especially the Falange, a fascist organization, and the Carlist Requetés of Navarre,

4. Arthur Koestler, *Spanish Testament,* p. 115.

5. Gabriel Jackson, *The Spanish Republic and the Civil War 1931–1939,* p. 386.

who were organized in military fashion and supported a reactionary Monarchist cause. The immediate occasion for the rising was the murder by the *Asaltos*, the police force loyal to the Republic during the war, of Calvo Sotelo, one of the leaders of the parliamentary opposition. Calvo Sotelo himself had been involved in a conspiracy against the state, and was murdered in reprisal for the murder by Falangist gunmen of Lieutenant José Castillo of the *Asaltos*. The murder of Sotelo, by regular police, was the culmination of two years of violence, plots, and counterplots which had plagued the Spanish Republic.

Since the establishment of the Republic in 1931 there had been three periods of parliamentary rule. The first, left-wing government had suppressed a military rising by the Right in 1932 and then had been defeated in the 1933 elections by a swing to the Right. The election of a right-wing government had resulted in 1934 in a left-wing rebellion of miners in Asturias, and a separatist rising of Catalans in Barcelona. Both risings had been brutally suppressed, and in the period between 1934 and 1936, both extreme Left and Right began arming and plotting to secure, by force if necessary, the political aims which were denied them by the parliamentary Republic. The right wing, hating working-class discontent, socialist aspirations, and the bewildering lack of a central ordering principle in liberal democracy, was plotting to restore conservatism in the form of a dictatorship, while the violent left wing was obsessed with the revolutionary ideals of Marxism, Trotskyism, and anarchism. Campbell's early poems predicting the coming of the cleansing sword are typical of the mood of threatening violence of this period. Even though international communism was going through a period of cooperation with radical democratic elements in the newly formulated Popular Front policy, the Spanish socialists were independent and divided enough for many still to be bent on revolution, while the anarchists were openly committed to violence. Nevertheless, the reality of the danger of a mass communist rising, inspired by an international communist plot, on which the military rebels based much of their subsequent propaganda, was highly questionable, particularly since the Popular Front had won the elections of 1936, and was legally in a position to carry out reform.[6]

The Falange was banned at this time for the turmoil it was provoking in a campaign of planned subversion intended to bring about the collapse of Spain's democratic experiment. In *Flowering Rifle* Campbell refers to the Falange as a nonfascist, Christian organization, and praises its founder, José Antonio Primo de Rivera, as well as making many laudatory references to the Falangist blue shirt, and their emblem of yoke and arrows. His description of José Antonio Primo de Rivera's death is typical of the tone of much of *Flowering Rifle*. After justifying the murder of García Lorca, he adds this footnote before launching into his praise of the founder of the Falange: "When the Nationalists entered Granada the unbelievable babooneries perpetrated by the Reds made them trigger-happy as they rounded up and shot all corrupters of children, known perverts and sexual cranks. A natural reaction, considering that the week before the Reds had slaughtered and tortured anyone who was under suspicion of any sort of decency at all" (2, 199). The curious assertion that the slaughter of "sexual cranks" is a "natural reaction" is typical of the futility of so much of Campbell's partisan writing. The verse in which he praises the son of the old Spanish dictator shows little more control:

> For One (whose Absence fills the land entire
> With one mad love to emulate his fire)
> At the same moment, to the firing squad
> Spurning his body, launched his soul to God,
> Whose epic line (no flourish of the pen)
> Was life and rapture, and whose words were men
> And though he died ere it was well begun
> Rolls flaming onwards to the rising sun:
> For in young Primo's grave his slayers stowed
> One fire-brand safe, a whole *mine* to explode,

6. See Madariaga, *Spain*, p. 472, and Hugh Thomas, *The Spanish Civil War*, pp. 95–109.

> And seldom such a triumph (since the Cross)
> Has glorified a single human loss.
>
> [2, 199–200]

In the light of this extravagant praise it is sobering
to remember that among the activities of the Falange was
a deliberate attempt to spread disorder throughout Spain,
and thus justify demands for a regime based on "order."
Falangist gangsters stopped at little in their efforts to create
chaos, and were even involved in church-burning, which
could be used to fan antianarchist sentiments. José Antonio
was arrested in March 1936 in an attempt by the government to maintain order before the outbreak of the rebellion. Campbell's unqualified praise for the Falangist leader
is part of his total political involvement, and obviously
one-sided. On the other hand, his scorn for those who
demanded the execution of José Antonio after the outbreak of the rebellion has a great deal of validity, and
illustrates the mingling of legitimate and highly personal
views in his propagandist writing. Even though José Antonio was obviously involved in the plot against the state,
his execution, after a trial, was an unnecessary example of
ruthlessness. When Azaña, the president of the Republic,
was asked by a friend to prevent the execution, he replied
that he was himself a prisoner who could do nothing
against the extreme element in the Republic. The Nationalists shot the son of the Republican prime minister, Largo
Caballero, in reprisal.

The turmoil was general after the election of the Popular Front government in 1936. Both the extreme Right and
extreme Left were fomenting chaos, while the military
perfected its plot to rise against the elected government
and restore old Spain. Campbell's defence of the rising
against a freely elected government shows many of the
characteristics of Nationalist propaganda. At times he states
that the elections were not democratic and that the Popular Front government was not representative:[7]

7. In *Light on a Dark Horse* (p. 334) Campbell alleges that he was
forced to vote in the elections.

> The votes, as if Democracy to slight,
> And show its rusted workings to the sight,
> Seated the left, yet counted for the right—
> And this in spite of violated urns,
> Shots at the booths, and falsified returns.
>   [2, 146]

Although the Popular Front did gain more seats than its proportion of the total vote would strictly warrant, its majority was attained by the electoral system of the country which had brought a right-wing government to power in the preceding elections, and which had been drawn up by all parties. The Popular Front gained a majority of votes over the National Front, and the assessment of the overall majority of total votes cast depends on an arbitrary estimate of the way the Centre was aligned at the time of the elections. Both Salvador de Madariaga and Hugh Thomas agree that the overall majority of votes cast favoured the Left, which also had the majority of seats.[8] Further, Thomas describes the conditions at the booths as "generally calm," and quotes the correspondent of the *Times* (London) as saying that the voting had been "generally exemplary." In two cases where it was alleged that disturbances had prevented a free vote, Cuenca and Granada, new elections were held and both seats were won by the Left.[9] Campbell's criticism of the elections in the passage quoted does not rely solely on allegations of the unfairness of the electoral procedure, however. A sense of the futility of democracy and its "rusted workings" underlies his complaint about the undemocratic nature of the 1936 elections. This belief in the falsity of the whole democratic system is that which he offers most frequently in *Flowering Rifle* as the reason for flouting its workings to establish "order" and control. "Devout style" is continually contrasted with the materialist values of democracy. The following lines are

8. Madariaga, *Spain*, pp. 339–43; Thomas, *The Spanish Civil War*, pp. 92–94; see also Jackson, *The Spanish Republic and the Civil War*, pp. 189–94 and pp. 521–23.

9. Thomas, *The Spanish Civil War*, p. 100.

typical, both in their lack of poetic distinction and in their
evocation of the mystique of the ordered and the uniform:

> Whether it's guns to fire, or bricks to pile,
> Matter is always sensitive to style
> (Which is the breathing rhythm of the soul)
> And shows itself Devout from pole to pole:
> In storms and shocks it always looks for order[:]
> The waves in uniform, with silver border,
> Still fight to keep in equidistant ranks
> As we against artillery and tanks:
> Happier still to worship than to grovel
> It shows in the Cathedral than the hovel,
> And there of centuries will take the polish
> Requiring tons of Nitre to demolish:
> But when democracy begins to soar
> To whom the jail, the brothel, and the store,
> Stand for the Church, and tries for like proportions
> Matter complies with sorrowful distortions.
>
> [2, 168]

The degraded values he sees in democracy are directly
linked with the decline, tolerated by democracy, of religious faith:

> And is the answer to each canting fool
> Who deems such drones were ever fit to rule,
> And shows the right hand is the hand of workers
> And the shut Left—of parasites and shirkers,
> And that Democracy has had its hour
> That shoves such sleepy scullions into power,
> Which only as a system could be borne
> When Christians held barbarity in scorn
> And, with the land-myths, nourished with the sod
> The voice of peoples was the voice of God.
>
> [2, 159]

The only thing that made democracy *bearable* was the
uniform Christianity of the good old days. From this point
it is an easy step to the standard reactionary position that

democracy, or democratic freedom, leads to and can be equated with communism. All political opponents are, as a result, "Red" in Campbell's propagandist poems.

When the right-wing rebellion broke out in the military garrisons and Civil Guard barracks in July 1936, the Republic, against which the military were rebelling, was virtually without armed forces to protect itself other than the *Asaltos,* many seamen who revolted against their rebellious officers, and part of the air force. The military rebellion was further supported by the Foreign Legion and the well-trained Moorish mercenary army that fought with them, both units being transported to Spain itself from Morocco shortly after the rising. In the face of this overwhelming military threat the Republic was virtually without defence, except for the armed factions within the Left of trade unions and political parties. They had been using their guns in the previous six months of gang warfare amongst themselves, and against the gangsters of the Right. The union arms were not enough, however, to withstand the rebellious army. On July 18, 1936, the people of Madrid came out into the streets demanding arms to oppose the rebellion. It was at this stage that La Pasionaria broadcast her first speech calling for total resistance throughout the country to the rebellion. Azaña and Casares Quiroga, president and prime minister of the Republic, delayed the issuing of arms until the prime minister was referred to by the crowd as *Civilón,* or civilian, after a bull who would not defend himself in the ring. Finally on July 19, in the early morning, Casares Quiroga resigned, and a new government composed of middle-class liberals, but supported by the communists and socialists, was formed. It immediately threw open the public arsenals to the trade unions and the masses.

Because of this step the rebellion was met by what amounted to a revolution. The armed crowds resisted the rebellious army, in many cases successfully, and embarked on a reign of terror against any supporters of the Right or known opponents of the Republican regime. The government lost control completely over the revolutionary masses, and what had begun as a rising against a military rebellion became a proletarian, antibourgeois revolution which the middle-class government was powerless to stop. Old enmities and hatreds fanned passions throughout Spain during this period, and terror and murder were the norm. This is the terror to which Campbell repeatedly refers in his Spanish writings. The violence and brutality were exactly as he describes them, but what he does not mention is that the revolution began as a defensive measure against the military revolt, and that in Toledo itself the revolutionaries were fighting to reconquer the town from the military rebels whom they finally forced into the Alcazar. Typical post-rising Nationalist propaganda was that they had risen to prevent the reign of terror, which they knew was imminent. Campbell accepts this argument completely, and in *Light on a Dark Horse* has a chapter entitled "The Coming of the Terror," while he gives the official Nationalist line in *Flowering Rifle*: "Since for five months we'd turned the other cheek / And only stalled the Terror by a week" (2, 163). The terror was, however, a result of the military rebellion, directly caused by mass opposition to the military rebels and their allies of the bourgeoisie, Church and Falange.[10] The arms which made the terror possible were issued by the Republic in self-defence.

Revolution and terror sickened many supporters of the Republic and changed the nature of the conflict. Through the revolution, and the fact that the only major power prepared to aid the Republic was the Soviet Union, the communists gradually gained control of most positions of influence within the government. By the later days of the war they had instituted a secret military police, the SIM, which behaved like its model, at the time engaged in supervising the great purges in the Soviet Union. Many Republican officials, including the last prime minister, Dr. Juan Negrín, were not communists, but cooperated fully with the Soviet regime because on it depended the flow of arms and supplies. Campbell's description of the military rising as antirevolutionary is not accurate, but he is justi-

10. See Thomas, *The Spanish Civil War*, pp. 139–64; Madariaga, *Spain*, p. 472; and Jackson, *The Spanish Republic and the Civil War*, pp. 276–92.

fied in many of his attacks on the totalitarian nature of the communism which was gaining a hold over his opponents.

What at times he takes pains to deny is that there were terror and persecution on the side of the Nationalists. The difference between Nationalist and Republican killings was broadly that the Republican murders were mainly committed in the first few months of the war by uncontrollable revolutionary forces. Apart from political persecution of individuals, there was virtually no mass killing in the Republic once order had been restored. On the Nationalist side, mass executions were part of a policy of repression in occupied areas, and were carried out throughout the war and after it. Gabriel Jackson is "certain that close to 200,000 men died in the years 1939–43," in the Nationalist attempt to exterminate the conquered "Reds" after the war. He goes on to say, "When Heinrich Himmler visited Madrid in 1941 in connection with the training of the Spanish political police, he disapproved, on practical grounds, the rate of execution."[11] The Nationalists were associated with terror tactics throughout the war. Systematic bombing of towns and civilians made its appearance in European history when the Nationalists systematically bombed Madrid, while the German officers of the Condor Legion watched "to see the reaction of a civilian population to a carefully planned attempt to set fire to the city, quarter by quarter. The bombing concentrated as far as possible on hospitals and other buildings such as the Telefonica, whose destruction would cause special panic."[12] The destruction of Guernica by German bombers on April 26, 1937, was caused by a mixture of military motives and the wish to observe, as an experiment, the effect of a devastating aerial attack.[13]

The horror of the war and the atrocities committed by both sides make Campbell's unquestioning support of the

11. *The Spanish Republic and the Civil War*, pp. 538–40.

12. Thomas, *The Spanish Civil War*, p. 329.

13. Campbell explicitly denies in *Flowering Rifle* that Nationalists bombed Guernica, and gives the official Nationalist propaganda line that the town was destroyed by the "Reds" themselves (2, 218). For a detailed account of the bombing, see Thomas, *The Spanish Civil War*, pp. 419–22, and Jackson, *The Spanish Republic and the Civil War*, pp. 381–82.

Nationalists difficult to accept, quite apart from any personal attitude the reader might have towards the sort of government it was the aim of Franco and the Right to establish. Campbell's persistent jeers at the deluded English nation, which seems to him to support the Republic, are partly justified in that the articulate English Left, including his composite MacSpaunday enemy, were active supporters and propagandists for the Republic. The support was not general, however, and apart from assistance given the Republic by British communists and by Anglo-Saxon left-wing intellectuals, Britain and the United States observed official neutrality towards the conflict. France was less strict in her neutrality, particularly in so far as the International Brigades were organized on French soil; but after the Non-Intervention Treaty was signed, there was no official French aid to the Republic. Western capitalists and conservatives were disturbed by the revolution within the Republic, and the Nationalists as a result enjoyed an advantage over the Republic in the amount of international capital they could attract. The support each side gained from the totalitarian powers was decisive. The Axis powers sent material and men on a large scale to fight for the Nationalists (the Italian troops even remaining for the victory parade), and probably provided the crucial assistance in the closing stages which actually won the war. The Soviet Union, with Mexico, was practically the sole source of Republican aid, and provided large-scale supplies of material, organizers, and advisers, although few combatants. For assistance in that field the Republic had to rely on the International Brigades, organized mainly by the Comintern, which again provided crucial assistance in the early days of the war and saved Madrid from the initial Nationalist attack.

Campbell's experience of the terror at first hand and his recognition of the totalitarian principle of communism give his attitudes towards the revolution a validity which was little recognized at the time. Nevertheless, his refusal to accept the need for reform in Spain and his passionate support of the Nationalists, which at this stage really amounted to an acceptance of fascist views, severely limit the range of his own insight into the failings of the Republic. The ex-Comintern agent, Arthur Koestler, has summed up, with a lucidity and humanity that elude Campbell, the attitudes of the intellectuals whom the poet so violently opposed:

> All this we know to-day, but we did not know then. We know now that our truth was a half-truth, our fight a battle in the mist, and that those who suffered and died in it were pawns in a complicated game between the two totalitarian pretenders for world domination. But when the International Brigades saved Madrid on November 8, 1936, we all felt that they would go down in history as the defenders of Thermopylae did; and when the first Russian fighters appeared in the skies of battered Madrid, all of us who had lived through the agony of the defenceless town felt that they were the saviours of civilisation.[14]

Campbell's uncompromising commitment to the Nationalist cause cuts him off from those who thought they were defenders of a new Thermopylae; yet his insistence that they were deluded, although scorned at the time, has been borne out by those intellectuals themselves. His views are only partially justified, however, in that he takes no account of the genuinely humanitarian and altruistic motives of most left-wing intellectuals and the sincerity of their support for the Popular Front. But the main reason that it is only half true to say that he saw through the deception of the Popular Front, when most intellectuals did not, is that his scorn for the "Reds" is based on his own passionate support for attitudes opposed to the humane principles in which many of the intellectuals believed, as well as to the totalitarian communism of their allies. Campbell's imperviousness to cruelty, his praise of the death-dealing militarism of Franco's legion, and his belief in a mystique of "order" and "style" are manifestations of his fundamental support for fascist movements which the

14. Koestler, *The Invisible Writing,* p. 325.

Popular Front was not deluded in opposing. The more obvious signs of this support for what became the Axis powers can be seen in his repeated attacks on the Jews, his scorn for the League of Nations, his sympathy for Mussolini's Abyssinian campaign, and his partial justification for Hitler's antisemitism, all of which can be found in *Flowering Rifle*.

Campbell's propaganda poetry is most fully illustrated by the long "epic," *Flowering Rifle,* which reflects every aspect of his political stand in Spain. The circumstances in which it was written made objectivity virtually impossible. After being evacuated from Toledo in 1936, the Campbells stayed with the Garmans in Binstead, Sussex, where the poet felt particularly ill at ease in the company of his left-wing relatives. Early in 1937 he returned to Spain as a war correspondent for the *Tablet*. After a short time in the country, however, he was asked to abandon any desire to enlist in the Nationalist forces and to use his talents as a propagandist for the Nationalist cause. As a result, he left Spain shortly after his return in 1937 and settled at Estombar in southern Portugal. His family joined him there, and he began working feverishly on *Flowering Rifle*, which shows all too many signs of the speed with which it was written. The personal involvement of the writer manifests itself not only in the one-sided tone of the political commentary, but also in many personal boasts. His friend C. D. Ley comments on the poet's assertions about his activities in Spain:

> He lived in Spain for four years in the 1930's, until evacuated at the beginning of the Civil War. He then retired to Portugal, visiting Salamanca as a war correspondent, until such time as it was possible to return to Toledo, where he lived till 1941. He then made several recent visits to Spain, during which I had the great privilege of being very often in his company. He said that he had sold vegetables from his farm in Altea and trafficked in horses in Toledo and Cuidad Real, but these activities cannot have provided a real livelihood. He was never a professional Spanish bullfighter. He

said himself in a lecture in the Ateneo, Madrid, that the Spanish authorities discouraged him from volunteering in the Civil War, because "there are enough rifles but not enough pens." . . . Campbell was, in fact, a very great poet, and, as such, naturally not in the least "genuinely a man of action," though his rich sense of humour made him love to mystify people by making them swallow as many of his more or less Munchausen stories as possible.[15]

Campbell's total acceptance of Nationalist propaganda and his complete identification with the Nationalist cause are apparent throughout the violent "epic" "from the battlefields of Spain." The fact that he had been outside Spain for most of the war might be the reason for his absolute acceptance of the official Nationalist point of view. His personal experience of the struggle was at its most intense in the very early days in Toledo when the revolutionary terror was at its height, as the "people's army" reacted against the military rebellion aimed at toppling the Republic. It is highly unlikely that he had an opportunity of observing Nationalist brutality, and, although he never admitted it, was probably deceived by the Spaniards about the realities of the situation, in much the same way as many left-wing writers found themselves deceived about the realities of their cause.

His defence of the poem was vigorous, and when the reviewer in the *Times Literary Supplement* suggested rather timidly that for the poet Right and Wrong were automatically Right and Left,[16] Campbell replied with a long letter, published on February 25, 1939. In the letter he defended his viewpoint with the same violence as in *Flowering Rifle*, alleging, amongst other things that he was illustrating his points "by tangible achievements, such as the surplus of a million tons of wheat and the surplus of half a million calves;" he adds, "every line that I write has in

15. *Times Literary Supplement* (November 22, 1957), p. 705. The letter expresses appreciation of the review of the second volume of *Collected Poems*.

16. *TLS* (February 11, 1939), p. 93.

real life several thousand tons of wheat behind it, and every word has twenty tons of beef or mutton."[17] Among the attacks on the work, Stephen Spender's review in the *New Statesman* possibly rattled Campbell as well as providing him with the title of his next volume. The review is headed "The Talking Bronco" and epitomizes the disgust felt by many English readers:

> There are several passages in this book which make me feel physically sick. Finally, the undiscriminating abuse of the enemy defeats its own ends, because if we are to believe Mr. Campbell, there can be little merit in defeating an army which never does anything but run. All sense of conflict is lost when his verminous adjectives culminate in the defiant:
>
> > The bronco, Life, with angry snort of fire,
> > Has ever boomeranged four feet entire
> > And stamped him like a cockroach in the mire.
>
> Mr. Campbell indignantly repudiates the accusation that he is Romantic. He is quite right, for the Romantics were distinguished by their disinterested passion for truth, equalled only by their love of freedom and justice. The bronco Life! Perhaps that phrase gets nearer the mark. Mr. Wyndham Lewis diagnosed the Dumb Ox in Hemingway's novels. Here we have the Talking Bronco, the Brute Life armed with abusive words and, most unfortunately, not with Mr. Campbell's Flowering Rifle, but with Flowering Machine Guns, Flowering Henkels [*sic*], Flowering Capronis.[18]

Although it is vitriolic, badly organized, and often poor in quality, there are many good moments in *Flowering Rifle*, which Campbell revised for publication in the second volume of *Collected Poems*. It is the final, revised version to which I refer. The main changes between the 1939 edition of the poem and the 1957 version are that the first book of the 1939 version is printed as a separate poem, "A

17. *TLS* (February 25, 1939), p. 121.
18. *New Statesman and Nation* (March 11, 1939), p. 370.

Letter from the San Mateo Front," in *Collected Poems,* and
that he has added his later poem, "The Vision of our Lady
over Toledo," as a conclusion to the final section of the
1957 version.

The epic and heroic qualities Campbell sees in Franco's
crusade are expressed with much of the zest with which
his perennial theme of heroic vitality had been expressed
in the past. But the hollowness at the core of the experience is apparent in his description of the new "epic
years":

> Spain was to them what scurf they could infect
> And flake away with their bought intellect;
> So with the Kominterners of the day,
> Mistaking both the slough and the decay
> In which as feeding parasites they lay
> When with the withered skin they peeled away—
> For the live python with revolving spires
> That from the tombstone of her mighty sires,
> Shedding the rags of winter-bitten skin
> With the snug parasites that housed within,
> Volted with solar glories and desires
> And wheeled upon a hundred spangling tyres
> To strip the Zodiac of its rolling fires,
> With gleaming helmets for her million scales
> From a long winter of inertia sails
> In a strong current of electric might
> Like a great river churning power and light
> From dynamos of valour and delight.

[2, 151]

This confusion and prolixity are typical of *Flowering Rifle.*
The same snake image is still doing duty on the next page,
some thirty-five lines later, where the picture of the re-
newal of the golden age of Spain's past is linked with the
idea of the health-giving surgery which is so often repeated
in Campbell's Nationalist poems:

> Which, too, may compensate for strangled vice,
> The feelings of such literary lice

That fell off with such flakes of winter skin
They could infect or loosen from within,
When Spain threw down her dominoes and dice,
And Franco bade the epic years begin,
Flying unarmed to dare the fiery zone
And shouldering the Impossible alone,
To lift three fallen centuries from the slime
Where they had bogged the ebb and flow of time,
Which is no one-way stream as we mischart,
But circulates, like blood, the solar heart,
And when the artery's stopped, to sap the vein,
The sword must slice the ligature in twain.

[2, 152]

The wordiness in each of these passages is not the result of routine imagery alone. It is the abstract quality of the thinking throughout passages like this that is the reason for the thinness and emptiness of effect, in spite of all the extravagance of image and metaphor. In the last passage alone Campbell tosses about the concepts of "Spain," (which is the most constant abstraction in the poem) "the epic years," "the Impossible," "the ebb and flow of time." Precision and accuracy of observation characterize all of his best poetry, and it is no coincidence that the flabbiness in texture is persistent in *Flowering Rifle* where the cause he champions is so often based on abstract values. Within *Flowering Rifle* itself the change is marked when he captures observed details and suggests real scenes:

Since the Real Spain was in the cloisters hidden
Beneath the fiery sun on mesas ridden
Where tourists would have fainted with the heat—
It was her dregs that filtered to the street,
Where communism hung around the bars
Among the dominoes and cheap cigars,
Where waiters, chauffeurs, menials were the guys
That headed on the infernal enterprise.

[2, 148]

"Real Spain" appears again here, but Campbell sets out to evoke the atmosphere of his real Spain, and succeeds in capturing the Spanish ethos which he supports. Even the "fiery sky" has a sensuous relevance as well as suggesting passionate values.

When there is no solid experience to justify an epic tone, he fails in his attempt to give epic proportions to assertions of Nationalist superiority. Theory is not heroic, and Campbell's arguments are often as theoretic as the abstract social dreams which he opposes. Nevertheless there are many moments when his unqualified scorn does rise above the level of undisciplined harangue:

> In him you have the Adversary, Man,
> Go Hammer him according to your plan
> And geld him with a Sickle if you can!
> And that he took not kindly to the chain
> Well may the baffled demagogues complain
> Who never knew the Eagle Heart of Spain.
>
> [2, 140]

Abstractions are still there, but the poet's disdain is convincing in these lines. His reaction itself is the experience underlying them. Even the play on the hammer and sickle is witty, in contrast with so many tedious attempts to ridicule the emblems of his opponents.

The mystique to which most of the theory in *Flowering Rifle* is subordinated is that of the "clean rejuvenated nation," led by one leader to a purer form of national existence which spurns both capitalism and communism. The influence of the views of José Antonio Primo de Rivera and his Falange are clearly noticeable in these passages, which show the chivalric and Catholic overtones that distinguish Spanish fascism of the period:

> It was not "liberty" that thus could level
> Mankind in common bondage to the Devil
> Nor yours, kind Labour, was this ghastly birth
> Of squalor—though to camouflage the stain,
> Our intellectuals take your name in vain;
> Only where Franco rules you seem to shine
> Whose influence reaches to our foremost line.
>
> [2, 230]

A sneer at false beliefs in "liberty," the compliment to "kind Labour," and the insistence on efficiency, when coupled with an assertion of the "shining" rule of the leader, are too close to the official fascist line to be accidental. Here is part of the speech made by Calvo Sotelo in the Cortes on June 16, 1936.[19] After attributing the disorder in Spain to the democratic constitution of 1931, he went on:

> Against this sterile State I am proposing the integrated State, which will bring economic justice, and which will say with due authority: "no more strikes, no more lock-outs, no more usury, no more capitalist abuses, no more starvation wages, no more political salaries gained by a happy accident, no more anarchic liberty, no more criminal conspiracies against full production." The national production will be for the benefit of all classes, all parties, all interests. This State many may call Fascist; if this indeed be the Fascist State, then I, who believe in it, proudly declare myself a Fascist!

After stating that there was no danger of a rising by Monarchist generals, and that no soldier was prepared to rise against the Republic on behalf of a Monarchy, he concluded:

> If there were such a person, he would be mad—I speak with all sincerity, mad indeed, as would be any soldier who, before eternity, would not be ready to rise on behalf of Spain, and against anarchy—if *that* should be necessary.

The similarity is obvious in both mood and vocabulary to Campbell's descriptions of the ideal state and his explanations of its necessity. This implied threat to the Republic was made in the Cortes a month before military rebellion actually broke out. In his paean to Calvo Sotelo in *Flowering Rifle* Campbell sees him as an innocent victim

19. Thomas, *The Spanish Civil War*, p. 7.

of revolutionary terror, while the Right was turning the other cheek:

> Though for five months we'd turned the other cheek
> And when we struck, with loss of blood were weak,
> Too late alas to stop the coward hand
> That struck the hope and honour of the land
> Who promised fair to parallel the Star,
> Triumphant, of the gracious Salazar,
> And only just in time to stay the wave
> That would have swept the country to its grave.
>
> [2, 147]

The number of semimessianic leaders in *Flowering Rifle* is surprising; here Calvo Sotelo and Salazar are celebrated in much the same way as Franco and José Antonio Prima de Rivera. In each case, however, the mystical qualities of the leader cult suggest the health and new life which are strongly contrasted with the "outworn," sordid conditions under which democracy provides cover for the red threat:

> Creative rhythm shuns their blistered hands
> And is a thing no Fiscal understands
> While style and unity and emulation
> Inform each clean rejuvenated Nation,
> Wherever there's a Leader to rebel
> Against the outworn socialistic Hell,[20]
> And muzzle up the soul-destroying Lie
> Which Lenin was the first to Magnify.
>
> [2, 225]

To found a clean rejuvenated nation in which all sectors of the population benefit from the central ordering principle of the leader—and which becomes an organic entity—is essentially the aim of José Antonio Primo de Rivera. In 1933 he wrote: "The country is a historical totality . . . superior to each of us and to our groups. The state is founded on two principles—service to the united

20. In the original edition the line reads: "Against the outworn democratic Hell" (p. 124).

nation and the co-operation of classes." In the next year his views showed even more of the mystical quality of the fascist dream: "Fascism is a European inquietude. It is a way of knowing everything—history, the State, the achievement of the proletarianisation of public life, a new way of knowing the phenomena of our epoch. Fascism has already triumphed in some countries and in some, as in Germany, by the most irreproachable democratic means."[21] Before the Asturias rising he had written to Franco offering support for a military coup d'etat to restore the "lost historical destiny of the country."[22] Even after his arrest in 1936 José Antonio continued in the same vein, and in May wrote an open letter from prison to Spanish soldiers in which he called for assistance to protect "the sacred identity of Spain," stating, "in the last resort, as Spengler puts it, it has always been a platoon of soldiers who have saved civilisation."[23]

Campbell's old devotion to what is heroic and distinguished in life modulates easily into political views of this sort:

The racket of the Invert and the Jew
Which is through art and science to subdue,
Humiliate, and to a pulp reduce
The Human Spirit for industrial use
Whether by Capital or Communism
It's all the same, despite their seeming schism,
In that for human serfs they both require
Limpness, servility and lack of fire.

[2, 212–13]

The heroic ethic in Spanish nationalism is intimately connected with a desire to resurrect the greatness of ancient Spain. As a result it is also connected with a belief in the Catholic character of the race and emphasizes the part religion played in its past grandeur. The aims of an early

21. Thomas, *The Spanish Civil War*, p. 70.
22. Ibid., p. 87. Compare Campbell's, "To lift three fallen centuries from the slime."
23. Ibid., pp. 106–7.

fascist movement, Juntas de Ofensiva Nacional-Sindicalista, the JONS, were embodied in the "sixteen points" of Valladolid in 1931. Hugh Thomas describes one of these aims: "Unlike Hitler, Ledesma and Onesimo Redondo [the two founders of the movement] gave a place to the Roman Catholic religion, which they named as embodying the 'racial' tradition of the Spaniards. Catholicism meant indeed the same to them as Aryan blood did to Hitler. But they nevertheless criticised the Church in Spain of the time."[24]

Campbell's Catholicism is, of course, central to his thinking from this period until his death, and is not in any way a convenient political concept for him. Nevertheless his religious beliefs become part of his concept of the ideal state. In particular, his belief in the unyielding militarism of his cause and its need for realistic and often self-sacrificing surgery is closely linked to the concept of the redemptive sacrifice which he presented so fully in "Mithraic Frieze":

> The Christ of Salamanca teaches this,
> The devil-routing Lord of the Abyss
> Who, till this time of men resigned and bold,
> Ignatius was the last man to behold—
> Since then, till now, men fought for greed or lust
> To seize the booty or to bite the dust,
> But the old world is "braver" than the "new,"
> Can use it as its foot-stool or its shoe:
> Or when it rots as it's begun to do,
> As a sharp knife can cut that Stilton through
> Cough though the scientist or squirm the Jew,
> Or stink, abjectly dead, the poets too.
> That God was never brilliantined or curled
> Who out of Chaos saw his battles won,
> And gave, like Moscardò, his only Son,
> To save the charred Alcazar of the world.
> For of all gods, he only breathed our breath
> To live the solar myths, and conquer death.
>
> [2, 174]

24. Ibid., p. 69.

Christ is the "christ of Salamanca," explicitly associated
with a Spanish religious leader in the devil-routing of the
unfaithful, and quite clearly "Lord of the Abyss." So close
is the identification of politics with religion that even the
central sacrificial experience of the Christian faith is presented in terms of the siege of the Alcazar. Colonel Moscardó, beseiged in the fortress, sent a telephonic farewell
to his captured son whom the besiegers finally executed
after failing in their attempt to blackmail the colonel into
surrender. The sacrificial element in Christianity is seldom
so bluntly equated with actual military events. But ten
lines later Campbell is still pursuing the comparison between Christ's sacrificial victory to save mankind and the
saving of "the race."

A sense of Christ's being the Nationalists' military ally
is repeated throughout *Flowering Rifle,* though when describing Christian persecution Campbell prefers to picture
a loving and harmless Church, only concerned with the
timeless and the eternal. At the end of the poem he describes Toledo and her claim to "queenly titles" in these
terms:

> And hers to none in history shall yield,
> Where Christ the sword, and Mary was the shield,—
> Lepanto, or the Catalaunian Field!
> For here the Tartar's dreams were put to flight,
> And Europe rescued in her own despite.
>
> [2, 255]

The approval which the poet gives to the slaughter of his
enemies is linked to his belief in the sanctity of his cause,
and its support from God. This inhumanity in *Flowering
Rifle* is to a large extent attributable to the god-like qualities Campbell sees in the Nationalist restorers of order. If
the Nationalists represent order, the inhuman and devilish
forces opposing them must—by logical necessity—represent disorder. In the poem God's vengeance is not often
tempered with mercy:

> And well may they abominate the Sword,
> The bared and naked vengeance of the Lord—

> And curse the Soldier, him, the human brand,
> That came to lop the sacrilegious Hand,
> And root the godless vermin from the land.
>
> [2, 170]

Slaughter in the poem becomes commonplace. Even when the poet is outwardly critical of crimes committed in the cause of "Humanitarian Progress," he describes his opponents' predilection for terror as a "fashion":

> For never yet was loafing such a passion
> Or murder, rape, and arson so in fashion
> As where conjoined in Brotherhood of "Labour"
> Humanitarian Progress loves its Neighbour,
> The bloated Caesars in their purple lists
> Out-Caesared by to-day's Philanthropists
> Who, in as many weeks as they took years,
> Trebled Rome's catacombs for blood and tears:
> Who slaughter ten times more their love to press,
> Than we for anger, vengeance, or redress.
>
> [2, 144]

At first Campbell is trying to suggest that the humanitarians are unconcerned about murder, rape, and arson, but the unconcern becomes a part of the poet's own attitude. When he turns to denunciation, the sense of outrage is in no way a presence in the empty list of crimes, and his whole case against slaughter disintegrates with his casual acceptance in the last line that "we" also slaughter, albeit ten times less, for the haphazardly nonlegal motives of "anger, vengeance, or redress." The same casual acceptance of Nationalist violence can be found in "A Letter from the San Mateo Front," where, in an almost identical passage, he writes:

> Though as "humanitarians" they write
> With greasy Tartuffades to slime the cause
> That has more victims in its murderous jaws
> Than ever were destroyed in mortal fight,
> Blasted with bombs, or heaved with dynamite,
> Or executed here, to serve them right.
>
> [2, 46]

His admission that Nationalist executions take place is made without any formal legal justification beyond the fact that it served the victims right. In the same poem he unconcernedly implies that the Nationalists slaughter prisoners of war, while decrying the cowardice of a unit from the International Brigades who wished unheroically to "crawl before a handful of Italians" rather than be killed by the Spanish. In a footnote he writes: "They were far too scared to surrender to the Spaniards who sent me over to interpret: they knew what they had asked for! They said they wished to surrender *en bloc,* to the Italians, but would otherwise 'have to fight' as they knew what they deserved from the Spanish!" (2, 42)

Campbell's dismissal of whole groups and races who do not share his sense of "style" or heroic resignation grows out of his own concept of an ideal, ordered world. A characteristic passage combines an assertion of the "mystic" with a racial sneer at its degraders:

> For Capitalistic lore, as Communistic,
> Must first of all discredit all that's mystic
> To sell the mind and body cheap for slavery
> Degrading them by slow hypnosis first,
> In which the Modern poets head the knavery
> In all the arts of degradation versed,
> The coolies and the agents of the Jew
> Whose only passion is to gripe the two.
>
> [2, 171]

This picture of the Jew as the perverter of the human spirit naturally leads to a partial justification of Hitler's policy of oppression. A long harangue against left-wing writers ends in this way:

> With a gold medal clanking at his neck
> To lure his fellows to their sale and wreck,
> When cheapened, hypnotized, unmanned and cowed,
> The gelded slave his "freedom" is allowed—
> A tyranny far worse than blamed on Hitler
> Whose chief oppression is of the belittler,
> The intellectual invert and the Jew.
>
> [2, 213]

Again, after describing the exile quality in Marxists and Marxism, and France "Karfunkelled through the nose" for the concept of a "New Jerusalem," Campbell continues:

> Marx's whole knowledge of the earth and sun
> Was of a boarding house for exiles run
> With dodging rent as the chief role of man
> And being as much a nuisance as one can:
> Which is why Hitler gives them leave to quit.
> [2, 223]

Not content with providing this insight into the workings of the Third Reich, he adds a footnote: "Compared with our beloved Russian allies, who never let dissidents escape or emigrate, even Hitler was, at this time, comparatively human, since he did not impede but encouraged the exodus of the emigraille which has cost England her empire and atom-bomb secrets."

Campbell's justification of Hitler in *Flowering Rifle* is only partly motivated by his racism. The other motive is that the Axis powers were allies of the Nationalists. This leads to condemnation of the hypocrisy of democratic countries who object to the new European dictatorships. Even the League of Nations, which had protested and had proposed sanctions against Italy and Japan in their expansionist invasions, is condemned as an instrument of international communism and freemasonry:

> So John Bull breathes in subterrene intrigue
> And hangs around the coffin of the League,
> That sheeny club of communists and masons
> Where Pommies' ears serve for spittoons and basins
> In which to wash the grime from bloody paws.
> [2, 220]

The ease with which Campbell can introduce slang into his derogatory political writing has been seen in the prewar political poems, and is a consistent feature of the harangue in *Flowering Rifle* and "A Letter from the San Mateo Front." Quite apart from the quality of his argument in *Flowering Rifle*, and the political realities on which it is based, the falsity of mood in so much of the poem is a direct result of the coarseness and exaggerations of his low style. He is never sure whether he is writing the great epic of the rebellion, or one enormous flyting of all its opponents. Each aspect of the poem limits the other. The epic pretensions are continually made to appear hollow when passages evoking the grandeur of the cause lead into nose-thumbing jests and insults at the expense of the "Wowsers,' "Pommies," or "Reds," while the epic moments give the impression that even the wildest insults and charges that follow are meant to be taken seriously, or at least are taken seriously by the poet himself.

A naive tone informs most of his attacks on Britain and her sinful ways. Many of the attitudes in the attacks are simply vulgar jibes, but many others are based on his firmly rooted Christian taboos, which give a curiously prim tone to passages in which the style is distinctly low:

> These Pickwickoid buffoons will smell you roses
> Where even dunghill rats would hold their noses,
> And though divorce was their first end and source
> Though Onanism's now their next resource,
> And next, who knows, to keep the same proportion
> These canting thugs will sanctify abortion?
>
> [2, 203]

The shock implied at the suggestion of abortion, and the obvious distaste at the sanctioning of divorce, although out of proportion in a poem which discusses slaughter with such unconcern, are still within the bounds of a morality which is general enough to have a relevance beyond the strict limits of Catholic canon law. However, when Campbell shows contempt for the British people for not only tolerating, but even advocating contraception, the sense of disproportion is obvious. Again the undertone of glee at making jokes about perished rubber adds to the sense of disordered value in these lines:

> Frustration the main theme of all their cults,
> They wash and war with similar results,

> Which makes their poets wish they'd not been born
> And hold their kill-joy parents up to scorn
> Whose error was not to abort them whole,
> In body, as they managed with the soul,
> For perished rubber dashed their early hopes
> As sponsored by their Church and Marie Stopes.
>
> [2, 209–10]

In moderation jests like this might be amusing, but the obsessive recurrence throughout *Flowering Rifle* of sneers and taunts degrades the author far more than the object of his insults.

He can articulate his scorn for the Left, however, and "A Letter from the San Mateo Front" opens with an extended play on the values suggested by the open palm of the fascist salute and the clenched fist salute of the communists:

> I introduce this sample to a Land
> Where all the sweet emoluments are thrown
> To that snug, sinister, and bungling drone,
> The fist-shut Left, so dextrous with the dirk,
> The striker, less in battle than from work:
> The weed of Life that grows where air is hot
> With "Meetings" for its aspidistra-plot:
> That leaves its labour to the hammering tongue
> And grows, a cactus, out of hot-house dung:
> A manual head-ache, fastened in a fist,
> And fed with fumes of foul carbonic mist.
>
> [2, 38]

The length of the attack—and it continues in much the same fashion for pages—becomes tedious, especially as the lack of any obvious ordering principle makes the closing lines appear simply a list of faults. Nevertheless Campbell is not merely being insulting. He is also explaining his dislike, and the basis for his onslaught is never submerged too far beneath the attack itself.

There are many successful moments in the later Spanish poems, in spite of the excesses into which Campbell's total

political commitment leads him. In particular there are
passages in *Flowering Rifle* where his rejection of the Utopian element in dreams of social progress is given sensible
and effectual expression:

> To shun the Actual nobody more smart,
> To dodge the Obvious is his native art,
> For both insult him with derisive grin
> From his environment and from within:
> Whose gluttony all mixtures can sustain
> Save what is actual, evident or plain.
>
> [2, 217]

An insistence on the abstract and theoretic nature of communism or socialism at the expense of the real is the criticism which he offers most consistently in the political
poems, and one in which he is often convincing. "To a
Pommie Critic" is typical of this genre in its down-to-earth
insistence on commonsense:

> I cannot "voice" your hesitations,
> Your difficulties or your doubt?—
> The rictus of your affectations
> Would sprain my jaw and knock me out!
> I see the obvious ten leagues off,
> The lighthouse of my little theme;
> It does not make me sneer or cough
> That things resemble what they seem.
>
> [1, 274]

Campbell's intentionally assumed manner of the plain man
is under control here as part of the norm against which intellectual affectations and hesitations are shown to be small
and unnecessary. The sense in the lines of experience being the basis of his scorn is what distinguishes even so
slight a poem as "To a Pommie Critic" from the vitupera-
tive passages in the war poems themselves. Even in
these, however, there are passages where he describes an
experience directly instead of writing a political harangue.
Almost invariably the poetry in such passages is of a totally
different order from that of his coarser sneers.

The subjective validity of his evocation of fear in
Flowering Rifle creates one of its most powerful moments,
and provides a far greater understanding of the horrors of
the terror than any of his attempts at objective denunciation:

> Cut off from the Alcazar as we lay
> With nothing save to listen and to pray,
> To listen and to start at fancied sounds
> While the Infernal searchers went their rounds,
> And life, a fly upon a rum-glass rim
> Was subject to the vilest drunkard's whim.
>
> [2, 193]

At the same time as his own fear and tension are being captured, the evil of the tormentors is being suggested as an
integral part of the horror of the scene. He goes on to
combine the impression of horror with a moving statement
of the total perversion on which terror is based:

> Abomination flawless and profound,
> Loathing turned joy, as if some fearful tumour
> Could find expression in the realm of sound:
> Or be translated by a rabid hound,
> With hoary mane erect and foetid breath,
> Into a cry whose echo in the gloom
> Would jog with fear the very bones of death
> And bristle up the grass upon the tomb.
>
> [2, 193]

A control of tone at moments like this is what most distinguishes them from the shabby histrionics of the greater
part of *Flowering Rfle*.

When Campbell's reflective presence is part of the
poetry, the passages are conspicuously superior to the rest
of the poem:

> Cooped in a trench, it was my chance to study,
> My neighbour for a day or two, a bloody
> Unburied arm, left lying in the snow

> Which melted now its attitude to show,
> Quite independent of its late discarder,
> Clenching its fist on Nothing, clenching harder
> Than to a stolen penny clings a child:
> But to the desert scene unreconciled
> That seemed so well to sympathize with it,
> With knuckles so inextricably knit,
> It seemed against the Universe to hit,
> As it would storm and hammer at the sun
> Knocking for entry till the world be done.
>
> [2, 245]

His detached observation in the opening lines and his unconcerned acceptance of the severed arm create an air of
objectivity. The value judgements which he goes on to
make appear as simply another element in the description
of the arm. They grow so easily out of the experience as a
whole, and are founded on such a clearly personal and
articulate reaction towards the communistic clenched fist,
that their effectiveness is independent of politics:

> But here his fury is external yet
> In frozen paroxysm fixed and set
> Constricted on the Nothing in its hold
> A clenched fist that Nothing can unfold
> Nothing can satisfy, Nothing appease,
> Though in its grasp that zeroid treasure freeze
> And there is Nothing more for it to seize—
> All that it wished to leave of the crushed world,
> Compassed, and in its grip of lock-jaw curled—
> And yet with its contorted boomerang
> Of hate, it seemed my vigil to harangue
> And on my mind, as on its table, bang.
>
> [2, 245]

A similarly subjective treatment of a political statement
characterizes one of Campbell's best known "war poems,"
"The Fight," which was in fact written before the war,[25]
and derives its central image of two fighting aircraft from

25. First published in *Time and Tide* (November 9, 1935), p. 1608.

a poem by Apollinaire. In "Les Collines" Apollinaire uses the description of a fight between two aircraft above Paris to portray the struggle between his youth and the future. The victory of the future leads the poet into a prophecy of the new world of the future and of the unexplored realms of consciousness and experience which await the sensitive investigation of the artist. The struggle between young and old in the French poem is related to artistic sensitivity and to the emergence of new art forms and theory, which are suggested in surrealist scenes in the closing stanzas. Campbell's aerial dogfight is part of his rejection of the humanitarian idealism of his youth for his Catholic faith. In the balancing of youth and the future the two poems share more than simply the image of aerial combat. But Campbell develops his poem in a typically personal fashion, and once again has used a French source as a stimulus to a similar, but distinctly original, poetic investigation of his own:

> One silver-white and one of scarlet hue,
> Storm-hornets humming in the wind of death,
> Two aeroplanes were fighting in the blue
> Above our town; and if I held my breath,
> It was because my youth was in the Red
> While in the White an unknown pilot flew—
> And that the White had risen overhead.
> [1, 155]

The aerial image occurs in the opening stanzas of "Les Collines," and here the similarity with Campbell's lines is obvious:

> Au-dessus de Paris un jour
> Combattaient deux grands avions
> L'un était rouge et l'autre noir
> Tandis qu'au zénith flamboyait
> L'éternel avion solaire
>
> L'un était toute ma jeunesse
> Et l'autre c'était l'avenir

Ils se combattaient avec rage
Ainsi fit contre Lucifer
L'Archange aux ailes radieuses.
                    [*Oeuvres Poétiques*]

Both poems share the same sense of detached observation
at their opening, but Apollinaire, in the secular poem, goes
to greater lengths to suggest the evil of the past and the
value of the future than does Campbell in his explicitly
religious poem. Once Apollinaire begins his announce-
ment of the art of prediction as his "youth" is shot down,
there is little similarity between his poem and "The Fight":

Où donc est tombée ma jeunesse
Tu vois que flambe l'avenir
Sache que je parle aujourd'hui
Pour annoncer au monde entier
Qu'enfin est né l'art de prédire.

In contrast with the breadth of vision implied in Apollinaire's declamation, Campbell's final religious statement
appears limited by his peculiarly intense Christian response:

The towers and trees were lifted hymns of praise,
The city was a prayer, the land a nun:
The noonday azure strumming all its rays
Sang that a famous battle had been won,
As signing his white Cross, the very Sun,
The Solar Christ and captain of my days
Zoomed to the zenith; and his will was done.
                                    [1, 156]

The formal and external quality with which the poem ends
is different from the more subtle and personal description
of the fight itself, but typical of the burnished finish of
much of Campbell's religious writing.

Although they do not all show similar control, the
Toledo sonnets in *Mithraic Emblems* are justifiably the best

known of his war poems, and embody this fervid response in its most condensed form. They give effective expression to his violent outlook, and their Goya-like scenes of horror are part of his homiletic reaction to the war. The opening lines of "Christ in Uniform" reveal the extreme nature of his picture of sacrificial fulfilment:

Close at my side a girl and boy
Fell firing, in the doorway here,
Collapsing with a strangled cheer
As on the very couch of joy,
And onward through a wall of fire
A thousand others rolled the surge.
[1, 154]

His uncompromising reaction has a conviction which is not marred by an attempt to argue the rights and wrongs of the situation. The same totality of response informs the lines from "Hot Rifles" in which he comments on the Toledo fighting:

Of all that fearful fusillade
I reckoned not the gain or loss
To see (her every forfeit paid)
And grander, though her riches fade,
Toledo, hammered on the Cross,
And in her Master's wounds arrayed.
[1, 153]

The concept of wounds "arraying" anyone is an unsettling aspect of his zealous application of the crucifixion mystique to his violent crusade. But the passion of his redemptive belief is realized with a rhetorical fervour and conviction which characterize all aspects of his political stand in Spain.

The reactionary views, the violence, and the peculiarly personal response of Campbell's Spanish period caused his work to be regarded with a distaste that left him more isolated and defensive than ever. The impression that he was a wild man with decidedly un-English values could only be strengthened. This hostility towards him was inevitable. His political utterances on Spain are often crass, cruel, and tedious. Nevertheless, the obvious weakness of so much of the propaganda poetry has obscured many fine moments in the work of the Spanish period. The fact that he advances so many false political values has tended to conceal both the validity of many of his attacks on Utopian dreams and the real strength embodied in his heroic view. Campbell himself tried to limit the question of his political values to one of courage and commitment when he later enlisted to fight the fascism to which his ideas so clearly tended during his life in Spain. But the question-begging flourish of his heroic gesture does not dispel the uneasiness created by most of the ideas in *Flowering Rifle*. This uneasiness is heightened by the fact that he stood by the values of his Spanish poems until the time of his death, and his revised version of *Flowering Rifle* was published posthumously. As a choric comment both on the confusion resulting from this retention of his old views after the realignment of his loyalties and on the equivocal nature of all propaganda, the propaganda talk he broadcast for the B.B.C. on the Overseas Africa Service on March 2, 1942, shows an enlightening and atypical statement on the reality of life in Spain in the *año seis de la Vitoria*:

> Compared with that sort of life which I had just left, the amazing bounty, wealth and freedom of English wartime life struck me very forcibly. For this man was grumbling about rations and food; and he was a very lucky man to have any rations to grumble about. Where I had come from we were reduced to stewed thistles and roasted acorns and we were fined, or imprisoned even for referring to the fact. Wherever the "Ginger Locust" appears (as the German is called in Spain), whether he appears as an invader or a friendly protector his voracity is the same—and he leaves you no bread to grumble about. It was a truly dazzling sight to see loaves of bread in all the bakeries here—stacks

of it. I had volunteered to come over and share in the privations and misery of the British as represented by Axis propaganda in Spain. But I found I had really come to share the bread and the laughter of the healthiest nation alive!

[KC]

CHAPTER 7

TALKING BRONCO

From his *Flaming Terrapin* days Campbell had been commenting as an outsider on the situation in which he found himself. His return to South Africa alienated him from his colonial background. *The Georgiad* excluded him from the British literary scene. When his Provençal and Spanish environments at last provided him with companions and values with which he could identify himself, his "anachronistic," "equestrian" outlook was still that of the outsider. Not only was he deliberately cutting himself off from "Pommie" ways; he was defying the twentieth century. The European war forced Campbell to abandon his Mediterranean havens. Even before 1939 he had found himself evacuated to Britain from Toledo, and then isolated from the realities of the Spanish war while he wrote propaganda in Portugal. By the end of 1939 he had to choose between remaining in Franco's Spain and finally excluding himself from his culture, or allying himself with that imperial culture, now threatened by a new barbarism which he was beginning to understand more fully. Throughout the first half of 1939 he was still a passionate defender of the Axis position, and intensely scornful of what he interpreted as British hypocrisy or gullibility. Once the Second World War broke out, however, he suddenly chose to end his estrangement from British ways, and although still a fervent supporter of the Nationalist cause in Spain, became pro-British in loyalties, determined to fight against the Axis powers.

Before returning to Toledo at the end of the civil war in 1939, he spent some time from late 1938 to 1939 in Rome, where he attended the funeral of Pope Pius XI. The quality of his commitment to the Axis point of view can be seen in the letters he wrote to his mother (who had been with him in Rome) on his return to Toledo. One letter, written at Avila, "on our way back to Toledo," describes favourable reaction to *Flowering Rifle* from the right quarters, and goes on to comment on the international situation:

> The British Press has tried to make light of the book as it brings such heavy charges against them. But this time I have lots of good people to champion me and the book spreads in England like fire. Several people like the Maxwell Scotts are never without a dozen copies which they pass round to their friends. I think I told you how favourably the Spanish Royal Family were impressed with my book and how they have had their gentlemen and ladies in waiting write to me to thank me. The Marquesa de Candara in Rome who is one of the ladies of court told me that Don Juan the Prince the [sic] Asturias was tremendously enthusiastic about the book and took it away with him. Signor Maraini who is the head of the Italian Ministry of arts and his wife an English woman had just ordered 20 copies of it when I left Rome: and I enclose a letter from Harold Goad to Miss Curry editress of the Weekly News in Rome. He is the head of the British Institute of Art at Florence. It is very nice to feel there are still some Englishmen who are not still sat on or hypnotised by the Jews. Don't be-

lieve your press about Hitler. Checoslovakia *[sic]* was
entirely under French and Russian officers planning the
bombardment of Berlin—so he just took it over as he
was asked to do by their own Government who had no
authority over the mob—it was the best thing that
could have happened. Now with the taking over of
Albania there are two storm-centres less in Europe, if
only the British Press would interpret right. As for
"breaking one's word," none of the dictators did so
until every promise ever made by the Democracies had
been violated so as to make it laughable to keep their
side of the bargain.

[KC]

In another letter, dated June 3, Year of Victory,[1] he writes:

I met many German Catholics in Rome and know all
about what you sent me in the Readers Digest, a paper
that has always suppressed any mention of the *real*
Persecution of Christians like in Spain where 500,000
were massacred by hand, including 60,000 children
under 15. Catholics are never afraid of the Big Stick
and will not change their religion for it as protestants
have done in Germany. What catholics realise is that
Hitler is a civilised and human adversary compared to
the only other alternative, and they suffer as cheerfully
as they can. That is what bravery is for. It is on the side
of the only other alternative that the Readers Digest
weeps these crocodile tears for German catholics; to
raise up ill-feeling against Hitler who has not persecuted or robbed a tenth of what the IIIrd Republic in
France has done, or even what England has done in this
XXth century with her black-and-tans in Ireland burning churches and killings. . . . It is the first thing that
one expects in being Christened a Catholic, to be persecuted, and it is a very cheap price to pay for being a
Christian Christian *[sic]*. What we realise however is
that the world is going to become either bolshevik or

1. Campbell means 1939, although the phrase is often used to refer
to the year in which the rising occurred, 1936.

fascist, and we know that with one exception the fascist states are eminently Christian and allow Christians to live whereas bolshevism simply kills and degrades everything—it is against morality, and against every form of religion.

[KC]

An interesting feature of the letter is that Campbell accepts implicitly that Spain is a fascist state, and, unlike Germany, "eminently Christian." His attitude towards the new Italy in another letter to his mother shows the same unquestioning sympathy. The inevitable attacks on the English with which it is coupled are typical of his almost hysterical need to explain away his own ostracism:

At the Popes funeral I had charge of two young Englishmen who came to do the broadcasting for England. They enjoyed everything in Rome so much and were almost in tears when they had to go. I said "Why don't you tell your friends (the ones that give the lying news) to come & see Italy?" They said that if they were to drop one word in favour of Italy or what they had seen there they would not only lose their jobs but every friend they ever had. It is terrible the way the Press has worked up England, it is impossible to reason with them.

[KC]

Campbell's feeling for the past, for imperial grandeur, and for "style" are all part of his attachment to Spanish and Italian fascism. The fascism of the Aryan master race was of a different order, however, and almost immediately after the outbreak of the Second World War he had decided to enlist on the side of the allies. In a letter to his mother dated 1939, and written in Toledo after the war had begun, his decision is already clear:

The consul will let me know the moment there is any opening for me either in the ranks or as an interpreter in France. In this war they only seem to want engineers, experts, doctors & aviators outside of young unmarried men, . . . I do not share your pessimism about Russia, that she is on the other side. But for that we would have had the rest of Europe against us—probably Italy if not Spain and Portugal. I thank God Russia is on the other side. . . . The present neutrality of Italy is worth 1000 times the friendship of Russia.

[KC]

The most interesting aspect of the letter is that soon after the outbreak of war he is already so closely identified with Britain in the struggle that Spain is now a possible member of an Axis alliance against "us." His instinctive wish to support Britain is not explained rationally, and is particularly amazing in the light of the letters written in the first half of the same year in which even the invasion of Czechoslovakia is regarded as "the best thing that could have happened."

Campbell's abrupt change in loyalty was not a unique phenomenon in 1939. Once war was inevitable many British writers critical of British democracy made similar decisions. Wyndham Lewis publicly revised his opinion of Hitler in 1939 when he published *The Hitler Cult,* and, on the other side of the fence, Orwell emerged as a "patriot" during the war. Even the cynical Evelyn Waugh was about to speak glowingly of a "Churchillian Renaissance." Patriotism was not dead, and Campbell's past was rooted in a British imperial tradition in Natal. When faced with the grim alternative, he instinctively supported Britain, and, since it was an instinct, he found his support difficult to rationalize. In "The Clock in Spain" he tries to explain both his pro-Nationalist and his pro-British loyalties, but can only make vague assertions of his own superior vitality. Its opening is urbane and poised. He begins by showing an amused superiority and indifference to what the British clock is proud of:

This Clock from England says he came
Where as a God he was revered.
His hours in length were all the same,

> And each departed whence it came
> The moment its relief appeared.
>
> To a great Firm his line he traces,
> Of manufacturers the aces,
> And if you don't believe it's true,
> The legend written on his face is
> "Birmingham 1922."
>
> [2, 58]

His bantering tone is ideal for capturing the foreignness to him of a petty life obsessed by time. When he describes the clock's arrival in Spain, however, his personal involvement destroys the earlier sense of detached contempt:

> Some Red Brigader, panic-shod,
> Abandoned here, on Spanish sod,
> This sacred fetish of his race
> He'd fought to substitute for God—
> So we took pity on his case.
>
> [2, 59]

This stanza is already less poised than the opening, and when the major change occurs later in the poem, the poet's urbanity vanishes completely. At this point, instead of Spanish scenery altering the manners of the clock, the sight of Campbell's lover turns its "notions outside in." The most remarkable feature of the change is not its unexpectedness, but its insensitivity. Not only does the irony disappear, but any sense is lost of the poem's growing out of real experience or any understandable adult emotion. Earlier, the unbounded natural world which the clock comes to know in Spain has been neatly introduced:

> But when, athwart an open door,
> He smelt the orange-trees in flower,
> And heard the headlong Tagus roar,
> And saw the white sierras soar,
> That moment cost him half an hour.
>
> [2, 60]

The detailed sensual description of Campbell's love, however, seems an end in itself, and only arbitrarily connected
with the central irony of the poem. Even the terms of the
physical description itself are arbitrary:

> Her hair that smokes with raven swirl
> To tell of banked and hidden fire,
> And golden dynamos that whirl
> To launch a battleship of pearl
> Into the rollers of desire.
>
> [2, 60]

The sight of the lover "clearing for action to the skin"
(with, among her other attributes, "breasts like bruised
and bouncing roses," and "haunches like a bounding
filly's") completely alters the rigid and restricted manners
the British clock. The intensity of Campbell's personal life
is thus established as the element that distinguishes his
Spanish ways from bourgeois British customs. British imperial heroics have always attracted him, however, and in
the closing sections of the poem his wit returns as he
cleverly identifies himself with the now altered clock which
is still basically British. Here the Byronic manner not only
preserves a feeling of sanity, but gives a public resonance
to his own heroic commitment:

> Although he may appear to you
> To have renounced his race and era,
> His steel is British, cold, and blue,
> As ever flashed at Waterloo
> Or held the line at Talavera.
>
> And if the dreadful hour should chime
> For British blood, and steel as grim,
> My clock will wake, and tick the time,
> And slope his arms and march—and I'm
> The one to fall in step with him.
>
> [2, 62]

The similarity between the poet's and the clock's
accepting the ease of Spanish ways until a moment of

crisis is shown quite clearly without the sexual incident. The whole sexual episode is introduced because Campbell cannot articulate his motives for siding with a nation whose attitudes he despised during the civil war. His intention in describing the mysteries of his emotional life is to suggest that he is beyond normal customs and reactions. In this way he can escape the problem of rationalizing the change from his assumed Iberian irony and mysticism to his support for the country of commercial materialism. The implication is that although his zest for living allows him to lead an infinitely fuller existence than his British contemporaries, this does not mean that he lacks British courage. The inability to say why he has changed his attitude or what he is now fighting for is implicit both in the unsuccessful evocation of transcendental passion, and in the simple, question-begging assumption that the new crisis only requires British courage. In the Spanish situation, we may note, British fighting potential appears as the panic-shod Red Brigader; but then that situation required the Spanish courage shown in the defence of the Alcazar.

Campbell returned to England alone in 1941, to be joined later by his family. The extreme isolation into which his fervour for the Nationalist cause had driven him can be seen from the reaction of his old right-wing ally, Wyndham Lewis, who had been delighted in 1936 to be hailed as "Moscardó to the whole of Europe."[2] In a letter in 1942 to Augustus John, who had seen Campbell with Nina Hamnett "in a Soho speak-easy," Lewis writes: "It was a great pleasure to get your letter, and therein to catch a glimpse of you in some smoky den in Soho (for if Nina was there, it must have been a den) exchanging iron fisted he-man salutations with our Vaquero—to whom please give, should you encounter him again, my best wishes. It is really capital news that he has got out of Spain, where he was liable, because of his over-fervent papist nature to get involved in all kinds of abominable nonsense."[3] In a letter to Mary Campbell, dated January 5, 1944, from Windsor, Ontario, where he was attached to Assumption College,

2. Wyndham Lewis, *Letters*, p. 239.
3. Ibid., p. 338.

Lewis again dissociates himself from Campbell's stand in Spain: "How long has R.C. been in Africa? Is he stopping there? Please give me his address. I was glad to hear from Augustus that he had exchanged his requeté uniform for that of the Home Guard. The best Catholic opinion now— and I speak from very near the horse's mouth—is that the requetés were on the wrong side in the land of the flowering rifle."[4]

By returning to England, Campbell both renewed his contacts with English life, and publicly validated his heroic image when he joined the British army. *Sons of the Mistral* was published in 1941, and proved to be a popular selection of his best work. In the following year, after serving for some months as an air raid warden in London, he enlisted in the British army as a private. After undergoing training at Brecon and Winchester he was sent to East Africa, where he served as a coast watcher in intelligence. Eventually osteoarthritis in his hip caused him to be invalided out of the service in 1944, with the rank of sergeant.

His soldiering was extremely important to him and provided him with both a sense of belonging and his last poetic role—that of the "old sweat" who has a down-to-earth, cynical insight into reality, and, like the vaquero in the poems of the thirties, shows the simple virtues of comradeship, courage, and endurance. The letters he wrote during his period of active service show that his own experience, far from glamorous or exciting, often involved tedium, strain, and discomfort for a man in his forties, suffering from an injured leg, and not in good health. In a letter to his mother dated August 12, 1942, and written at a training camp in Winchester, he writes: "The I.T.C. recommended me for a commission (though I am happy in the ranks) but I don't think I'll get it as I am a bit long in the tooth and they wisely prefer youth. . . . I was by some years the grandfather of our platoon—and I think I have stood the wear and tear pretty well. I managed to disguise my lame leg through forced marches when many younger men fell out, and I did very well on the shooting." (KC) A

4. Ibid., p. 374.

similar impression of strain and diffidence is apparent in another letter written from the Intelligence Corps Depot in Winchester to his daughter, Tess: "In spite of everything I said in my letter to Mum about being in a blue funk most of the time it is really very exciting and interesting. Oh I forgot to tell you I wear one of those crash-helmets that you say you like—like half of a melon on top of my own melon: and a huge pair of goggles." (TC)

During the early days of his return to England, he was extremely sensitive about the unpopularity his Spanish position had caused him. Before his wife had joined him, he wrote to her: "You would be surprised what people think of me over here 'sober hard-working good-natured etc.' I seem to have got out of a groove. But Spain did me a lot of good. The Spaniards are (for all their faults) far better than we are individually. I am considered a sort of goody-goody over here and in Spain I was supposed to be a sort of rake."(MC) His simple wish to be good and to be liked shows an element of real pathos in his isolated situation, and presents a very different picture from that of the he-man literary persona. In a letter to his wife from his training camp he writes: "Everybody among my friends Pearson Keller and others are quite surprised at the sort of extravagant affection (! may it last!) that I enjoy on all hands. Everybody calls me by my Christian name including even the female cooks. It is quite a change after being so eminently unpopular as a writer. I only hope it lasts—and spreads!" (MC)

The army did provide Campbell with many new boon companions, and the firm and varied friendships he made helped him to feel accepted, and even to remain cheerful in Africa, where his work was tedious and lonely. Quite apart from his arthritic hip, he suffered frequent attacks of malaria, which often necessitated hospital treatment. A letter to his daughter, Tess, written from Nairobi after a spell in hospital gives an impression of his life in the army:

> In answer to your questions I am quite as contented as one can be in such a God-forsaken spot and so far from my loved ones—but I think that absence has been

a good experience since I appreciate you all three even more when I miss you so badly and long for you so much. Your letters do make me so happy for hours and hours after I get them. . . .

You can see from my letters (how dull they are now!). Well may be it will give me something new to write about when I get down by the sea. This is my last day in Nairobi.

If we were all here together I dare say it would seem a wonderful place. . . . I can tell you the country outside of Nairobi is almost unbelievable—it is like Walt Disney's "fantasia" only it bears the signature of the Creator in his more humorous mood nothing in the way of Noaks *[sic]* Ark's or Flaming Terrapins comes up to the reality of the scampering droves of zebras, giraffes, etc. But here we are more or less in the suburbs and apart from the flowers and birds and an occasional glimpse of Mount Kenya in the distance you might just as well be in Petersfield.

Even my pal Mick Fenlon has done nothing funny enough to recount in a letter for at least six weeks. And if this place makes him dull, it would make any one dull. But I read a lot and will soon be resigned to being a B III man. I liked it far better when I was down in Tanganycka *[sic]* in the bush.

[TC]

The solitude in the bush was not always attractive, however, and in December 1943 he wrote to his wife in these terms:

I hope I dont repeat myself too often since life on a post like this is uneventful though I never feel the monotony being kept busy and having plenty to read. Many people can't stand this sort of job—the solitude drives them almost out of their wits. But Ive got fairly good company with your photo and my books. Luckily Ive got a good imagination and memory and if I cant be with you at least I can remember you almost as if you were here and imagine everything we're going to

do when we meet again—That meeting is the one thing
worth living for to me.

[MC]

   Campbell was invalided out of the service in 1944, and
returned to England. After working for a time on the War
Damages Commission he became a talks producer with the
B.B.C. in 1946. In the same year *Talking Bronco* appeared,
the last volume of original poems to be published. The
Spanish civil war and his support for the Nationalist-
Christian cause reappear in *Talking Bronco* with a different
emphasis from that in the intensely Spanish poems of the
1930s. Since he himself was enlisted in an antifascist army
from 1942 to 1944, his assessment alters of the qualities
for which the Nationalist rebels stood. The war is used by
him as an example of his stand against the totalitarian persecution of Christians by communists, just as the Second
World War is an occasion for the humble worker and
ranker like himself to make a personal stand against the
totalitarian persecution of Jews by fascists. The commitment to fight against this persecution either in Spain in the
1930s or Europe in the 1940s confers a personal integrity.
Such integrity contrasts with the compromising and equivocal position of the politicians and propagandists who
"farm this carnage from the rear," leading others to fight
for ideals which are being betrayed by the very men who
promulgate them. His scorn for left-wing writers who had
not enlisted is particularly virulent, and he coins for them
the composite name, MacSpaunday.[5]
   The persona of the humble "old sweat" is often obtrusive, and the recurrence, in many of the war poems, of
the trappings of the Sergeants' Mess creates an effect of
disproportion similar to that created by the recurrence of
the Tagus and Toledo in the poems from *Mithraic Emblems*.

   5. MacNeice spent most of 1940 in the United States. At the end
of the year he returned to England. In 1941 he joined the staff of the
B.B.C. as scriptwriter and producer. Spender was co-editor of *Horizon*
until 1941, and then joined the London Auxiliary Fire Service. Auden
left England in 1939, and remained in the United States after the war.
Cecil Day Lewis was in the Home Guard in 1940, and from 1941 to
1946 was editor of books and pamphlets for the Ministry of Information.

The symbols, which have such a marked personal importance for Campbell, do not carry the same significance for
the general reader, and in the war poems often suggest an
element of banality when the poet insists on introducing
his chevrons, his rifle, or his rations:

> Through rusty grooves, a four-by-two,
> Your luck till now has pulled you through—
> But chance ignores the rules of chess.
> The skyte-hawk falls, the swoop of fate,
> And swipes your rations off your plate
> Between the cook-house and the mess.
> [2, 66]

The down-to-earth tone does not make the down-to-earth
moral any more significant. There is a contrived simplicity
about the sergeant's world. By accepting its terms of reference so completely, Campbell ignores his own sophistication and wit because they cannot be easily subsumed in
gnomic noncommissioned verse. A similar limitation can
be seen in his simple acceptance of military values:

> What's more majestic underneath the sky,
> Than when a British Regiment marches by
> With rolling drums, and pipes, and colours spread,
> And gravel crunching to the rhythmic tread,
> The conscript, with the volunteer beside,
> Lifted three inches by contagious pride,
> And all by comradeship, with ghostly ply,
> So harnessed, that the worst for all would die.
> [2, 80]

In this passage from "Jungle Eclogue" the poet himself
is not speaking, and the visionary "Nat" who makes the remarks is describing the virility of the British regiment in
order to show that even this withers and faints at his touch.
Nevertheless Campbell himself clearly believes in the
majesty of a British regiment marching by, and expects the
reader to attach the same unequivocal value to the scene.
The military details which he describes often carry little

general significance or suggest anything more than a specifically military skill or utility. In a passage from "Talking
Bronco" he boasts of his own military prowess at his training camp near Brecon in this way:

> And if I'm talking bullshine as you reckon,
> Then go and ask the Billygoat at Brecon
> Who broke the record of his I. T. C.
> With rifle, tommygun, and L. M. G.?
> And on the targets wrote his number, name,
> And unit with an autograph of flame?
>
> [2, 86]

The use of army abbreviations and terms like "bullshine,"
as well as the comradely self-effacement of an identity
established by number, name, and unit are all part of the
role Campbell plays in *Talking Bronco*. The role itself is of
limited interest, however, and Campbell seldom succeeds
in conveying to his reader the importance or value of the
N.C.O. world which he himself takes so seriously. When
his war poems are immediately successful, he has usually
transcended the specific world of the N.C.O. and captured
a wry or cynical attitude that has a general significance far
beyond the limit of the barracks, even if the original impetus comes from the poet's identification with the
unprivileged mass of the "other ranks." The brilliant little
epigram, "Snapshot of Nairobi," depends on the military
world's being placed in sardonic perspective by the humble
ranker:

> With orange-peel the streets are strown
> And pips, beyond computing,
> On every shoulder save my own,
> That's fractured with saluting.
>
> [1, 282]

Wit of this kind in itself raises the poet above the military
trappings in which, for once, he has no vested interest.
There is no suggestion of an inherent value in his noncommissioned status. A lack of pretension in the poem is one

of its most attractive features, and one that distinguishes it from other war poems in which Campbell ostentatiously uses his status of common soldier as part of a polemic against politicians and Utopian left-wing writers. The strain in these poems derives from the illegitimate use to which the poet puts his status as a volunteer. The physical courage and commitment which he associates with the volunteer in the ranks do not automatically entail a superior insight into the political realities behind the war. His charge of cowardice against the antifascist writers who did not enlist when the war came does not necessarily entail the refutation of their earlier insistence that fascism should be fought.

Although Campbell's dislike of socialist movements did not alter after the outbreak of the Second World War, his opinion of fascism and the Axis powers did. The mask of the cynical ranker who knows he is exploited by all politicians is adopted largely to enable him to abandon his previous political statements about Hitler, Mussolini, democracy, and even at times the Nationalist cause in Spain, without having to contradict himself. All politics are now nasty and treacherous. All political values are meaningless. In this way the poet does not have to criticize the quasi-fascist theory which crept into his own writing in the thirties, but can maintain his attack on socialist theory and the left-wing writers who continue, in his view, to deceive the nation at war, just as they did in peace. "Talking Bronco" itself is closest to the Spanish poems of the thirties in tone, and adds little either in the way of invective or argument to his position in *Flowering Rifle*. The poem is similarly low in style, and derives its impetus from the poet's personal animosity towards left-wing writers. As a result, his overt intention is often to sneer and ridicule:

> They left no redder stain their faith to write
> Than what they sweat or piddled in their fright
> In drops as yellow as their oaths were red—
> And as they've written so shall they be read,
> With all who try to stutter their apology
> (From Duffduff down to Spaunday's last anthology)

> And all who farmed the carnage for good pay
> Though from the firing they kept far away.
>
> [2, 84–85]

Although his assertions here vary little from those in *Flowering Rifle,* his view of himself has changed, and the cynical, laughing, lone-wolf sergeant is the image he presents to shame the cowardly MacSpaunday:

> So History looks the winner in the mouth
> Though but a dark outsider from the South,
> A Talking Bronco, sharked from ear to ear
> With laughter, like a running bandolier,
> With teeth, like bullets fastened in their clips,
> To chew the thunder and to spit the pips,
> Ejecting from the breech, in perfect time,
> The shells of metre and the shucks of rhyme,
> Yet drive the thoughts with perforating aim
> Like tracer-bullets on their threads of flame.
>
> [2, 85]

A detailed description of the actual mechanics of firing is typical of Campbell's military preoccupations at this period. And inevitably such preoccupations have a mechanical effect on the texture of his later satirical poems. As the cavalier sergeant he consistently presents himself in an aura of moral superiority:

> And why the Talking Bronco in the front
> With Recces and Commandos takes the brunt
> Though by his age, race, domicile, description,
> Exempted from all service or conscription?—
> While joint MacSpaunday shuns the very strife
> He barked for loudest when mere words were rife,
> When to proclaim his proletarian loyalties
> Paid well, was safe, raked in the heavy royalties,
> And made the Mealy Mouth and Bulging Purse
> The hallmark of Contemporary verse.
>
> [2, 87]

Although the Talking Bronco's own claim to be in the front with Recces and Commandos is not accurate, his war service as a coast watcher was a tedious task, involving much privation, from which his age, race, domicile, and description would normally have exempted him. Stephen's Spender's work as a London fireman seems to have been not very different, however, and was possibly more dangerous, although, of course, as an Englishman he was under a *de facto* obligation from which Campbell, as a South African, was free. The admiration Campbell has for Reconnaissance-men and Commandos, to the point of suggesting a connection with them, is part of his obsession with military values, which offer the appearance of solidity in contrast to political values. His rejection of all political values is only partly a result of the embarrassment of his old political atitudes, however. It is also a natural development of his heroic, "anachronistic" world-view. To the extent that his sergeant's persona is really based on a personal revulsion against politics, it does enable him to present with conviction a consistently cynical picture of the motives behind war.[6]

He constantly contrasts the left-wing poets' behaviour during the Second World War with their "bloodthirsty" antifascist writings in the thirties. During the Spanish civil war their insistence was on action:

A more ferocious, bloodthirsty poltroon
Has never howled for blood beneath the moon
Than joint MacSpaunday, when his leash of heads
To murder, rape, and arson roared the Reds.

[2, 89]

However, in the major antifascist struggle in which Campbell himself is taking part, those writers who were most vociferously and belligerently antifascist during the thirties, are inactive:

6. The pervasive quality of Campbell's cynicism at this time can be seen in a letter written to his wife from his infantry training camp. After describing his delight at a speech by Smuts, Campbell goes on to say, "He is a sly old fox and knows the value of rhetoric, and words, words, words—the less meaning they have the better."[MC]

For where was he, when England stood alone?
This Bogus Proletarian, the Drone
Who stood beside the Worker (*while it paid*)
Seeks every ruse his Gospel to evade
Appeals to privilege of class and wealth,
To save his pockets and preserve his health.

[2, 88]

He keeps his attack on the personal level, and does not make any political deductions from the situation which he describes. The integrity which MacSpaunday has sacrificed by his unwillingness to fight is the only value which Campbell considers in his overt rejection of politics. His insistence on courage and action during the Second World War, and his dismissal of any overriding political considerations, or even of the possibility of an overall view of the political situation, are typical of his own brand of instinctive, heroic consciousness. Because he deliberately dismisses politics, however, he cannot see the political motives behind the attitudes of the Auden group during the thirties, and the way their world had collapsed with the outbreak of war. In his autobiography, *World within World,* Stephen Spender gives articulate and convincing expression to the predicament of these writers:

The background to these personal events was the victory of Franco in the Spanish Civil War, the Munich settlement, and the occupation of Czechoslovakia. Of these, the fall of the Spanish Republic symbolized the end of an epoch. The other events were the beginning of a new one—the beginning of the war. . . .

After this the emotions and the arguments used by the anti-Fascists were taken over by the democratic governments in their war against Hitler. Journalists sometimes complained in the Press that the anti-Fascist writers who had shown such zeal in 1936 and 1937 seemed perversely uninterested, now that the action against Hitlerism for which they had been clamouring, was really taking place. But the fact was that the anti-Fascist battle had been lost. For it was a battle against

totalitarian war, which could have made the war unnecessary. The war certainly produced its heroes: pre-
eminently the fighter pilots who won the Battle of
Britain. But their flame-like resurgence of a quality
flowering throughout English history was something
different from the individualistic anti-Fascism of the
1930's. [pp. 261–62]

The resigned and restrained tone of an attitude like this
towards the Second World War itself is foreign to Campbell's passion for heroic action and to the great value he
attaches at all stages of his life to simple physical skill and
courage. His insistence on the values for which he is fighting appears extremely naive in contrast to Stephen Spender's statement:

> As now today I'm fighting for the Jew
> (Since Poles or Finns subsided out of view
> Though once the pretext for this war, it's true)
> So I have fought for Christians, and my steel
> Is always pointed at the tyrant's heel,
> Whether from Right or Left he dares to clout
> His Maker's image with a butcher's knout.
> For Blacks I've done as much, and risked my life,
> As since for Jews or Christians in the strife.
>   [2, 93]

This oversimplification of issues is made in characteristically generalized racist terms. The political attitude which
makes possible the persecution of Jew, Finn, or Pole is
never discussed, as if the Second World War were fought
over the specific issue of Jewish persecution, and the
Spanish civil war over the persecution of the Church.
Campbell mirrors the simpleminded reaction of the English
public even as he jeers at their naive enthusiasm when the
democracies seemed at last to be rallying to the defence of
little nations in 1939. The rabbit did not run; washing was
not hung out on the Siegfried line, and an absurd scheme
to aid Finland against the Soviet Union came to nothing.
Nevertheless, in these lines Campbell can only substitute

another victim for those that have faded out of view. He is no closer than the deluded phoney-war Britons in coming to terms with a situation in which he now depends on the Soviet divisions to tear the Panzers apart. The sergeant's uncompromising faith in his blow for the underdog is simply not convincing as a faith which makes the war worth fighting, particularly because of the insensitively racist terms with which the underdog is described. In "Jungle Eclogue" the British N.C.O. opposes these ostentatiously rough and ready values to the demoralizing insinuations of the hallucinatory "Nat":

> . . . One must be deft
> When liberty's attacked from Right and Left.
> With my left fist the Nazi though I fight
> I've banged the bloody Bolshy with my right,
> With his own captured arms, his guns and tanks,
> Which first we had to rustle from his ranks.
> Between the Jewish Fascism of Russia
> And gentile Bolshevism farmed on Prussia,
> I see no difference save in their salutes.
>
> [2, 83]

Campbell does show a change in attitude here from that he held in the thirties, where he actually praised the values symbolized by the fascist salute in Spain, and opposed them to the grasping outlook suggested by the communist closed fist. At the same time, however, his old instinctive dislikes are still lurking under the surface. For all the outward fair-mindedness of his attempt to show the similarity between two different forms of totalitarianism, the idea of the "Jewish Fascism of Russia" is not very far removed from the anti-semitism of his Spanish period. Because his motives for enlisting in the British army really do not grow out of political conviction, but are related to his own personal feeling for what is magnanimous and heroic, Campbell is most convincing when he refrains from attempting a homespun political philosophy of the sort just quoted, but expresses a personal disillusion with political ideals:

I'm fighting for no better world
But for a worse—the blasted pit
Wherein the bones of this were hurled—
And our hegemony of it!
I'm fighting for a funkhole-warren
Of bureaucrats, who've come to stay,
Because I'd rather, than the foreign
Equivalent, it should be they.

[2, 68]

The impression that the disillusion is real, and that he is speaking with sincerity, grows when he goes on to include his Spanish crusade among those in which the victory has been bathetic:

For I have lived, of three crusades,
The heroism and the pathos,
Seen how the daft illusion fades,
And learned of victory the bathos.

[2, 68]

There is no suggestion whatever of special pleading in the lines, and this reinforces the impression that his attitude grows genuinely from experience. Campbell's commitment to fight now in spite of his awareness of the falsity of the political values behind war is explicitly linked, a few lines later, with his similar commitment in Spain, and, by implication, with his disillusionment with the politics of that struggle:

Let me be there to share the strain
And with the poorest pull my weight
As in the catacombs of Spain
When all the world was Red with hate!
I know that all ideals miscarry,
That cowards use the blows we strike,
That liars aim the guns we carry
Screeching their hatred on the Mike.

[2, 69]

When he relates his overall sense of political futility to
his own situation, the cynicism rings true. As a result the
corresponding value he places on simple integrity and
courage is a convincing part of the poet's own response to
the war. The poetry which arises out of his subjective attitudes towards the struggle, and the futile-seeming experience of his own soldiering, has a genuine quality far
superior to anything in the objective polemical attacks.
His own experience clearly informs a fine passage from the
uneven "Jungle Eclogue."[7] The "Nat" is speaking:

> Mine are the suns of slow miasmal pomp;
> Peril, without adventure, in the swamp;
> The green reef creaming through protracted calms,
> Dhows passing through the screen of dusty palms,
> The rigmarole of Jambos and Salaams:
> The solitude of coast-watches who've died
> Of their own company—those hollow-eyed
> Anchorites of the bush, through wounds or illness
> Thrown out of fighting ranks, to face the stillness
> Of jungle days. . . .

[2, 81]

Even the unobtrusive inclusion of dialect words is part of
the authentic quality in the whole East African rigmarole.

In his preface to the Cape Town edition of *Adamastor*,
published by Paul Koston in 1950, Campbell describes his
deliberate attempt to use colloquial words in his later
poems:

> In *Adamastor* the language is still somewhat formal and
> "poetic" and the verse somewhat loose, but I think
> that the process can be detected, in some of the poems,

7. Compare the extract from "Jungle Eclogue" with this passage
from a letter written to Mrs. Mary Campbell from East Africa, dated
September 19, 1943: "It is very tantalising to see the sea and not be
able to go to it or to do any fishing, which I believe is marvellous here.
One sees dozens of dhows fishing. They are lateen-rigged like the bettes
and tartanes of Provence, Spain and Portugal—and make me very
homesick for the Mediterranean. But the resemblance is only in that
towering triangle of sail with its long antenna. They are probably full
of wogs and Arabs, and stinking fish." [MC]

which was to lead to the blending of the everyday vernacular with classical verse-forms, which I have almost
attained in poems like *The Skull in the Desert, The
Clock in Spain, Dreaming Spires, The Carmelites of
Toledo,* and *The Moon of Short Rations,* which in the
opinion of poets and critics as different as T. S. Eliot,
Dylan Thomas, Desmond MacCarthy, William Empson,
Wyndham Lewis, C. S. Lewis, Edith, Osbert and Sachev-
erall [sic] Sitwell, Graham Greene, and John Betjeman
represent my best work so far. What I eventually aim
at is the restoration of the vernacular to its true place
as the vehicle of poetry; and to be able to combine the
comic, the poignant, the satirical and the lyrical in a
style flexible enough to carry them all, and to contain
and control the most sudden transitions from one to
another without internal disruption.

In the best poems of this period the vernacular does modu-
late into the lyrical or the poignant without strain, especially when the vernacular is so essential a part of the whole
experience of the poem as the dialect words quoted in the
last passage. As we have noticed, however, army slang and
abbreviations can become obtrusive in Campbell's war
poetry when introduced more or less for their own sake
and with an exaggerated emphasis. In the successful war
poems, on the other hand, his wit reasserts itself. It is his
wit which gives a sense of proportion to poems where he
describes his own wartime privations, and his scorn for
those who stay safely away from it all, without himself
appearing too pious or self-satisfied.

In "The Skull in the Desert" Campbell insists on his
ranker's knowledge of hardship, taunts the "hyena-bellied
muses / That farm this carnage from the rear," and describes his own capacity to recover from disaster and distress. What could be merely a stale reiteration of old
attitudes is transformed by his wit into one of his most
successful late poems in which his belief in the spiritual
insight resulting from suffering, his religious faith, and his
scorn for any "poet of the breed we know" all appear as
legitimate parts of a subjective and imaginative response.

> I found a horse's empty cranium,
> Which the hyenas had despised,
> Wherein the wind ventriloquised
> And fluting huskily afar
> Sang of the rose and the geranium
> And evenings lit with azahar.
>
> Foaled by the Apocalypse, and stranded
> Some wars, or plagues, or famines back,
> To bleach beside the desert track,
> He kept his hospitable rule:
> A pillow for the roving bandit,
> A signpost to the stricken mule.
>
> [1, 160]

The paradox, that the skull is both a worthless husk and an object which "sang" of things romantic, exotic, and beautiful, is organic to Campbell's final, heroic moral. It is the inextricable linking of the worthless and the valuable, of pain and beauty, which he points to. The background of chaos, death, and disaster which surrounds the skull becomes part of its passive, catalytic nature. In its total assimilation into the life of the desert Campbell sees a total natural harmony:

> He served the desert for a Sphinx
> And to the wind for a guitar,
> For in the harmony he drinks
> To rinse his whirring casque of bone
> There hums a rhythm less its own
> Than of the planet and the star.
>
> [1, 160]

The wind in the skull suggests the possibility of beauty growing out of horror, and this leads easily to a typical assertion of the poet's own ability to recover from distress:

> All I had left of will or mind,
> Which fire or fever had not charred,
> Was but the shaving, husk, and shard:

> But that sufficed to catch the air
> And from the pentecostal wind
> Conceive the whisper of a prayer.
>
> [1, 162]

There is no sense of staleness in the stanza. The assertions and exotic experiences are not being dragged into the poem as an inevitable part of whatever the poet has to say. His wit and verbal dexterity give real vitality to that combination of the colloquial, extravagant, and serious which he describes as a conscious goal.

In several *Talking Bronco* poems, the lyrical and the colloquial are similarly balanced. "One Transport Lost" is built around a sudden change of mood and style. The opening stanzas describe the violence and confusion following the torpedoeing of a crowded, garish troopship, "Where, packed as tight as space can fit them / The soldiers retch, and snore and stink." Once the ship has gone down a sudden shift of perspective occurs, and the elegiac calm of the sea becomes the centre of interest:

> For them, the wave, the melancholy
> Chant of the wind that tells no lies:
> The breakers roll their funeral volley
> To which the thundering cliff replies.
>
> [2, 64]

The futility of human activity remains the same both before and after the change; the central shift does not bring with it a complete break, but shows two different aspects of the lot of constantly impotent humanity.

Skill of this kind in manipulating tones and styles reaches a peak in "Dreaming Spires," which is also a "war" poem, deriving from Campbell's East African experiences. Like "One Transport Lost," "Dreaming Spires" is built around a sudden change of mood, which contrasts two worlds, two modes of existence. A group of raucous riders on motor bikes crash through the confused and terrified African landscape until pulled up by the serenity of a herd of giraffes. In many ways the mood of the opening ride is that of a motor mechanic's spree, and it is a tribute to the range of the poem that this sense can exist side by side with the wit of a Marvell:

> Respiring fumes of pure phlogiston
> On hardware broncos, half-machine,
> With arteries pulsing to the piston
> And hearts inducting gasoline:
>
> Buckjumping over ruts and boulders,
> The Centaurs of an age of steel
> Engrafted all save head and shoulders
> Into the horsepower of the wheel—
>   [1, 279]

Once the artisan guffaws are hushed, like the rumbling machines, at the otherworldliness of the unperturbed giraffes, the change in mood is complete:

> We close our throttles, clench the curb,
> And hush the rumble of our tyres,
> Abashed and fearful to disturb
> The City of the Dreaming Spires—
>
> The City of Giraffes!—a People
> Who live between the earth and skies,
> Each in his lone religious steeple,
> Keeping a light-house with his eyes.
>   [1, 280]

The world of the giraffes is one of solitary, ponderous tranquillity, and at the same time includes vivid visual details. When Campbell's reverie on the giraffes ends, the harsh reality of the machines reasserts itself, and the mechanical turmoil of the first part of the poem exists side by side, for a moment, with the phantom world of the animals before they disappear to the grating of gears:

> Into the dusk of leafy oceans
> They fade away with phantom tread;

And changing gears, reversing notions,
The road to Moshi roars ahead.
[1, 282]

This mingling of styles and moods in "Dreaming Spires" is typical of Campbell's most mature work, in which there is no weakening of poetic intensity. The best poems in *Talking Bronco* show a new dimension with his growing tendency to balance the vernacular and the lyrical. But this tendency is not really a major development, and the volume as a whole does not show the poet about to take any new move or direction. The tiresome polemical interest that dominates the early poems in the volume is the result of an increasingly institutionalized, down-to-earth reaction to complexities which irritate him. In spite of its share of successful poems growing from an inward and personal response, *Talking Bronco* is spoiled by the mechanical nature of so many of the poet's political utterances. Predictable polemic was to continue to occupy much of his attention after the war, and the lyrical fervour of his early poetry never returned. The fervour of the polemic itself, however, was only partially subdued.

CHAPTER 8

THE LAST PHASE

By returning to England in 1941 Campbell ended the
period of his most intense alienation from English culture.
His pleasure at being accepted as a man among men in the
British army both restored his confidence and renewed
many of the loyalties of his youth in the fiercely pro-British
colony of Natal. There, staunchly imperialistic values per-
sisted long after the colony became a province of the
Union of South Africa in 1910. His persona of the old-
sweat sergeant reflects a Kiplingesque tradition as well as
his own political disillusion. As the cynical N.C.O. he was
able to identify himself with a group, and, at the same time,
continue to make comments as one outside the conforming intellectual herd. After the war, however, the detested
coterie of left-wing writers was no longer either a coterie
or particularly fashionable. And Campbell himself was no
longer ostracized, but again accepted in the British literary
world. As symptoms of his return to respectability there
were his position with the B.B.C. and the fact that it was

Faber and Faber who published *Talking Bronco*. His role as the lone wolf became institutionalized, and although he did not cease to play the part of the rugged individualist after the Second World War, his work lost the intensity that real isolation in the past had given it. As he grew older he became increasingly attached to biographical assertions and anecdotal details which would confirm his he-man image. As part of this flamboyant persona, his conservative views dominate the occasional writing of his last years, when his work as an editor and his popularity as a lecturer gave him many opportunities to indulge his polemical verve.

In 1949 the first volume of *Collected Poems* appeared, and the general praise with which it was greeted re-established Campbell's reputation. Writing in the *New Statesman*, G. S. Fraser commented:

> And I think that his personal feuds sometimes rob him of a craftsman's sense of proportion. Yet, when the dust has settled on these quarrels—and on wider political quarrels on which I have not touched—Mr. Campbell's place, I would think, among the dozen or so more important poets of our time is assured. . . . Is there another lyrical poet of our time who combines, just as he does, vigour, directness, technical control, and the most vivid sense of beauty?[1]

The *Times Literary Supplement* published a full page review which ended: "Mr. Campbell's best performance has been to extol, in memorable and shining words, all sorts of bravery—and in an age of versifiers far more justly described as croquet-playing than the noble Tennyson."[2]

With his poetic standing higher than it had been since 1931, he left the B.B.C. in 1949 and took up a new position as joint editor, with Rob Lyle, of *Catacomb*, a journal which appeared monthly from April 1949 to May 1950 and then made eight appearances as a quarterly from the summer of 1950 to the winter of 1951 to 52. He published several of his translations from the French and Spanish in *Catacomb*,

1. *New Statesman and Nation* (December 17, 1949), p. 738.
2. *TLS* (March 24, 1950), p. 184.

which presented a militant right-wing attitude. The "Preamble" by Lyle and Campbell to the eighth number (November 1949) gives a good indication of the editorial tone:

> Unlike so many reviews which pass as intellectual, we don't confuse creative ability with pacifism; nor do we think that a nodding acquaintance with foreign cultures entitles us to despise our own country. If they only used their eyes, our comrades of the Left-*Behind* would find it unnecessary—as our foreign correspondents in these regions assure us—to go further afield than Hampstead or Swiss Cottage, to enjoy a surfeit of foreign culture.
>
> Parting company with them again, we must confess our dislike of *all* classes and categories, being interested solely in men and women. Our staff is composed indifferently of ex-officers, rankers, A.T.S. and W.R.N.S.; and, since we are reactionary enough to love and to have served our country, we have found the views of experts in naval and military matters necessary to maintain the proportion of our review. [p. 169]

In a later "Editorial Note" (May 1950) to explain the change from monthly to quarterly publication, Campbell's own tone is unmistakable:

> One of our first objects has been, and will be, to bring together Faith, Intellect and Action; "The Priest, the Soldier, and the Poet," who, in every civilised age, are the natural leaders of the community; but who, in modern barbarism, have become separated by the growing philistinism of men of affairs, and by the spiritual treason and cowardice of intellectuals. This object must fail if its setting cannot make clear the natural unity of this Triumvir. [p. 352]

It is not difficult to see why Rob Lyle should have reacted defensively to a reference in the poetry magazine, *Nine*, to the "swashbuckling Catholic Right."[3]

3. See the "Editorial Statement" in *Nine* (Autumn 1950), p. 279, and Rob Lyle's reply in *Nine* (Winter 1950–51), pp. 93–94.

Campbell's continual work at translating, from this period on, resulted in the publication in 1951 of *The Poems of St. John of the Cross,* which was awarded the Foyle Poetry Prize, and in the appearance in 1952 of his translation of *Les fleurs du mal.* In the same year he published his short study, *Lorca.* Later he was to publish two translations of Portuguese novels by Eça de Queiroz: *Cousin Bazilio* in 1953 and *The City and the Mountains* in 1955. Five translations by Campbell appeared posthumously in 1959 in *Six Spanish Plays* (the third volume of Eric Bentley's *The Classic Theatre*), while the third volume of *Collected Poems* contains only translations.

In 1952 the Campbells moved from England to Portugal where they settled on a small farm in Sintra with the Lyles. His second autobiography, *Light on a Dark Horse,* had appeared the year before. In it the tall stories are even taller than those in *Broken Record,* and the insistence on personal prowess verges on the obsessive, although the best passages show imaginative strength. A boys' story set in Natal, *The Mamba's Precipice,* was published in 1953. The pervasive influence of his youth is evident throughout the book, in which the fictional narrative dwells on incidents that are recorded in the two autobiographies. In the same year the Lyles returned to England, leaving the Campbells alone on their property, Quinta dos Bochechos, in Sintra. Their life in Sintra was not as isolated as their life in Spain in the thirties. The development of communications in the intervening twenty years made it much easier for Campbell to keep in touch with other friends and writers. He made overseas lecture tours and returned to England with his wife at Christmas. Portugal was cheap, and he was more relaxed in the sun, away from English life to which his reaction was such a complex combination of attraction and discomfort.

In the autumn of 1953 he made a lecture tour of Canada and the United States. His personality made a deep impression, not always favourable, on his audiences, and in many cases the accounts of his behaviour are already verging on the legendary. He made another tour in 1955. A letter written to Mary Campbell from Toronto in October

1955 gives a vivid impression of the mood of the poet's
North American trips:

> My dearest one,
>
> I received your most loving and beautiful letter at
> Halifax where there wasn't a moment to spare before
> catching the train to Toronto. It was only on asking
> Canadians on the ship the fare to Toronto (1500 miles
> or so from Halifax!) that I realised that I hadn't enough
> for my fare so I sent a radiogram to Dalhousie Uni-
> versity "Arriving tomorrow Saturday" and said my
> prayers. Sure enough Professor Bennett turned up and
> worked like a fiend to raise the 100 dollars required
> (the banks were shut) we rushed round various offices
> buying train tickets etc. Meanwhile my box in the
> Customs not having been claimed was put back on the
> Saturnia which sailed off to N.Y. with it apparently—
> there is just a chance however that it was among some
> other boxes on the platform if so it will be sent on
> here. But we've wired the Purser of Saturnia to send it
> to Regnery if still on board.
>
> . . . I have just arrived after three days in train (I flew
> part of the way). I never realised it was so far. Excuse
> this wretched pen. I am well. All day yesterday I only
> had 1 whiskey and 2 bottles of beer—but what beer! I
> should say the best in the world. Everything so far has
> gone with ——— (except for the box which should be
> quite safe) John Sutherland, in hospital with T.B. for a
> year at least, lent me an overcoat. . . . I must break off
> to write tonights lecture as I lost all my papers in the
> box.
>
> [MC]

Campbell was now more than merely respectable in
South Africa. He was proudly claimed as a South African
poet of international standing. Public recognition of his
stature came in 1954 when he flew to South Africa to receive the honorary degree of Doctor of Literature from the
University of Natal, and was thus acclaimed, like so many

of his family, in his native province. Returning as a distinguished guest to the city he had left with such bitterness in
1927, he reacted with a combination of humility and panache typical of his outwardly exhibitionist, yet inwardly
defensive, nature. During his stay he showed an almost
childlike gratitude for the public recognition he was receiv-
ing. His political views had changed considerably since the
Voorslag days. Abandoning a prepared script half-way
through his graduation speech he showed his colours with
this spontaneous defence of the South African regime:

> Now the Brazilians and Spanish Americans may have
> some right to criticise us as colonists, but not the Eng-
> lish nor the Americans. Their concern at the plight of
> our *ten million* natives seems to me a hypocritical alibi
> for the guilt of having sold two hundred million of
> their own race, to a far worse form of baboonery and
> tyrannous barbarism than that from which we under-
> took the last war to deliver them. . . . The two hundred
> million "natives" of Europe—victims of the Yalta
> Booby-Trap—were sold there for a bottle of Vodka,
> by people whom one would not have thought capable
> of such utter gullibility. It is true the victims were mere
> Europeans, and therefore could be sold into abject
> slavery without causing any indignation amongst the
> intellectuals.[4]

A similarly extreme conservatism informs his last prose
work, *Portugal,* written in 1956 and published in 1957, after
he had travelled through Portugal as the guest of the Portuguese government. In 1957, when returning to Sintra
with his wife from an Easter visit to Spain, Campbell was
killed outright in a motor accident on April 23.

The last years of his life had been comparatively tran-
quil and serene. In spite of the fact that he was drinking
heavily before his death, and had suffered a minor break-
down on his second trip to North America, the fifties were
free of public controversy. Although his aggressive literary
persona had been carried over into real life when he

4. "Poetry and Experience," *Theoria,* no. 6 (1954), p. 37.

punched Stephen Spender at a public meeting in London after the war, his bearing towards his family and those he knew well was essentially mild and kindly. It is this accommodating aspect of his often lonely private life which is most consistently concealed by the obsessive quality of the assertions made through the poet's public mask.

The personal assertions themselves dominate Campbell's prose works written during the fifties. Their charm, panache, and lyrical moments provide an interest which still holds readers. The total effect of the books is, however, marred by recurrent tall stories, obsessive personal boasts, and an often scornful insistence on the absurdity of any attitudes which do not conform to Campbell's world-view. He is seldom a good theorist, and usually less convincing when communicating ideas rather than emotions. In his prose writings he often expresses ideas, and almost invariably these passages are less successful than those in which he gives free rein to his imaginative and descriptive powers. The carefree mood of his best prose is that which informs the earlier *Broken Record*: "I am so passionate a spectator of action that I have often found myself taking part in things which do not come in the way of most other poets, and a series of disjointed romantic adventures have been the result, some of which project into my imagination, but for that I can make no excuse, as my memory and imagination work as one; by force of recounting them they have assumed more elegant shapes, and I am not the one to bore you with a list of facts" (p. 11). The idea of facts being boring is in perfect keeping with the charming impudence of the whole passage, as is the graceful superiority of "I am not the one to bore you"; but at the same time the attitude itself has hints of the know-all manner in many parts of *Light on a Dark Horse*. In the best passages from *Light on a Dark Horse* and *Portugal* his imaginative involvement can give a sense of wonder and excitement to the scenes he describes. His childlike fascination with things mysterious or exotic, coupled with his poetic imagination, is often compelling and appealing. For this reason his prose still attracts readers. The general reader is perhaps puzzled by Campbell's unevenness in tone, by his straight face in retelling tall stories, and by his personal boasts, but the fascination is caused by a momentary, total imaginative involvement.

A different kind of involvement, and one that detracts from Campbell's prose, is the desire to show inside knowledge, or to be associated intimately with selective groups. This urge to demonstrate expertise recurs continually in the later books. Even the children's adventure story, *The Mamba's Precipice*, contains many descriptions of his own specialized knowledge. There is a lengthy digression on the correct throttle and clutch drill for motorcycle rough-riding, and two Iberian cattlemen explain the finer points of their lance and cape work to the children on the Natal coast: "Then Antonio adjusted his garrocha, placing the haft under the sole of his boot and aiming the point straight at the bull's muzzle: 'Ha, Ha, toro!' he called in his own language—which is also the language of all cattlemen" (p. 89). In a boys' adventure story these details are merely demonstrations of technical knowledge.[5] Still not satisfied with these precepts for his young readers, Campbell adds a footnote: "Almost every word relating to cattle and horses—rodeo, lazo, corral, etc.—derives from the Spanish." The same assertion is made in all his writing on horses and cattle, and the fact that he should repeat it in *The Mamba's Precipice* is an indication of his personal involvement in suggesting both encyclopaedic knowledge and his membership of a privileged group. This desire to show himself a knowing member of different groups and societies often gives a curious ring to his writing. His first voyage to England is described in *Broken Record* as aboard "the cargo steamer S.S. *Inkonka* (Captain Barrow)," (p. 23) where the naming of the captain sounds knowing enough. In *Light on a Dark Horse* the atmosphere of nautical authenticity would do credit to Gulliver: "The breakwater was the last thing I saw of Durban on my first remembered transoceanic voyage on the S.S. *Inkonka*, 2,000 tons (Captain Barrow) of the Harrison Rennie Line" (p. 173).

In *Light on a Dark Horse* the pedagogic tone is beauti-

---

5. The technique described in *The Mamba's Precipice* has already been described in detail in *Taurine Provence*, pp. 41–42.

fully captured during a description of a bullfight: "The strongest muscles of most animals are weak in the reflex. Note how a blacksmith can paralyse the terrible hind hoof of a horse, by bending the leg upwards, and how fish-mongers keep the powerful claws of lobsters from opening with a flimsy loop of paper-elastic" (p. 309).[6] The bullfight which this digression interrupts in *Light on a Dark Horse* is itself an involved piece of personal assertion, showing both Campbell's delight at belonging to or being noticed by certain groups and his tendency to exaggerate his own deeds of prowess. He describes the occasion as the "open-championship of Provence for the free course of bulls, and for the steer-throwing championship." He continues, "It was on that afternoon, in honour of my wife and in an arena crowded with French military and naval aviators, that I gave my supreme performance of 'mancornar,' or hurling a bull by the horns, not from the saddle but from the ground" (p. 309). In *Broken Record,* closer to the event, and without his persistent need for glorification, the incident is described in more humble terms. The bull is an ox in the earlier account, and Campbell is clearly a novice at the game, grateful for the help which has somehow vanished in the second version:

> When I put down Ferraud's fighting ox six years old, I found Raoux swinging by its tail. . . . I was very surprised at the ease with which he came down. Before that I had never tried anything but steers and cows and some domestic animals in the abattoir, and sometimes with the *toros-emboulés*—sheath-horned bulls of the festivals. It happened to be on the tenth anniversary of my meeting with my wife. As I knelt on the horns, Raoux came and sat beside me and showed me how to take off the cocarde, as I had no hook to clip it from its tight knots on the hairy forehead of the bull. I sent the cocarde from hand to hand up to my wife, and she had an ovation from the crowd. [p. 183]

6. The lesson is repeated almost word for word in *Portugal* (p. 113), except that "look" replaces the earlier, more pedantic "note."

Seventeen years after this account the story is retold without mention of Raoux. By this time, too, the aviators, who have already been specifically mentioned, are given the additional description, "truly valiant people": "When I had thrown this bull, I sat on its neck, took off the cocarde, the 'gland,' and the rosette, and received an ovation from a crowded arena of truly valiant people" (p. 309). The only time the aviators are mentioned in *Broken Record* is at the end of the description: "After this as my clothes were not in a fit state, I was wrapped in a cloak as in the Burial of Sir John Moore, and passed up after the cocarde to my wife by the spectators, who were mostly aviators and were very cordial" (p. 183).

The whole description in *Broken Record* has an air of sanity about it, whereas that in *Light on a Dark Horse* seems strained and unreal. This is caused partly by the too bland tone with which the heroics are mentioned and partly by the unnatural interest Campbell shows in the spectators, those "truly valiant people." The quality of spectators who offer applause affects the quality of the applause itself, and in this case his valour is praised by those who really know what valour is. At the same time, his eagerness at being accepted by the airmen shows his sense of being an outsider, delighted at any suggestion of belonging to or being accepted by an enviably homogeneous group. The hero of the bull ring is "honoured" at being wrapped in an aviator's cloak: "As my pants were ripped, on that occasion, to tatters, I had the honour of being wrapped in a French aviator's cloak and of being presented, jointly with my wife, with several thousand francs (worth a lot then) for the three cocardes, and a bottle of champagne" (p. 309). It is a sense of childlike awe at being associated with glamorous things or with conduct generally admired that creeps into his work at moments like this. The group loyalties and pride which result from this attitude are particularly marked in his references throughout *Light on a Dark Horse* to his school or army experiences: "Then we had the finest history master in the world, Captain Blackmore, M.A. Oxon. He had a really colossal historical insight" (p. 74). "Our excellent Natal Cadet training concentrated chiefly on drill and marksmanship. In that respect we were the best school in the British Empire at that time. We took the Schools of Empire Shield off the Edinburgh Academy, and held it for years" (p. 71). The tiny world which it is the aim of esprit de corps to bolster is often accepted unquestioningly by Campbell, even down to the superiority of Iberian barracks over their British counterparts because of the lack of "toe-jam."

A similar sense of pride informs his frequent remarks on how good an N.C.O. he was. *Light on a Dark Horse* is filled with the arcana of the Sergeants' Mess retold by a "senior N.C.O." who knows the ropes. And the assumption that all readers share his concept of the ideal regimental wag leads him into empty anecdotal slapstick. He often sets out to appear both a muscular rake and a wily old soldier. After recounting an incident in which he allegedly threatened with his rifle butt an old friend of the twenties, and frightened the man into giving him a "tenner" ("though he owed me twice as much"), Campbell suddenly becomes proud of his professional skill at getting away with his escapades: "I accepted the compromise since I was loth to lose my stripes, or deviriginate my charge-sheet, which I kept stainless throughout the war, till my discharge with 'Military Conduct: Excellent' " (p. 231). The independent mind of which he is so proud is surprisingly abject before the sort of rigid authority symbolized by military discipline. It is remarkable not only that he should be so proud of preserving the appearance of what officers regard as excellent conduct, but also that he should wish to exhibit his barrack-room bravado: "I would have smashed the till-machine to bits with my rifle-butt (and himself included) and taken the contents." In *Portugal*, Campbell again mentions with pride his pay-book, officially stamped with excellence, although he has already boasted of "trading in poached rhino-horns when supposed to be coast watching as a sergeant in the last war": "Is it any wonder that my British uniform, battle-dress, bush-hat, medals, with the pay-book in the bum pocket of the battle-dress (bearing witness to exemplary military conduct) have been bleaching and fraying, now almost unrecognizably, on the scarecrow in my wheat-field, ever since I was disabled and read of the suicidal 'benders' of Roosevelt and Churchill at Casablanca and Yalta" (p. 43). Official approval of his conduct really is important to Campbell. In his often futile gestures of defiance at the stupidity of authoritarian figures like Roosevelt and Churchill he shows the feeling of impotence and smallness before authority, which is the reason for his pride in authoritarian approval.

A childlike quality in his coterie-talk and reverence for skilled groups, such as fishermen and cowmen, emerges clearly in *The Mamba's Precipice*. The boys' adventure story contains many incidents and details incorporated from Campbell's account of his childhood in *Broken Record* and *Light on a Dark Horse,* and with little or no alteration the sense of awe and excitement in these passages suits the tone of the boys' book perfectly. A childhood smugness and cosiness in the description of Moonsammy, the cook, affords a simple example of an irritating mannerism of the other books which is in place in *The Mamba's Precipice*: "Moonsammy was the best cook in Natal; but he liked his comfortable kitchen in Durban, and he hated going away to the ramshackle old cooking-hut which had been built on to the Beach Cottage in the bush" (p. 14). "The best cook in Natal" is a childish boast which is quite inoffensive in an overtly juvenile book, whereas the similar insistence in Campbell's other books on his having known the best history master, the best rugby coach, the best cadet corps, is tedious.

So involved is he with the magic world of his youth that not only does he often rewrite the same incidents in *Broken Record, Light on a Dark Horse,* and *The Mamba's Precipice,* but in the children's story the world he creates is clearly that of the first decades of this century. The outboard motors and motorcycles, which appear towards the end of the book, are anachronistic intrusions into a world where, in the opening chapter we are told: "Tom was the faithful old servant who had worked for Dr. Jackson's father since he was ten years old. He drove Mrs. Jackson's horse carriage when she went out shopping in Durban, and very smart he looked in his white suit with a red fez on his

head" (pp. 13–14). This is a detail from Campbell's autobiographies, as is the carbide lamp with which the boys
go fishing, and which is admittedly placed in the story as
"old fashioned." The mood in which Beach Cottage is
described in *The Mamba's Precipice* is also clearly that of
his youth: "When they were at the cottage Michael would
have to ride to the station-store six miles away to fetch the
provisions and the post. He would have to provide them
with venison or guinea fowl for the larder" (p. 13). The unquestioning excitement with which Campbell describes an
unclouded outdoor life reflects the idealized nature of his
childhood memories. His total involvement in describing
sardine fishing or opening up a lagoon is the involvement
of carefree youth.

The mannerisms are inseparable from the themes in
Campbell's prose works. His expressions of passion for
equestrian tradition and hatred of socialism, "progress,"
or humanitarian scruples are facets of the self-portraiture
which is always either explicit or implicit. When the views
expressed are convincing, they are both based on defen-
sible principles (such as a reasonably cynical attitude towards the possibility of unrestricted progress) and free
from the obsessive self-aggrandizement that spoils his
wilder attacks. The most consistent pattern behind those
attacks is that of defence. His feeling of being an outsider,
and the correspondingly desperate loyalty towards any
group which he can feel is his, are often the basis for
Campbell's theoretic boasts, just as they are the basis for
his boasting on matters of fact. It is difficult to separate his
loyalty to a group (whether South African, Provençal, or
Iberian) from his loyalty to an idea. The way his group
loyalties urge him on to the attack and the genuine confusion created by his immediate personal feelings are
clearly suggested in a passage from *Portugal*:

> The British hatred of "dagoes" due to the thundering
> defeats, routs, and surrenders at the Antilles and
> Buenos Aires and Oriamendi, of Raleigh, Drake, Hawk-
> ins, Cobham, Brooke, Beresford, Lacy Evans, etc. (if it
> did not date from the resounding thump that the Black

Prince took back with him to die of chagrin and fright
at Bordeaux) has resulted in a voluntary misunder-
standing and underrating, in England, of this superb
literature, only paralleled by the Hebrews, the Greeks,
and the English themselves—those perishers!—who in-
fatuate and exasperate me equally (wonderful soldiers
—utterly ignorant diplomats, and destroyers of the
Universe!). [p. 203]

Campbell's extraordinarily defensive reaction to an imagined group hostility can only last as long as he has the
feeling of being an outsider. The collapse of his hostility is
inevitable once he turns from discussing Portuguese literature (as a lonely Anglo-Saxon connoisseur) to the English
literature with which he himself is intimately connected.
The coupling of infatuation and exasperation as the two
forms of his association with the English is an exactly
truthful assessment of the two moods which characterize
the opening and closing of the paragraph, and offers a real
insight into the emotions underlying many of his quasi-
historical or sociological sallies.

Apart from broad, commonly accepted beliefs in tradition, valour, and the futility of Utopian schemes, all
Campbell's theoretic arguments vary like this from moment to moment according to his mood. Almost invariably
the wild attacks he launches at other groups or beliefs
have their origin in the defence of some attitude or activity
which he cannot really defend logically. The recurring
theme of the traditional superiority of those closest to the
soil and the bare necessities of life is a prolonged defence
of a group and a world he knows and likes, just as his
attacks on modern industrial civilization are an only half-
reasoned sneer at a world to which he cannot belong.

In the poems written during Campbell's last years
there is an autobiographical element similar to that in
Light on a Dark Horse and *Portugal*. The tone of the personal poems of this period is often restrained, as in "Félibre," even though the personal assertions are not modest:

I, too, can loose my Pegasus to graze,
Carouse with drunken fiddlers at the Fair,

And with the yokelry on market days
Jingle in spurs and sheepskins round the square.

They say it is a waste of time. I differ.
To learn should be as easy as to look.
You could not pass examinations stiffer,
Nor sweat a deeper learning from the book—
                                        [2, 111]

Bald statements of the poet's own accomplishments and
values are surprisingly insistent in the late poems, and
made consistently in these explicit terms. There are still
successes among the last poems, however, and in them
Campbell shows his mature skill with an easy modulation
of tone. "Rhapsody of the Man in Hospital Blues and the
'Hyde Park Lancers' " grows out of real experience and
shows him discussing an acute personal problem, his growing lameness, with ironic insight and wit. From the opening
line the poem has a direct verbal crispness:

From Notting Hill to Prince's Gate
I'd started breaking-in my stick
And of my new, three-legged gait
Acquired the quaint arithmetic.

No more to canter, trot or trippel,
Where dandies pranced along the Row,
I coaxed the strange unwieldy cripple
I had become yet feared to know.
                                        [2, 100]

His sardonic awareness of his own absurdly limited appearance ("No last-man-in has ever batted / With a more desperate intent") gives the poem a manly detachment which
he only achieves in his best work. Its success is occasional,
however, and represents no new turn in his writing or
thinking.

His repetition of earlier themes in the last poems and
his several autobiographical assertions among them indicate that he was probably not about to enter a new phase
of original writing at the time of his death. The satisfying

poems of this last period show that his technical skill was in no way affected by the absence during these years of any insistent need to express a central theme or problem. Nevertheless there is no thematic topic in the poems published after *Talking Bronco*. It was probably this lack of a central theme, coupled with the fact that his technique was not affected by what might be called his loss of inspiration, which drove Campbell to translation. The success of the translations indicates how supple and flexible his poetic talent remained.

The second and third volumes of *Collected Poems* appeared posthumously in 1957 and 1960 respectively, and in each case were given considerable attention from reviewers. Since the publication of volume three, however, interest in Campbell has dwindled. Although the political quarrels in which he played so passionate a part lost their popular interest during the prosperous fifties and sixties, he still suffers from the political reputation he gained in the thirties. Not only was there, until recently, little interest in the issues which shaped Campbell's political life, but also there is a common, subliminal reaction that, in any case, he was politically wrong. In this respect he has suffered from a reaction almost exactly opposite to that enjoyed by MacSpaunday. MacNeice was not doctrinaire, and therefore had little to recant. But Auden, Spender, and Cecil Day Lewis all changed their attitudes radically by the end of the thirties, and yet the glamour of their commitment during that decade still hangs about them. In spite of their own statements to the contrary, there is a common, subliminal reaction that they were politically right. Like Campbell, however, their most successful work is usually that in which they transcend political issues and dogma. Certainly they could be at least as doctrinaire as he, and at least as smug. Few readers can find in Marxist platitudes or Mortmere fantasies any more serious comment on the complex world they know than in Campbell's defiantly "anachronistic" equestrianism. As the polemics which figured so largely in these poets' lives assume an increasingly historical rather than living interest, the accompanying prejudices should also fade. Campbell's best poetry has an independence of fads or fashions. The fact that his lyrical gift is at its most intense when he is striving to express subjective values or personal emotions ensures the living interest of his best poems. This timeless, self-contained element gives his finest work a poetic validity which eludes most twentieth-century poetry.

The case for Campbell as a lyric poet does not have to be belaboured. And to say that much of his later polemic is the result of a stock response can hardly be regarded as incautious. There is an area of his work, however, on which opinions will invariably differ. The effectiveness of his humour is intricately connected with questions of taste at a level on which argument becomes most subjective. One shares all Campbell's tastes or one does not. In particular, the slapstick in his well-rehearsed anecdotes appeals to a specialized taste only. A sense of the frontier and of the fantastic, un-Western world of the African bush still does attract readers of Campbell's wilder sallies. The waggish raconteur, teasing a sober-minded and gullible audience with Munchausen-like tales, is an appealing figure to a certain kind of reader—often one who is old enough to remember the yarns and yearn for the freedom of a wilder, unstandardized Africa. Old soldiers' tales have a similar appeal, mainly to old soldiers. The wit which Campbell can use with such beautiful poise is not a part of his broad anecdotal clowning. To those (like myself) whose tastes in humour are more cerebral (or "solemn"—depending on one's viewpoint), the delicacy of wit which he can achieve, and the sense of exhilaration which is produced by all such displays of intelligence, make many of his exaggerated jokes appear doubly flat and tawdry. It is in terse, epigrammatic jests that his major claim as a humorist lies. In them his ability to sustain a conceit, his intelligence, and his virility all find natural and satisfying expression. "On Some South African Novelists" has, surely, secured a lasting place in the canon of English literary jokes:

> You praise the firm restraint with which they write—
> I'm with you there, of course:
> They use the snaffle and the curb all right,
> But where's the bloody horse?

[1, 198]

Campbell did not fulfil the promise shown by *The Flaming Terrapin* or *Adamastor*. It is tempting to suggest too simple a reason for his neglecting his real lyrical talent to be dominated by an excessive polemical urge as he grew older. His colonial background, and the isolation which resulted from his uneasy relations with both English and South African life, certainly had a decisive effect on his development. An inherent defensiveness in his personality could only have been exaggerated by his almost continual sense of being an alien. It is, however, an oversimplification to think of Campbell's life as a case history of a "colonial exile" who found himself cut off from all roots. His exceptional childhood and family life in Natal cannot be typed, and yet were crucial in forming both his own aristocratic instincts and his idealized view of a vital, outdoor existence. A basic intellectual limitation is also a distinctive feature of his literary life. Campbell is not an original thinker. He takes over others' causes and ideas; several original poems derive from Romance sources, and when he turned almost exclusively to translation in his last period, he was really only continuing a lifelong habit of basing poems on other works. There is a basic difference, however, between the two kinds of borrowing. Most of Campbell's poems based on French works are transformed by his poetic genius, which often appears most vivid and original in free adaptations. In his polemical writing the arguments and theories are not transformed by his lyric power.

The limited range of his interests becomes an obstacle in reading his work as a whole, and the perversity of several of his fervently defended beliefs becomes tiresome. Nevertheless, for all the insensitivity of many of the poet's polemical utterances, his consistent scorn for the smallminded action, and his continual celebration of the heroic, the magnanimous, and the colourful, do have a compelling total effect. As a reviewer wrote of his first poem: "It is something, after all, to have the courage to be damnably poetical. It is something to be unafraid of the ample gesture, the upswung arm, and the frenzied eye, of the cloaked figure standing prophetically out against the horizon and wind-driven clouds, of lone defiance flung shatteringly up to Heaven and downwards to the ruck of the ground-lings."[7] There is a bigness about Campbell's work, in spite of its moments of crassness. The delight, vitality, and colour which he so consistently captures have as distinctive and personal a note as that struck by any major poet of this century. He does not have the range or the intellectual subtlety of a Yeats or an Eliot, but his own particular talent is refreshingly vigorous and challenging in an age noted for its scepticism, weariness, and hesitance. He can dismiss, with unintelligent insensitivity, whole groups or classes who do not share his heroic code, but the panache with which he expresses that code has a ringing, rhetorical con-viction. It is a notable literary personality that informs the lines:

> For none save those are worthy birth
> Who neither life nor death will shun:
> And we plough deepest in the Earth
> Who ride the nearest to the Sun.
>   [1, 136]

7. *The Dial*, 77 (November, 1924), 423.

APPENDIX

D. R. Gillie's Translation of Kuhlemann

Gillie sent Plomer a "still very rough version of the first two verses"[1] of Johannes Kuhlemann's poem, "Tristan d'Acunha." The translation of the first verse is the more striking:

> Behind thee will the cities all grow cold,
> Their locks of flame will fall away and die;
> But as the sea wraps round thee fold on fold,
> Wind from thy hair lifts ashes, passing by,
> Thou, Captain of Aurora, true of old,
> A "Farewell" from the masthead lettest fly.
> Yet will declare itself one sorrow more—
> Not all the seas are thine for sailing o'er.

The likeness of these lines to Campbell's poem lies mainly in the general concept of the position of the island as the lone vanguard of the world and in the adoption of an occasional phrase:

> Your strength is that you have no hope or fear,
> You march before the world without a crown,
> The nations call you back, you do not hear,
> The cities of the earth grow grey behind you,
> You will be there when their great flames go down
> And still the morning in the van will find you.
>
> You march before the continents, you scout
> In front of all the earth; alone you scale
> The mast-head of the world, a lorn look-out,
> Waving the snowy flutter of your spray
> And gazing back in infinite farewell
> To suns that sink and shores that fade away.
>
> [1, 41]

The closest parallel between the two poems occurs in the shared concept of a farewell from the masthead, and in

1. Mr. William Plomer kindly copied for me these words from Gillie's letter and the text of his translation.

Campbell's lines: "The cities of the earth grow grey behind you, / You will be there when their great flames go down," which resemble Gillie's opening lines: "Behind thee will the cities all grow cold, / Their locks of flame will fall away and die."

Gillie's "still very rough version" does not have the polish of Campbell's poem. Quite apart from the difference in finish, the major difference is between the vigorously energetic qualities associated with the island's lonely "march" in Campbell's poem, and its static and passive nature, wrapped round by the sea and blown upon by the wind, in the Kuhlemann version. This active role associated with Tristan da Cunha by Campbell is an essential part of its capacity to outlast all other earthly things. Campbell attributes a total self-sufficiency to the island:

> You fish with nets of seaweed in the deep
> As fruitlessly as I with nets of rhyme—
> Yet forth you stride, yourself the way, the goal,
> The surges are your strides, your path is time.
>   [1, 42]

This concept has echoes of the second of Gillie's translated verses:

> Not over all the seas—thou farest ways
> Long woven out in thee.
> Thyself way to thine end, whate'er the maze,
> Thy path through thine own waves will ever be.
> Yet but a lust for a long vaunt and blaze
> Of trumpets will salute and colour free—
> Thy squadrons that are looking toward Death
> And only know what their poor wanting saith.

The similarity is marked between "Yet forth you stride, yourself the way, the goal," and "Thyself way to thine end, whate'er the maze, / Thy path through thine own waves will ever be." As Plomer remarks in *Double Lives*, the original creative impetus which the reading of the two translated verses sparked off in Campbell is a "good example of collaboration in the Crocean sense" (p. 167).

A SELECTED BIBLIOGRAPHY

Works by Roy Campbell

Collected Poems. London: Bodley Head. Vol. 1, 1949; vol. 2, 1957; and vol. 3, 1960.

Separate Volumes of Poetry
The Flaming Terrapin. London: Jonathan Cape, 1924.
The Wayzgoose. London: Jonathan Cape, 1928.
Adamastor. London: Faber and Faber, 1930. Republished by Paul Koston in Cape Town, 1950.
Poems. Paris: Hours Press, 1930.
The Georgiad. London: Boriswood, 1931.
Flowering Reeds. London: Boriswood, 1933.
Mithraic Emblems. London: Boriswood, 1936.
Flowering Rifle. London: Longmans, Green and Co., 1939.
Sons of the Mistral. London: Faber and Faber, 1941.
Talking Bronco. London: Faber and Faber, 1946.

Works in Prose
Taurine Provence. London: Desmond Harmsworth, 1932.
Broken Record. London: Boriswood, 1934.
Light on a Dark Horse. London: Hollis and Carter, 1951.
Lorca. Cambridge: Bowes and Bowes, 1952.
The Mamba's Precipice. London: Frederick Muller, 1953.
Portugal. London: Max Reinhardt, 1957.

Translations
The Poems of St. John of the Cross. London: Harvill, 1951.
Baudelaire: Poems: A Translation of Les Fleurs du Mal. London: Harvill, 1952.
Eça de Queiroz: Cousin Bazilio. London: Max Reinhardt, 1953.
Eça de Queiroz: The City and the Mountains. London: Max Reinhardt, 1955.
The Classic Theatre: Six Spanish Plays, vol. 3, edited by Eric Bentley, New York: Doubleday, 1959 (Five plays translated by Campbell).
Paço d'Arcos: Nostalgia, a Collection of Poems. London: Sylvan Press, 1960.

Articles

"The Significance of 'Turbott Wolfe.' " *Voorslag,* no. 1 (June, 1926), pp. 39–45.

Review of the collected works of T. S. Eliot. *Voorslag,* no. 1 (June, 1926), pp. 59–62.

Review of *The Worship of Nature. Voorslag,* no. 1 (June, 1926), pp. 62–63.

"Fetish Worship in South Africa." *Voorslag,* no. 2 (July, 1926), pp. 3–19.

" 'Eunuch Arden' and 'Kynoch Arden.' " *Voorslag,* no. 2 (July, 1926), pp. 32–38. [Signed Lewis Marston]

"The Mental Traveller." *New Statesman* (August 27, 1927), p. 623.

"The Emotional Cyclops." *New Statesman,* Supplement on Christmas Books (December 3, 1927), p. X.

"François Villon." *New Statesman* (March 24, 1928), pp. 765–66.

"Contemporary Poetry." *Scrutinies,* London, 1928, pp. 162–179.

"White Laughter." *New Statesman* (July 20, 1929), pp. 473–74.

"Reviewer's Preface" and "A Rejected Review." *Satire and Fiction,* London, 1930, pp. 13–16.

"Editorial." *Catacomb,* no. 8 (November, 1949), p. 169.

"On To Methusalah." *Catacomb,* no. 8 (November, 1949), pp. 171–73.

"Persecution of Spanish Communists in Russia." *Catacomb,* no. 9 (December, 1949), pp. 219–21.

"A Screw-Tapey Letter." *Catacomb,* no. 10 (January, 1950), pp. 245–49.

Review of *Spain* by Sacheverell Sitwell. *Catacomb,* New Series, 1 (Summer 1950), pp. 421–23.

"Epitaph on the Thirties." *Nine,* no. 5 (Autumn 1950), pp. 344–46.

"Apollinaire Trismegistus." *Catacomb,* 1 (Winter 1950–51), pp. 547–52.

"A Poet." *Catacomb,* 2 (Spring 1951), p. 64.

Review of *Fifty Spanish Poems* by Juan Ramón. *Catacomb,* 2 (Summer 1951), pp. 126–28.

"Poetry and Experience." *Theoria,* no. 6 (1954), pp. 37–44.

Works by other writers

Aldington, Richard. *Introduction to Mistral*. London: Heinemann, 1956.

Apollinaire, Guillaume. *Oeuvres Poétiques*. Paris: Gallimard, 1956.

Baudelaire, Charles. *Les Fleurs du Mal*. Oxford: Blackwell, 1942.

Benson, Frederick R. *Writers in Arms: The Literary Impact of the Spanish Civil War*. New York: New York University Press, 1967.

Brenan, Gerald. *The Spanish Labyrinth*. Cambridge: Cambridge University Press, 1943.

Campbell, Ethel. *Sam Campbell: A Story of Natal*. Privately published in Durban, 1946.

Corbière, Tristan. *Les Amours Jaunes*. Paris: Gallimard, 1953.

Cumont, Franz. *The Mysteries of Mithra*. New York: Dover Publications, 1956.

Cunard, Nancy. *These were the Hours: Memories of My Hours Press, Réanville and Paris 1928–1931*. Edited with a foreword by Hugh D. Ford. Carbondale and Edwardsville: Southern Illinois University Press. 1969.

Ford, Hugh D. *A Poet's War: British Poets and the Spanish Civil War*. Philadelphia: University of Pennsylvania Press, 1965.

Goldring, Douglas. *The Nineteen Twenties*. London: Nicholson and Watson, 1945.

Graves, Robert, and Riding, Laura. *A Pamphlet against Anthologies*. New York: Doubleday, 1928.

———. *A Survey of Modernist Poetry*. London: Heinemann, 1927.

Hoskins, Catharine B. *Today the Struggle: Literature and Politics in England During the Spanish Civil War*. Austin and London: University of Texas Press, 1969.

Jackson, Gabriel. *The Spanish Republic and the Civil War 1931–1939*. Princeton: Princeton University Press, 1965.

John, Augustus. *Chiaroscuro*. London: Jonathan Cape, 1952.

Koestler, Arthur. *The Invisible Writing*. London: Collins with Hamish Hamilton, 1954.

———. *Spanish Testament*. London: Gollancz, 1937.

Lewis, Wyndham. *The Apes of God*. Penguin Books, 1965. First edition, London: Arthur Press, 1930.

———. *The Art of Being Ruled*. London: Chatto and Windus, 1926.

———. *The Letters of Wyndham Lewis*. Edited by W. K. Rose. London: Methuen, 1963.

———. *Satire and Fiction*. London: Arthur Press, 1930.

———. *Snooty Baronet*. London: Cassell, 1932.

———. *Time and Western Man*. London: Chatto and Windus, 1927.

Madariaga, Salvador de. *Spain*. London: Jonathan Cape, 1942.

Marsh, Edward, ed. *Georgian Poetry 1920–1922*. London: Poetry Bookshop, 1922.

Miller, Fey. *First Line and Title Index to the Poetry of Roy Campbell*. Johannesburg: University of the Witwatersrand School of Librarianship, 1961.

Miller, G. M., and Sergeant, Howard. *A Critical Survey of South African Poetry in English*. Cape Town: Balkema, 1957.

Mistral, Frédéric. *Mirèio*. Paris: Bibliothèque-Charpentier, 1924.

Murry, J. Middleton. *Aspects of Literature*. London: Collins, 1920.

Plomer, William. *Double Lives*. London: Jonathan Cape, 1943.

———. *Turbott Wolfe*. London: Hogarth Press, 1965. First edition, Hogarth Press, 1925.

Rimbaud, Arthur. *Oeuvres*. Paris: Garnier Frères, 1960.

Ross, Robert H. *The Georgian Revolt 1910–1922: Rise and Fall of a Poetic Ideal*. Carbondale and Edwardsville: Southern Illinois University Press, 1965.

Sackville-West, Victoria. *The Land*. London: Heinemann, 1926.

———. "The Poet." *Life and Letters* (April, 1931), pp. 259–68.

Sitwell, Osbert. *Who Killed Cock Robin?* London: C. W. Daniel, 1921.

Slater, Francis C. *The Centenary Book of South African Verse*. London: Longmans, Green and Co., 1925.

Spender, Stephen. *World within World.* London: Hamish Hamilton, 1951.

Squire, John C. *Poems in One Volume.* London: Heinemann, 1926.

Temple, Frédéric Jacques et al. *Hommage à Roy Campbell.* Montpellier: La Licorne, 1958.

Thomas, Hugh. *The Spanish Civil War.* London: Eyre & Spottiswoode, 1961.

Valéry, Paul. *Oeuvres.* Paris: Gallimard, 1957.

Vermaseren, M. J. *Mithras, The Secret God.* Translated by Therese and Vincent Megaw. London: Chatto and Windus, 1963.

Wolfe, Humbert. *Dialogues and Monologues.* London: Gollancz, 1928.

————. "The Ranciad." *New Statesman* (June 27, 1931), p. 646.

Wright, David. *Roy Campbell.* London: Published for the British Council by Longmans, Green & Co., 1961.

Articles on Campbell

Abrahams, L. "Roy Campbell: Conquistador—Refugee." *Theoria,* no. 8 (1956), pp. 46–65.

Bergonzi, B. "Roy Campbell: Outsider on the Right." *Journal of Contemporary History* 2 (April, 1967), pp. 133–47.

Davis, E. "The Spoilt Boy in Roy Campbell." *Trek* (March, 1951), pp. 12–14.

Delius, A. "Slater and Campbell." *Standpunte,* 33 (1954), pp. 64–70.

Gardner, W. H. "Poetry and Actuality." *Theoria,* no. 3 (1950), pp. 19–31.

————. "Voltage of Delight." *The Month* (January, 1958), pp. 5–17, and (March, 1958), pp. 133–47.

Harvey, C. J. D. "The Poetry of Roy Campbell." *Standpunte* (October, 1950), pp. 53–59.

————. "Roy Campbell and 'Les Fleurs du Mal.' " *Ons Eie Boek,* XX, 117–18.

Jurgens, H. "Behind the Poetry of Roy Campbell." *Lantern* (June, 1965), pp. 27–35.

Kirk, R. "Last of the Scalds." *Sewanee Review* (Winter 1956), pp. 164–70.

Krige, U. "The Poetry of Roy Campbell: A Few Aspects." *Poems of Roy Campbell Chosen and Introduced by Uys Krige*. Cape Town: 1960, pp. 1–32.

———. "Profiles: Roy Campbell." *Trek* (October, 1951), pp. 3–5.

———. "Roy Campbell as Lyrical Poet." *English Studies in Africa* (September, 1958), pp. 81–94.

Opperman, D. J. "Roy Campbell en die S.A. Poesie." *Standpunte* (March, 1954), pp. 4–15.

Paton, A. "Roy Campbell: Poet and Man." *Theoria*, no. 9 (1957), pp. 19–31.

Plomer, W. "*Voorslag* Days." *London Magazine* (July, 1959), pp. 46–52.

Povey, J. F. "A Lyre of Savage Thunder: A Study of the Poetry of Roy Campbell." *Wisconsin Studies in Contemporary Literature* 7 (Winter–Spring, 1966), pp. 85–102.

Sergeant, H. "Restive Steer: A Study of the Poetry of Roy Campbell." *Essays and Studies* (1957), pp. 105–22.

Seymour-Smith, M. "Zero and the Impossible." *Encounter* (November, 1957), pp. 38–51.

INDEX